.DGING THE ESTUARY

PETER FINCH
EDGING THE ESTUARY

SEREN

Seren is the book imprint of
Poetry Wales Press Ltd
Nolton Street, Bridgend, Wales

www.serenbooks.com
facebook.com/SerenBooks
Twitter: @SerenBooks

ISBN 978-1-78172-084-4

A CIP record for this title is available from
the British Library

The publisher works with the financial assistance
of the Welsh Books Council

Printed by Bell & Bain Ltd, Glasgow

Contents

Foreword

This is not a walker's guide. But then you probably guessed that when you picked it up. It's a book about the Severn Estuary, about the place where Wales rolling south towards England finally runs out. It's a book about the great water highway of the age of the saints, of the trading Middle Ages, of the world-beating Industrial Revolution and of the slow-sailed leisured present. It's about the coasts and communities that cluster along it on both the Welsh and the English shores.

As a conceit it uses the Tudor enhancement of the port of Cardiff's customs-collecting authority to embrace every creek, inlet, landing and quay from Chepstow to the very tip of Worm's Head on Gower. Cardiff is that big. Economic planners have suggested that, given advances in technology and communications, future cities may no longer need to cluster in ovals, lozenges, and epicentred sprawls. They may instead fill whole valleys, crowd mountain tops or run in lines along the coastal edges. The Tudors were well ahead with Cardiff. I chose to walk the distance and to report back.

Despite this not being a walker's handbook, walking has been my principal method of travel. Slog on foot and see the world. But I have interspersed my rambles with spells on a bike and briefly by boat. I haven't crossed the territory in one single journey either. This was not an epic, continuous walk with a tent and everything I owned in a pack on my back. I took things in stages, drove out, walked, turned round, drove back. Got collected, walked the route in reverse, looped inland, went home, made my notes, went back out. The book took a year to do. Rain, snow and sun. Largely it was done in the right order. And always the travel was from east to west.

Edging The Estuary is no amorphous ramble, no constant delving into my own memories, no hunt for the lines of energy, nor academic search for history. It's a journey with a goal, a linear walk, a book of adventures, a quest.

Around about the time I was starting Assembly Member Jane Davidson, with the backing of First Minister Rhodri Morgan, had evolved a plan to create an All Wales Footpath, a route open to walkers of all kinds that would traverse the coast of the Welsh nation. The new path would be as near to the water's edge as possible, would use current pathways and, where those did not exist, would have new ones created. Industrial areas would be navigated around. Feet would never get wet.

I met with local authority footpath officers, the on-the-ground implementers of the plan, and discussed progress with the Countryside Council who were drawing the various components into a satisfying whole. Getting in at such an advanced stage in the planning process was invaluable. I was ahead of them, of course, often crossing territory where they were yet to negotiate access, climbing fences and crossing the edges of industrial wastes, ports, power stations, stores, aggregate deposits and private caravan parks where public access was not yet and often never would be put in place. The path, wonder that it is, now strikes inland to avoid obstacle. Not my way. Don't use this book as a guide to the south east Wales component of the All Wales Path. We cross the same territory often, but we also deviate. For me deviation has always provided the interest. You'll find a lot of that in here.

With the path in place I wondered if I should now go back and walk again, travelling along surfaced paths, way marked, and without obstacle. Crossing the city of Cardiff along the coastal edge, for example, is certainly easier with the path in place. But *Edging the Estuary* is not a pasteurised travelogue. It's a journey. I decided not to go back.

For a lot of the trip I've walked in the company of my partner Sue. She's read the sections as they've been written and provided me with a constant stream of advice and observation without which this would have been a much poorer book. We've discussed, as we've travelled, just what this Estuary might be. Is it river or sea? Where do its tides take it? How saline are its waters? What decides its designation?

Those we've met think of the Severn, if they think of it at all, as water. Sea where there are white-topped waves, river where there is mud. Before locks and weirs were constructed, the daily tides ebbed and flowed right up as far as Worcester. Today they regularly get as far as the northern reaches of Gloucester. With high Spring tides when the weirs get topped, the tidal waters can even reach Upper Lode Lock near Tewkesbury. The salinity shifts. The coastal edge bends and blurs. This is a great river, the Welsh Mississippi. It's the river that made Wales, that brought invaders, that took away goods, that carried away Welsh iron, coal and steel to the far reaches of the world.

But if you are standing on the coast at Portishead, watching the ships sail in to the Port of Bristol, as they still do, then this is an English place, a waterway that connected England with its Empire, along which the slavers operated, the pirates worked, and the discoverers of tobacco imported their goods. From the Estuary's southern coast, Wales was seen as a distant, difficult land populated by malcontents and barbarians. Trade was slight and connection sporadic. until the Industrial Revolution changed everything of course.

On the tip of Worm's Head, in full sun and with visibility almost the whole way to America, or so it seems, I try to decide if my goal has actually been reached. Do I now know the Estuary? Have I found out just what it is? Behind me, sea mist descends again covering Rhossili. Looking west the waters shift and blur. The Estuary is too big to contain, impossible to know completely. My understanding is much greater now than when I started. But up ahead there's always more.

The Land and the Water

Inexorably they move together. You can't see it but land here is sinking. It has been since the last ice age when the great sheets, miles thick, that pressed the northern parts of these islands into the ground began to melt. Freed of their encumbrance, the rock below began to lift – post-glacial rebound as it's known – and Scotland began being pushed up into the air at the rate of a centimetre a year. But at our island's other extremity, down here where the Cornish peninsular and the fringes of Wales face the withering Atlantic, the land is subsiding, descending slowly among its shales, mudstones and limestone sheets. Going down.

I've walked it, nearly all of it, along this enormous Estuary, at some time or other. It was just land meeting sea when I first encountered it as a child, taken to the pebbles of Penarth to watch the brown waves crash on the grey rocks under a sun reluctant to shine for too long. Did the ground move? Who could imagine such a thing?

Recent decades, however, have seen the results of additional slow and irrevocable change. Fiercer seas, higher coastal walls, flood water on the streets, sandbags where there were never sandbags before. The globe warms and the ice caps return their waters to the oceans. The land sinks as the seas rise.

Coming up the Estuary is a waterway so wide that all sense of land containment has vanished. There is no hint that this ceaseless rippling expanse of grey-brown sea might be a harbinger of our collective future. J.G. Ballard in *The Drowned World*[1] postulates a water-locked, dystopian land, barracked with silt and entangled with Jurassic plant life. His drowned, future London is a "nightmare world of competing organic forms returning rapidly to their Palaeozoic past". The planet, but not quite as it is now. Stephen Baxter, in *The Flood*[2], has a different take. Here the waters rise, predictably at first, and then unaccountably not ceasing. They drown the towns, the cities, and then move on to the hills. The Welsh mountains and the moors of the West Country become islands. Tors and peaks emerge from the advancing seas as last bastions for civilized life. Eventually all that is left are the high peaks of Snowdon and the crowning rock outcrop of Scafell Pike, phone masts on top. They bear the flags of their nations, a last hurrah to who we were. Then they vanish under the unrelenting waves.

Already the Severn has shown what it can do. Four hundred years ago flood waters swamped the levels on both sides from Carmarthen to Gloucester (see p.85). Farms, castles and turnpikes went under. There was great loss of life and, among a God-fearing Christian population, the idea that this was retribution, the work of the Devil. The land was filled with dread. From out there on the choppy oceans it could come again. The defences we've since built along the coastal edges are testament to our continuing fears. Build a wall. Keep the sea out.

And we could build and build those walls, a great water-repelling stone and iron fence surrounding our countries. The sea risen a hundred metres, the land surface languishing in the dark swampy shadow a hundred metres below. We could save ourselves and, like Malé, capital of the Indian Ocean Maldives built large, hang on as we were. We could do that. But we probably won't.

Architects, being the visionaries they sometimes are, have proposed alternative futures. Already in Holland, houses float. They sit on watertight basements and when the waters flood they rise on their tethers to bob on the water's surface. When the waters recede they return to hard land. Each dwelling has a floating front path and a small boat. There are also proposals out there for whole retreating cities. Conurbations will be built hard on the coast's edge but sitting on rails. As the waters advance, these new retreating villages with their buildings mounted on concrete skids and iron rails, will be dragged back up the coastal plateau to higher ground. Whole urban complexes will shift inland. Architects from the London-based firm, Smout Allen, have made proposals which suggest that threatened future cities will move as if they were boats being hauled from the waves.

And if our Welsh estuarial conurbations and structures cannot be hauled away from the sea on rails then they could be made to hover. Architectural fantasists have suggested structures that can be attached to air balloons and allowed to move upwards into the skies. Cloud City has already been proposed as an emergency solution for New York should Manhattan succumb to rising water and hurricanes. Somehow though, in the Severn Estuary's prevailing westerlies, I can't see that quite working here.

What might be the Estuary's nearer future? As of 2011, following the collapse of part of Fontygary Caravan Park onto the beach below, the Welsh Government has put in place a new flood and coastal erosion strategy. It calls it that and it's good politics to be seen to be responding to events. In reality, however, it differs little from that which held sway on both the Welsh and English sides of the Channel before. Hold the line and where that's not possible step back[3]. There's a future out there of rising water and steady withdrawal. As the walls are threatened and topped by the sea, first on exceptional days and then increasingly far more regularly, they are left as they are. Managed retreat.

The Severn Estuary and the Severn Sea are such an attraction to those who live nowhere near them. Water has such an enormous pull, which is something I, who live right by it, find hard to understand. On a trip to the USSR, back in the days of the country's communist bid for world domination, my state-allocated female minder took me on a trip south to the Caspian

14

Sea. I was on an exchange visit, a young writer the communists clearly wanted to influence. We'd started from land-locked Moscow, where she lived in a regulation tower block among the vodka-drinking masses and babushkas with fat bellies and empty baskets hanging on their arms. My minder was used to life in the cold land-locked northern cities. It was all she knew. We flew south across the great and endless lands of the Soviet Union. When we eventually reached the Caspian, a flat and oil-scummed pool on the sand-coloured Steppes, with no rock edge nor wave action, no seaweed, no wind-blown white horses, no seaside paraphernalia of donkey rides and whelk stalls, none of that, she rushed forward and on her knees washed her face in the bitter waters. The sea, the sea. She'd never seen it before. The coast was a place to which she had never been. Despite the oil derricks stretching out across the waters and the presence of the ugly smoking city of Baku to our backs, for her this was a revelatory and holy moment. For me it was just a visit to a distant pond.

On the Severn's coasts I get the sense that despite its omnipresence and categorically certain rise, our sense of the sea is in retreat. In the city ports of Bristol, Cardiff, Newport, Barry, Port Talbot and Swansea the docklands are being engulfed by gentrification. Fine new apartments. Places to dine on lobster and duck with black bean sauce. Dock traffic is a fraction of what it once was. There are so few ships at sea. The dock labour force has shrivelled. Men do not leave port in trawlers looking for fish. The docklands themselves are surrounded by high security fences, the short cuts down port roads are no longer open, the truncated Royal Navy visit less frequently. They don't have the ships. The whole sense of us as a maritime nation is in retreat. City dwellers and, increasingly, those who live further out in the dormitory coastal towns and villages, are losing their sense of being by water. They take no part, they do not look. Seafaring words like *offing* and *anchor* no longer litter their language. They do not toe the line. They have never slung their hooks. There are those in Gloucestershire who do not know their county has a coast line. I've met students in the centre of Cardiff who do not regard the capital as a port city, are unaware of the true extent of its water front and, in any event, do not recognise the sea for what it is even when standing at water's edge. Flat Holm and Steep Holm lie out there on the real sea. The island beacons proof that these maritime places are seen as a sort of wallpaper. If they are seen at all.

But tell this to the sea fishermen who occupy the difficult to access coastal rocks with their rods and their hip flasks and you'll get a very different answer. So too, from the increasing number of coastal walkers and those who sail from the honey-pot marinas or the muddy pills that dot both English and Welsh coasts. It's not all lost.

French sailors from a port visit by one of their navy's coastal minesweepers were seen wandering the capital's nightclub streets. They looked very French and extremely maritime in their whites, their bell bottoms and their red bobble-topped sailor's hats. But among the drunken revellers dressed as vampires, schoolgirls, lumberjacks and characters from super-hero movies they came over more as a stag party who'd spent a bit more than usual on their costumes. The sea, the sea. Not anymore.

How Big is the Estuary?

Where does it begin? Where does it end? The Severn is tidal with ebb and flow detectable as far north as Maisemore, above Gloucester. But that far inland, the waters are clearly riverine. As an estuarial landscape the Severn doesn't really begin until it flows under the Severn Bridge at Aust. Here the river is two miles wide and has cut down through the Triassic Marls to gouge a channel deep into the underlying Carboniferous Limestone. This marks where the river once flowed, two hundred and fifty million years ago, in Permian times. The rock layers are all visible in the cliffs here: the limestones, the shales and the marls. The deeper Permian gully now forms the Severn's shipping route up through the Shoots, over the Tunnel, under the two bridges and on to the small ports upstream.

Most of what we see today is a drowned river valley in a place where the hard and older rocks of limestone Wales meet the younger and more readily erodible shales. Limestone outcrops form the islands of Flat Holm and Steep Holm, and the cliff promontory at Brean Down. They are the hilltops of the land as it once was.

If the Estuary begins at Aust then it ends either at a line drawn between Brean Down and Lavernock, or between the Doone Valley and Sker Point. Further west, the Estuary becomes the Bristol Channel and beyond that the Celtic Sea. In extent the region covers 55,684 hectares of water and has 353 kilometres of often fragile coast.

This is the place that everyone quotes as having the second highest tides in the world. The victor in this contest of moving waters being the Bay of Fundy in Nova Scotia, Canada. There the gap between flow and ebb can be as much as fifty-three and a half feet. The Severn Estuary's maximum is forty-six. Every place I've been along these coasts has claimed the record for their own: Cardiff, Barry, Newport, Penarth, Portishead, Burnham-on-Sea and Severn Beach. The record holder is actually Avonmouth. At Barry the tidal range reduces to thirty-three feet while at Cardiff it's slightly less again. Not that any of these gaps between high and low tide are a walk in the park. They are all dramatic to witness and have far-reaching effects on the shape and life of the lands they rise between.

Upstream of the two Severn bridges, the inward rush of the tides rising through a narrowing estuary becomes a moving wave known as the Severn Bore. This carries boats, swimmers, bodyboarders and surfers north from Overton near Fretherne to Maisemore in Gloucester. In the Estuary proper the effect of the tides are no less intense. The wide and slowly flowing river, moving at the pace of a glacier, so it seems, becomes mudrock and emerged land at the snap of the fingers. Green coastlines expand outwards in a rush to join with their fellows on the other side. The river shrinks down towards its prehistorical original course, a deep watercourse lost in a wide and brown landscape. The Severn world now looks like the moon or Mars, or at least as we imagine those places to be.

Who Runs It?

Free space, common water, the open sea. How can anyone own this place? The beaches are ours, the rocks that lie below the reach of the tides belong to no one and everyone – if we conveniently skip, that is, the bit about tidal waters and geopolitical ownership of the continental shelves and those things we've heard about the Russians, leaving a specially waterproofed national flag on rocks below the ice of the arctic seas. Despite there being no uniformed patrols nor evidence of authority, these waters still have to be managed. Someone must look after where they go, what's in them, and how they impact on the lives of those who live on and around them. That's a lot of people – more than a million at the last count.

There are fragile environments here – saltmarshes, intertidal mudflats, sandbanks, landscapes rich in drowned archaeology, places where wading birds still hold sway. Someone needs to protect these places from the advances of sand dredgers, the builders of power stations and those who want to establish new holiday villages among the shining mud stretches. Those who wish to dig ever down to create new deep water ports for the next generation of Ultra Large Container Vessels (ULCVs), the new sea leviathans, coming this way soon.

And someone does. Stretches of the water and much of the coastline have already been declared as special. There are Special Protection Areas, Sites of Special Scientific Interest, Special Areas of Conservation, a European Marine Site, and areas designated by the Ramsar Convention as Wetland of International significance. These designated areas – the SPAs and the SSSIs and the rest, there are so many of them – are policed by just as many agencies: the English Government and the Welsh Government's Environment Agencies[4]; local government; the River Authorities; the Drainage Boards and the Port Authorities; the harbour masters; Trinity House; the water companies; Natural England; and the Countryside Council for Wales.

The agencies band together. It's the only way they can make their multi-faceted and overlapping requirements work. At the offices of the Severn Estuary Partnership, a loose confederation of interested parties, I meet Paul Parker, their officer and guiding light. The Partnership[5] is based at the School of Earth and Ocean Sciences at Cardiff University and acts as a research base, meeting place, neutral platform, consultation body and information exchange for its hundreds of members. The Partnership has thrown its net wide and opened itself to everyone from the expected government agencies, commercial interest and national concerns to local interest organisations, fishermen, sailors, environmentalists, walkers and individuals with an interest in these waters.

"We have no formal powers," Paul is quick to tell me. "We currently have no desire to become any kind of designated authority. We do not represent a single viewpoint. We bring people together and identify the issues that collectively face us." And for this great Estuary what are those? Renewable energy, marine planning and climate change. The Estuary has two new nuclear plants under proposal for construction at Hinkley Point and at Oldbury. There are calls for more. Tidal power is an obvious developing area. The barrage is an issue. The recent Maritime and Coastal Access Act requires there to be a marine plan. We don't have one yet. For once Wales will have to co-operate with England in production and we'll end up with two documents. They'll snuggle up against each other along that line where England meets Wales, running down centre channel. The Welsh Government has already said that for all kinds of reasons there cannot be a joint plan, but that as a nation, Wales will contribute to planning jointly. Civil servant speak at its best. But then again the Estuary is big enough.

Climate change is the Partnership's biggest concern. Flood defence, managed retreat, resource vs. need, the economics of working where advancing water threatens to undermine whole communities. What's the future? That's the future. In thirty years' time it'll be the same major concern. Rising water, warming air.

The Partnership began in 1997 by issuing a joint report[6] that listed some 360 issues that faced the Severn Estuary and identifying more than 300 potential partners. By 2001 the group had published a response: *The Strategy For The Severn Estuary*[7]. Maps, concerns, questions, solutions. It's a vast work in progress. Everything is in there – from the need to undertake periodic surveys of drainage outfalls and sluices to responsibly expanding our ports – from accessing the value of heritage fisheries to coping with the water's rise. It's work that will not end as the Partnership's recent comprehensive summary, *The State of the Severn Estuary Report*[8] (Autumn 2011), is testament.

I push Paul for a view on the viability of the now much touted proposed barrage but like the good administrator he is he stays silent. The Partnership encompasses views from all sides. The greens vs. the industrialists. The environmentalists vs. the extractors. The historians vs. the builders. The pleasure seekers vs. the river employed. The Welsh vs. the English. Is that a problem? I get a smile but no answer.

Walking Again

There are only two real ways to view the Estuary. To sail on it and to walk along its sides. Some might argue that standing on a surf board in your wet suit doing twenty-one kilometres an hour towards Gloucester is the only real way, and that's certainly an exciting one. I've chosen, however, to get most of my experience by walking. Foot before foot. Cars can never hack it. Bikes are good but the walls, gates, stiles and mud stretches slow them down. Sometimes the route I follow is official, often it is not.

I want to see just where it is that Wales ends and how the world is right there. Are there whirlpools, waters falling over the edge of the map and sea monsters breathing fire? Does the air change its shape? Are the ley lines clashing here? Or do they simply ignore the artificiality of nationhood and, like the tectonic plates, roll on across the ground?

I'll do this mostly from the Welsh side but I'll also visit England. I want to look out and I also want to look back. I want also to sail and to paddle. Y Hafren, as it is in Welsh, Sabrina, which is what the Romans called it, the Severn. This is water, after all, I need to get wet.

Sailing on the Waters

As long as there have been boats they have sailed on these seas. In the age of the saints, in the dark ages, after the Romans had left and before the Vikings came, these waters were a sort of motorway. They offered a safer passage between Wales and England, Wales and Ireland, and on to Brittany and Scotland. In currachs and wickerwork ships, people traded, travelled and the saints went with them. St Petroc, St Cadoc, St Gwbert, St Brioc, St Breaca, St Dyfrig, St Ninian, St David, St Samson and St Carantoc all spread their brand of independent Celtic Christianity across the Western lands. They sailed on, west, out to sea where there's nothing between the old world and the new, bar serpentine monsters, to discover America. So many of them did this, setting off from each of their Celtic nations, that it is no wonder the United States has the independence of spirit and the wild accents it currently does. Brendan and Madoc, see what you've done.

To judge by the number of marinas, quays, boat clubs, pill pull-ins, and other protected landings on both sides of the Estuary, from where it starts way up river to where it runs out at the end of Devon and the promontories of Pembrokeshire, you'd imagine the Severn to be permanently full of plying yachts. Sails endlessly turning, men in denim captains' caps standing at their tillers, women in striped tops bracing themselves before the Atlantic breeze. As a leisure activity boating on these waters has increased more than tenfold since the war. But it remains a leisure activity. More time at mooring, for waiting the tides than out there facing the waves. Longer being repainted, thought about, scraped, polished, having the engine replaced, and sails fixed than actually at sea. Stand on the coast, anywhere you like. Count the sea-borne craft you see. You'll be hard put to spot more than you can manage on a single hand.

Add on the commercial traffic: the container ships, the tankers, the bulk carriers, the ferries, the dredgers, the occasional visiting warship (destroyers never aircraft carriers), the odd submarine (but you don't see them, other than in port), the pilots, and the increasingly rare coastguards, and what you get is sparse, spare activity. It's a slow place despite the winds and the wild tides. If you want to see ships go to Singapore and Hong Kong, watch them cluster those ports in their hundreds. Out here, in the west, our nations are only just still maritime.

In boats, of course, you do not nip. There's no quick launch and cross immediately to where you are going. Unlike the car, which will get over the bridge and back in a morning, trips by water need to be planned. They are slow things requiring access to the mooring, safety checking, good forward planning as to where you are going and then some consideration of the tides. In fact, huge consideration of the tides. Tides here can make or break any travel. Arrive at the wrong time and you can be stuck for twelve hours. Pick a stormy day and you can either never leave where you are tied up or, alternatively, not be able to land at the place you are going. Visitors to Lundy get stranded and have to be taken off by helicopter. Travellers to Flat Holm find their trips abandoned when the water turns out to be too rough. Health and safety regulations prevent mariners from doing what they once did. "You're okay mate, just leap, we'll catch you." Can't do that. The passengers may slip and then there'd be a court case and so much money would change hands that the boat would need to be sold. Best not to do it. Best not to even set out. Flat Holm, who wants to go there? But hundreds still do. The Severn is not always choppy.

Ports

The Estuary is rich with docks, a residue of the Industrial Age, of the times when people sailed the world in great liners and coal ships chased them around. Of the age when iron and steel from these islands went right across the globe. When our exports beat those of contemporary China and India combined. When south Wales was the world's Saudi and the West of England its America.

The principal docks we built then hang on, but almost all of them reduced in size and ambition. The main players[9] are still Bristol with its twin docks at Avonmouth and at Portbury and the once coal metropolis, Cardiff. Add on the commercial docks at Newport, Swansea, Barry and Port Talbot with perhaps the odd sand wharf at places like Briton Ferry and lay up at Bridgwater, plus the still operating landings at Sharpness and Gloucester and that's it. At first glance more docks than shipping. Bristol manages more than seven million tonnes annually[10]. Port Talbot, delivering coal to the steel plant, handles nine million. Cardiff just over two. Everywhere else handles far less. Bristol is the largest in size at over two thousand acres, Cardiff follows at just below a thousand.

Ambition, however, is not dead. Swansea is looking to a future trade with cruise ships and has already had the white ghost, *The World,* moored out at sea in Swansea Bay. Port Talbot and Bristol are developing deep water, super container ship facilities with Avonmouth already granted permission to construct a new Deep Sea Container terminal[11]. All this Western world needs now is an end to depression and a return of growth. We tread water while we wait.

The Water

The waters themselves are not Mediterranean blue. Far from it. In fact the nearest they ever get to blue is a sort of rich slate-grey. They are thick with silt in suspension, soil emulsified, translucent but never transparent. Put your hand below the surface and it will vanish. As the waters come down the Severn River and its tributaries, they bring with them eroded earth in quantity. Sediment solubility is low. The particles stay suspended. This gives the Estuary its distinctive grey-brown sheen, its look of polluted despondency, its air of unhealthy radiance, and its glistening brown banks. The days of genuine pollution, when industry spilled its waste into the waterway in quantity, are now largely over. Today I wouldn't say you could drink from the Severn without impunity but you can certainly wade through it without having your skin burn off. Myths of the Severn Estuary – it is full of poison. It is not.

Gulls

At my house I am being interviewed by a student from the journalism college. She's interested in the gull menace. I had no idea there was one. "You don't read the *Echo*?" "No, I don't." "Well, if you did you'd know. There are too many of these birds, they are everywhere." I'd never considered that a problem; that the gulls having found a way to live where industrialisation has wrecked their natural habitat and pollution has destroyed their food sources is a victory for natural adaptability. Eco eco. There's one out there on my flat roof now, a huge thing. I can hear it as it walks across the grey fibreglass, a clatter of webbed feet, a skittering. It's eating chicken it has found at the landfill site at Lamby Way to the east of here. Whoever threw it away didn't want it. Gulls, the great recyclers. They don't bother me. "Have you written about them?" "No, not yet, but I will now." Sure indicators of the sea, gulls. Portents of the Estuary. I like them a lot.

The Port of Cardiff – Where It All Begins

When did I discover that Cardiff, the place where I was born, was a port? From where I lived I couldn't see the sea. There wasn't a sea. You went on trips to the beach at weekends on a rattling train, smoke streaming back across the fields, smuts in your eyes. You had no idea of geography or distance. No idea about the way that in this world everything was connected to everything else. If Cardiff was a port then Cardiff would be on the sea. If Cardiff was on the sea that meant Cardiff had a coast. It had to. Yet those beaches I'd been taken to at Barry Island, at Lavernock, at Porthcawl, they could have been on Mars. You stood at the top of Penylan Hill, near the disused quarry with the pool at its centre and the folk myth about how a lorry and load, a whole horse and a cart, a Roman and a chariot, had tumbled in and vanished under its still and glinting waters. You stood there and gazed out across the Estuary. To Weston Super Mare, to Clevedon, to Burnham. On Sea. Burnham-on-Sea. But that wasn't a sea you saw, just mud. Unpalatable. Water.

On clear days you could touch the Somerset coast. See the buildings, the greenness, the line where the sea hit sand and there were donkeys in lines you could ride on. Deck chairs. Brown and red striped windbreaks. Men with handkerchiefs knotted on their heads and trousers rolled up. Tea on trays. Castles and forts built against the incoming tides. You sat in your trunks and you smiled and smiled and shivered. That's what you did where the land met the sea. On the coast.

That this place could have been seafaringly vital just never occurred to me. This estuary of the Severn, with a great river's mouth marked on the map, a whole sixteen miles across, had once been an industrial waterway of massive distinction. And it still was during my childhood, just.

Ships to me, to most Cardiffians, were specks. Unless those Cardiffians lived at the bottom end of Splott or Grangetown where the docks loomed and the masts could been seen rising between the houses. Or actually worked there, as dockers, as loaders, as coal cutters, as men with black faces and callused hands. But most Cardiffians simply did not.

Cardiff, capital, dirty port, once holder of the honour of being the greatest coal exporter in the industrial world. Most of its inhabitants knew it was thus. But few of them walked the streets whistling jaunty airs, wearing captains' hats, sailors' bell bottoms, tight knitted navy blue Guernsey sweaters, tattooed chain and anchors on their arms.

I moved on in my ignorance, floating wind-up battle cruisers in the bath and taking toy yachts to sail down in the Roath Brook. Stayed like this for years until my father took me down the great length of Bute Street, passed the cafes, the bars and the bustle, to enter the Dock gates on Bute Place and walk in among the trains and smoke and great noise to see the ships. Dozens of them. Merchant men. Tramps. Steamers. Tankers. Masts and iron ore, coal and dust. Yep. This was a port all right. Men as dirty as I'd ever seen a human. Iron boots. Hard faces. The real Cardiff.

Cardiff, it turned out, had been a port for a long time. These docks my father was walking me through, full of cranes and captured water, were a comparatively recent arrival. There was nothing here much older than one hundred and fifty years. The canal from Merthyr reached the town in 1798, terminating in a great canal basin and lock (now mostly a park and the sea lock lost). In the Bute Docklands, before that, there was little but slurry. The Town of Cardiff had a wharf running beside the Taff where Quay Street now intersects with Westgate Street. The Taff flowed in a different cut back then. There were minor quays also on the Rhymney and the Ely where small boats could pull up to offload salt, wine, pottery and fish in return for hides, butter, flannel, kelp, and knitted stockings. Before the Quay, the Normans had been here pulling their ships up loose onto the banks. Before them the Romans had built a fort at the place where the Tamion met the Fluvius Sabrina[12], and landed boats on the foreshore in the mud.

In 1559 with the entire Glamorgan coast controlled by the Earls of Pembroke and Worcester, the Crown moved to designate Cardiff as a Head Port. This was a device which enabled the King to collect Welsh customs revenues by wresting financial control of the ragged south Wales trade from his courtiers, thus bolstering the Royal treasury. Royal customs officers were appointed and given command of every dock, pill, creek, quay and navigable inlet running the whole distance from Chepstow to Worm's Head on Gower. At this time both Sully and Aberthaw were sub-Ports of some significance with several dozen small vessels attached to them. But Cardiff had a castle and was geographically more central. The officers were known as the Customers, Searchers and Surveyors. John Leek was the first Customer and he was welcomed everywhere much the same way that VAT inspectors are welcomed today. The sea world, like the rest of creation, runs on tax dispute, avoidance and collection. Did then. Does now[13]

Cardiff at that time, in those green, sixteenth century thinly peopled days, might have only maintained a population edging at two thousand but as a sea port it was vast. Sixty miles wide as the crow flies. Several hundred if you track the edges of the bending coast. Most of it eroding shale, limestone stacks, alluvial flood plain, or reclaimed flats sunk behind seawalls, notched by inlet, places big enough for a coracle and the odd fishing smack. Hardly anything of sufficient width to tie up a brig of more than fifty tons.

This town of Cardiff, this city, the one I knew, had always been a port, had made its life that way. Owed everything to trade by sea. The early Christians sailed here. King Arthur landed on the Wentlooge flats and made Cardiff his first royal stop. The Vikings raided us. Left streets here with Danish names. The Norman French. The Flemings. The Irish came in their thousands. The Bretons. The Somalis. The Norwegians. The rest of the world on their tails.

From Chepstow, where Welsh influence thins, to Gower, where English has held sway for a thousand years, Cardiff, port of the Welsh capital, runs across lands that struggle with their identity. Lands that switch and change. Lands that loom and fade.

Cardiff is as big as this. Bigger. The estuary it sits upon does not stay still. It erodes and fills, advances by soil deposition, is worn back by rising water and running tides. It's a place of both certainty and of constant change.

At the bumpy start of 2011, I sat down and thought about all this. Given my personal history I knew a bit about this waterway, but considering how long I'd lived right next it, not a huge amount. I knew what it looked like but not how it fitted together. I knew some parts intimately but others not at all. I ought to go out and investigate, and on foot. Of the ways of travel this one is always the best.

I drove out to Chepstow and parked near the town's Welsh-subduing Norman Castle. Pack on back, camera slung, I headed towards where the Celts thought the otherworld began, the Buddhists located enlightenment, and the Egyptians saw the portal to the netherworld – the west.

The East: Chepstow to Redwick

Chepstow

There's a bend in the river here, an *ystraigyl* Wikipedia calls it, from the Welsh it says, as these anglicised reference works often do. It's how it was listed in the Domesday Book. This is a word not included in my Collins-Spurrell[1]. (I still use that little red book. Down the years it's served me well.) We've found the Wye by standing on the platform of Chepstow Station. The tracks are thick with traffic despite this being a Sunday. A high pressure ridge, blue-sky day. Families out walking. Women with toy festooned pushchairs. Men with dogs in the park.

Chepstow, from the Anglo-Saxon *Chepe Stowe*, means a market place. Most of it is on the Welsh side of the river with the English border running right up the centre of the water. On my map this is depicted as a dotted line with spikes. The old Welsh name of *ystraigyl* had become *striguil* by the time the Norman's built the castle. But that appendage didn't last. In contemporary Welsh the town is known as *Cas-Gwent*. Castell Gwent, or Gwent Castle, is a name that only ever seems to get used by the recorded Grahame Davies sound-alike voice reading out the train times at Cardiff Central. *Y tren nesaf syn cyrraed a platform dau yn mynd i Gas Gwent.* O yes.

This is the far eastern end of the Estuary and not really even that since Chepstow lies mostly on the Wye rather than sitting on the Severn. It is a place of linguistic thinness and political uncertainty. A border town that in Ireland would have gun towers and armoured police stations. In Mexico it would have tank-trap defended customs points and razor wire fencing. Here the B4228 quietly rolls east. It passes houses called 'Pen-y-Coed' and 'Afon Gwyn'. It crosses John Rastrick's 1816 cast-iron and elegantly arched Wye bridge to vanish unremarked, other than by the small Welcome to England road sign, into the depths of Gloucestershire.

On the Wye's carboniferous limestone cliffs, on the English side, just above the waterline, a bold Union Jack has been painted. Done by the English, I thought, much as the Greeks do on the Turkish seaboard, laying claim with their flag to the tiniest of rocks. But this is Chepstow and nothing much of historical interest stays dark for long. There's a plaque. The flag was painted in 1935 by "some Chepstow salmon fisherman" to mark King George V's jubilee. The opening next to it is the Gloucester Hole, an entrance to a much larger chamber once used to store the tea of Shirenewton Quakers and explosives for Brunel's railway building. Accessible only from the river side. Equipped with chain and crane.

I'd never much liked Chepstow, passing through it on coaches bound for Heathrow, in cars destined for Gloucester or the Midlands. A hilly place of narrow streets and ancient walls. But today with the sun falling on its unreconstructed ancient-ness and refreshing lack of high-rise apartment and superstore redevelopment, I can see its charms. This is a town and not a city. In Wales such places rarely change.

Things to like:

Sun
No graffiti
Information everywhere

Largest and best equipped Tourist Information Centre I've ever been in, which included an assistant who can't do enough for you, and a Seren Books spinner containing, in quantity, at least four of my books
Dozens of pubs
Live acoustic music billed all over the place
Places that are open on Sunday
Readings of poetry

This last is a poster advertising William Ayot's latest in his ambitious 'On The Border' series presented at the town's Drill Hall. Next month: Oliver Reynolds and Douglas Dunn. I've done one of these, splendidly presented one winter evening by the colourful, castle-living[2] Ayot. I read with poet and children's author, Kit Wright. Possibly the tallest poet on the planet. We'd been equipped with radio microphones clipped to our waists and lapels, tested their clarity and range and been told to turn them off until we were announced on stage. Neither of us quite did this. We strolled to the gents talking about past times, the fractiousness of the poetry scene, our views of our host (good), opinions on the bookseller (plenty of Kit's books, not enough of mine) and considerations of the audience (large, middle-class, undoubtedly book buyers, one man in a luminous blue track-suit who would probably leave half way through, no hippies). We touched on politics, discussed women and then drinking, and both peed diligently in parallel and echoing urinals. The entire discourse was, of course, broadcast at full volume to the assembling poetry-loving crowd. We got a small cheer when we came out. On stage I got more laughs but Kit sold more books.

Not that life is all book sales. Even though some people might imagine it to be so. At the Tourist Information Centre at the side of the Castle Car Park (free on Sundays), the assistant asks me if I'm thinking of moving to the area. I've been pumping her with questions. "No, I'm writing a book about the Estuary. The Severn. This place where Wales meets England." "Really. Will you be including anything on the Aust Ferry?" This was the ramshackle, seventeen vehicles at a time, predecessor to the first Seven Bridge which opened in 1966. Famously Bob Dylan appears in Martin Scorsese's film, *No Direction Home,* standing at the Aust terminal, waiting to cross to Beachley on the Welsh side. The electrified Judas, dark glasses, John Cooper Clarke hair, a surrealistic prophet of all our futures, plays the Cardiff Capitol. For reasons I can now not understand (although probably money), I did not attend.

The *Severn Princess*, last of the Aust ferries, is being restored. Local school-teacher Tim Ryan found it abandoned at a remote wharf in County Galway, Ireland, and brought it back. It's in dry dock near the Bridge Works, I'm told. Awaiting restoration. Being repaired. After a brief lope across Riverside Gardens, we discover it on a patch of wasteland where Brunel's broad gauge-carrying Great Tubular Suspension bridge (manufactured by Edward Finch and Company in 1852) once stood. It's pulled up on the bank below the Brunel Bridge replacement, rusted to buggery, with no name visible, cabin doors red enough for the Kalahari Desert, wooden deck unravelling, deck rails vanished, and holes in her hull. It's hard to see how anything here might now ever be salvageable. Or, indeed, what work might have been done by the restoration group reported hard at it in the mid-2000s. Fixable now, I'd say, only by replacing every single part.

Outside La Bodega Susan (grilled sardines £5.95) on Riverside Walk another of the town's myriad plaques announces that in 1840, from this very spot, John Frost, William Jones and Zephaniah Williams, convicted leaders of the Chartist march on Newport, were transported to Van Diemen's Land. Tasmania. Other side of the known world. Below it a small brass plate tells us that historical novelist, the late Alexander Cordell, unveiled the plaque in 1985. April. We are precise in our recollection. Although in reality the past bends, melds, swims and flows.

There has been a port at Chepstow as long as there's been a river here. Ships running from the wilds of the outer estuary could find calm at the town's many wharfs. The Wye bends here. It loops around the Piercefield Cliffs, a rocky salient carrying an iron age fort, around the limestone promontory on which the Normans built a castle and then the town itself, to slope past a second fort at Bulwark and finally meet the sea and the Severn two miles to the south. Trade at the wharfs at the end of the eighteenth century was greater than that of Swansea, Cardiff and Newport combined. Wood, coal, hides, tea, meat, iron.

Edward Finch, who came to Chepstow from Liverpool to build Brunel's bridge, stayed. His works along the Wye, south of the walled town made wrought and cast-iron bridges, dock gates, gasometers, masts, and then, in the later 1800s, actual ships. The *S.S. Rovigo*. The iron screw tug *Red Rose*. The *Radyr*. The *Rougemont*. The *Carcavellos*. The *Royal Briton*. At its height the company had twelve berths and operated on both sides of the river. His works subsequently became part of World War One's National Shipyards and were succeeded by Fairfield-Mabey operating from the same site. Today, Mabey are still very much a going concern. They build footbridges, panel bridges, road bridges, rail bridges and gantry towers at a clean smoke-less site on low Welsh land between the rail line and the Wye water. They've recently opened a wind turbine tower manufac-turing facility capable of turning out more than 300 annually and have started winning contracts. The future is tall and it spins. Green but thick with controversy.

Coming in on my iPhone is the news. Governments are still lying. The radiation leaks in Japan are controlled. The truth is something they hold back lest we riot in the face of it. The population cannot ever be told what's really happening. The politicians say what the world wants to hear, enough anyway to get themselves voted back. The rads are rising. From here I can touch Oldbury, feel Berkeley trembling, sense Hinkley A and Hinkley B pressing in on my skin. Yesterday I was only dimly aware. Today I have concern. Where next in the rush for energy? Following Fukushima the future nuclear option clouds. Instead the world will turn to less effective renewables: river generators, tidal rotors, solar panelling, biomass briquettes, biomass gasifi-cation, artificial photosynthesis, twig burners, heat pumps, wind turbines reaching for the sky from every hillock. Few here yet, in the southern marches. And when there are more what will we get? 4% of our energy needs, Severn Barrage excepted, if we are lucky. Hinkley C, they'll build you yet.

Walking south from the heart of ancient Chepstow is not as straightforward as it might seem. The river banks are dense with the same glossy boot-sucking, impossible-to-remove sinking mud as the estuaries of the Taff, Ely and Rhymney back at base. Tracks are sparse, blocked by cliff and entangled bramble, and then there's the hazardous, great mass of the Bridge Works itself. The town is a soft unzoned mix of the gentle and the industrial, living proof that mix is better than separation. You walk to work. You can see the gates from your window.

Bulwark is the first place we reach. It's where two thirds of the local population reside and sits south of the Castle's old town. It runs a post-war, traditional council-build mix of semi and terrace right down into the next river place, the private development at Thornwell further south. Thornwell's Brookside houses sit directly opposite the Army apprentice barracks at Beachley Head. That's the spot, co-incidentally, where J.K. Rowling allegedly went courting. Above flies the first Severn Crossing. A world wonder when opened but now just a creaking bridge.

We zip through these overparked streets, narrowed by retracted wing-mirror and rear lights. As you roll, the populace stare, those who are up. They hang on their bikes and regard you. Watch from their front gardens. Look up from changing the oil or rebandaging leaking exhausts. Pause in their pavement conversations. You've ridden in, stranger. What do you want? You are not from here.

At Warren Slade, in the Chepstow district of Thornwell, we descend through Park Redding Woods to slip under the rail tracks and hit the Wye River Path. Amazingly there is one. It runs south along the top of a flood defence, an earth embankment that wouldn't stop much more than a metre rise in average high tides.

Trains pass. Six car units with numbers I might have captured in my youth when I collected such things. Kept in a book. Underlined in my guide to British rail rolling stock and loco units. Data. Unextended. Unformed. Aimless. But in that very lack of purpose is somehow a sign of the future. Ahead is a line of sheep, tracking the same muck as we are. To the west the setting sun casting great shadows, making the river mud gleam like polished chrome.

The borders all meet out there in the water. It's a place of endings, of blendings, of changings. Green over. Transparency finishes. Hard becomes soft. Mon turns to Glos. Wye becomes Severn. Wales becomes England. Out there where St Tecla[3]'s ruined chapel and its holy well sit on rocks off

Beachley. End of an Alfred Watkins ley. The finish of power, or its start. From overhead, up on the bridge walkway, someone waves. Hello, goodbye. The essence of this place.

The Gwent Levels

Beyond the relative density of Chepstow is the start of an empty space. The Gwent Levels. The flatlands. Replicas of them surround the entire northern reaches of the Severn Estuary. From Gloucester to Cardiff and from Slimbridge to the Somerset Levels south of Brean Down. It's an entirely artificial landscape. If it were not for human intervention this land would not be here. It is reclaimed from the waters, hidden behind seawall, and drained by a complex system of channels. A new sweet land. Sunk slightly as the water went from it. Water blown out to sea by gouts[4], one-way valves that open to let the land water drain away at low tide, that close again when the sea comes sweeping back.

The coast here has migrated a considerable distance over time. The water level today is at least two metres higher than it was when the Romans came. It was lower again before that. On that lost land there were once forests, Mesolithic trackways, Iron Age housing, Bronze Age huts, fishing henges, shaped flints, medieval boats, posts, poles, wattle fencing, farmland, bush, scrub, discarded pottery, coins, the remains of metal working, and palaeochannels that flowed millennia back. All now vanished below layers of alluvial gunk, peat, stone, and grey-green, mud-brown water.

Over time, sea walling and attendant channelling has drained great sections. Only to have them inundated again when the walling became abandoned, or was breached by storm. New sediment was deposited, new peat formed. The Romans began the draining process. It was continued by the Normans and, through a succession of rise and fall, ran on through the medieval period right up to the nineteenth century. No Roman remains are extant apart, perhaps, from the lines of some fields, but there are relics of medieval building – west of Collister Pill near Caldicot is a listed section. The present walls largely follow the sixteenth century line, straightening it where twentieth century sea level rise enhancements have been created. Near Chepstow, where I am right now, the sinuously snaking walls are barely wide enough to have a sheep walk on top. As they straighten towards Newport you can fit on a car. Sea fishermen do.

Behind the bund, the fields are drained by a hierarchy of ditches. Ridge and vurrow on the surface running to larger gullies known as grips and then on into a network of ditches at the fields' edges. The ditches then empty into minor water channels known as lesser reens. These outspill into the major reens which take their burgeoning content seawards. Here they either breach the wall itself or empty into an existing inlet or creek. The inlets are called Pills. From the Welsh, *pwll*, transliterated to English, as these things often are, by a population who recognised no standard spellings or ways of writing down sounds. Water management is aided by pens constructed among the reens. Here wooden planks, called stanks, are raised and lowered to control levels.

The system is a finely balanced co-operation between landowner, the Caldicot and Wentlooge Levels Internal Drainage Board, the Environment Agency and the local authority. Fail in your part and land gets lost. Water starts to lap the rail tracks. The world ends.

This process of sea rise, wall build, land reclamation, wall abandonment, further sea inundation, wall rebuild and land re-reclamation has resulted in a land surface rich in layered alluvium. Beyond the present wall the salt marsh steps down at least three times towards to water. The landscape here is rich in peat islands, grassy hummocks separated by pooled salt water, mud channel and reed. In summer, livestock are grazed here. The occasional fisherman digs for bait. There are drifted stacks of sea-washed brushwood. Wading birds predominate. There are no wrecked cars, dumped hard-core or abandoned shopping trollies. If there were, you wouldn't see them. Nothing much stays on the surface for long. The peat layers extend downwards for ten metres.

Archaeologically the area is as rich as anywhere in Britain, thanks to the Severn's importance as a seaway. Over millennia its course has altered. What was once coastline can now be found miles inland. The enormously wide tidal range of the river along with its breadth has led to archaeology by wader, zipping out with shovel and apparatus between inundations. Lifting blocks of mud. Digging pits. Plank walling. Mud flat walking. Finding the marks we make on the landscape and the things we leave behind. Photographing, mapping, recording. Watching the tide come back to cover everything once again.

When I was a kid, back in Cardiff's big city, no one came to this place. No one had heard of the Gwent Levels. No one except Martin Flanner. Flanner was alleged to come from somewhere beyond Llanwern, out there on the flatlands. East of Newport. Although Flanner never quite told us where.

Not that they were called the Gwent Levels then. Apart from in the history books there was no Gwent. East of Newport lay the rural green hinterland of Monmouthshire. Foreign lands. The Marches. England perhaps. Not Wales. The Levels were places with which the Capital had no connection.

At Martin's house, weekdays, we raided his elder brother's record collection. Roy Orbison, Bobby Darin, Everly Brothers. His brother was learning guitar and quite fancied himself as a sort of Welsh-version of Phil Everly. Sang in the bathroom. 'Bye Bye Love'. Among the echoing porcelain, harmonising beautifully alone.

Flanner's family, it turned out, was Plymouth Brethren. His father, who worked for the water board, was a strict adherent. The world rolled during the week but as Sunday approached it would begin to stumble and, when the great day came, fell. There were sequences of services all day at the Brethren's meeting hall and the Flanner household would attend every one. At the end of a full eight hours of constant praising they would still not be done. They'd finish by visiting the houses of Brethren friends for fish paste sandwiches and tea, and stand round the piano to sing with shining faces just a few more hymns to round off the day. There were no Sunday ball games, no fiddling with your stamp collection, no comics, no newspapers, no idle talk of worldly matters. The radio was kept off. Guitars stayed in their cases.

You became better people. Martin told me this as we stood in the lane smoking a cigarette before heading off to school. Consulate Menthol, cool as a mountain stream. The only tobacco I could manage without coughing. "Are you better than me then?" I asked him. "My mother says so," he replied. No answer to that.

Imagining the Levels riddled with Gospel Halls and Brethren Meeting Rooms, I decided this must be a flatlands thing.

St Pierre

I'm in the car now, on the M48, heading back to the coast. I've been home, regrouping, cleaning my boots, checking my photographs, writing up my notes. I've got Martin Sheen on the radio. It's been more than a decade since he served his second term on *The West Wing* but he still sounds like Potus. Josiah Edward Bartlett, forty-third President of the United States. Right now he's on *Desert Island Discs*.

He's not really called Martin Sheen, it turns out, but Ramón Gerardo Antonio Estévez. Half Irish, half Spanish. A mixture which sits perfectly in the landscape I'm crossing. Borderland. Half English, half Welsh. Part Norman. Ravaged by Viking. Infiltrated by the Irish. Settled by West Englanders. A place that's forever uncertain of where its heart actually beats.

Actually getting to the sea wall from the roundabout where the M48 has dumped us turns out to be no simple matter. The road takes us down onto the New House Farm Industrial Estate, a badlands of giant container shed and artic loading bay. Asda, B&Q, Tesco, Zenith, Alphamax. The Seven Crossing Distribution Park. Logistics. Order fulfilment. Sort and load. Store and sell. The articulated trucks roll like whales with flapping sides, like windowless ocean liners. The road is now the sea. The past reversed.

At the south end there's a set of unmanned railway crossing gates over the track to Gloucester and a path out onto the levels. Another border zone. Here, bright, two-toned, flat-roofed corrugated industrial storage sheds, stacks of wooden pallet, numbered bays and uncoupled containers meet the green and virulent regrowth of the wayside. These are the places where mattress and hard-core meet teasel, agrimony, fleabane and hogweed. Where work dislocates into leisure. Where urban ends. A line on the ground.

And here it is literally, that line, the railtrack. Seawards we are on the intertidal flats, this section known as Caldicot Moor and the Mathern Oaze. The Severn river west of its confluence with the Wye. Records show that not much has changed here in a hundred years. The shoreline is stable, the low marl cliffs of Beachley Point holding back the river's current. On the wall, the sea wall, it feels like we're striding through the swamps on thick soled shoes. Everywhere there are traces of water. Landward, the mesh of reens draining the flats. Seawards abandoned pools amid the grass. Tide drift of flotsam. Wood in quantity: trunks. Salt-washed brush. Blue boat rope. Plastic containers. Islands of grass. Brown-grey silt riddled by puddle. So much green. The line between land and water wavering. Rock dumped against erosion. Lines of posts where the wall once was, or might have been, but is no longer.

The seawall is no wall in any conventional sense but a wide-bottomed bund. An elongated, snaking and spongy earth mound, grown green on its sides and top. Sheep tracks run its length. Sheep themselves are perambulating up ahead. They move with that wobbly, skittish walk they have. If the wall was breached their fields would drown. But today the tide is out. There are miles of mud and stone separating shore from the Severn's grey, brown shimmer.

St Tecla recedes. Up ahead St Pierre beckons, in this land of river saints. The bund turns landward, twists, bows, bends, returns again to the sea. Its builders follow no plan that I can discern. They roll their line of humped mud as if it were a length of string randomly tossed down a stairwell by Marcel Duchamp. We pass gouts, with, now that the tide is out, water pouring through them. Yellow notices telling the sheep of the precipitous drop on the seawards side. Up ahead is a white tower, a direction beacon illuminated by a bank of purple strip lights, blazing permanently like some wild surrealistic disco. This is Red Cliff, and this beacon, together with its strip-lit repeater high on a four-storey pole up near the railway, marks the entrance to St Pierre Pill. From out at sea, line up these leading lights and you'll find the entrance channel. Sail straight in.

Above a pair of ducks quack and circle in a ritual dance. The distances they cover in their furious flapping are vast. Head to tail they do five circuits, then land only to take off moments later, refreshed, to circle once again.

On the glistening surface of the pill are small boats, half a dozen at least. There's a battered pontoon, a slipway and some sort of pilot house that looks abandoned but probably isn't. The pill, site of a medieval harbour, is incredibly silted. There are records which show it in use by seventy-ton barges as late as 1860. Today it's base for the Chepstow and District Yacht Club. Their web site makes the place look as sophisticated as the south of France. But read closer. The pill is a mud creek. There are no access roads. Signs warn of overhead electric cabling. Nearest drink is a mile and a half across the fields. Bring your own.

Inland is the manor of St Pierre. Norman. Home of Urien de St. Pierre who died in 1295. By 1380 it was in the hands of Sir David ap Philip, knight of Henry V. The name of his son, Lewis, was later adopted by the family. They remained in ownership for centuries. Sir David became the Governor of Calais and once, in lieu of the cash Henry owed him, held the crown jewels in the Church tower. They were redeemed in 1447. Many Lewises married wealth and became parliamentarians. One owned the New Passage ferry service that ran from Black Rock. The mansion, boasting a deer park and sixteenth century gatehouses, was sold by the Lewises in 1925. It was converted to a country club. Meic Stephens brought the master of a theatre of the absurd, Eugene Ionesco, here for lunch with Sir William Crawshay in 1974. Ionesco ate poached egg and spoke at length, in French, about the war. His had been good, apparently. So much for Pataphysics[5] and the less ordinary. Today the mansion is the Marriot St. Pierre Golf & Country Club. An undulating swath of watered green and exclusivity. Four hundred acres. At its heart, geographically at least, is the church of St Peter.

St Peter's church is tiny. I arrive to find the graveyard taped off with fluttering striped plastic as a warning against the danger posed by an unpollarded willow in the yard's far corner. There's a funeral tomorrow, of Margaret Finch. My name again, following me through life.

Inside are the medieval grave slabs of Urien de St Pierre, his name inscribed in Norman French, and that of William Benet, rector, who died in 1240. There's a prayer on the wall that says that to touch Benet's hand would bring good fortune. It's there on the grave slab, in worn stone relief, a cartoon hand holding a cartoon floriated cross, surrounded by cartoon coins. For generosity. There's a cartoon lion for bravery and cartoon doves for piety. I touch their roughness, my boot on Urien's sword as I stretch.

I'm a sucker for cures. I've tried them all. Holy well water against failing eyes. Against eczema. Against depleted strength. To fix bones, to fix muscle, to help breathe. Pinning cloth to bushes to ward off evil. Salt over shoulder. Never walk under ladders. Now a touch of Benet's fist to make my lot better. On the trek back to the coast it does not rain, I do not fall, I have not left my camera beside my chair in the Marriott bar, my phone's battery stays solid. And when we reach the car, hours later back in the New House Farm Industrial Estate, it has not been stolen. In a box in the boot are two bread rolls containing salami and salad. There's coke and an orange. Wm Benet you are a wonder.

Mathern

William Ayot has a theory, plausible enough, that when Brunel built his Broad Gauge railway lines through here in 1850 he cut St Pierre permanently from its Pill. The inlet that remains, the yacht-dotted inlet that I've just visited, is a shadow of what it once was. The earlier Pill[6] was a tidal lake that would have swamped the present golf course. You can see the remains in the fishing ponds that dot the fairways. It was fed by the fast-running Meyrick brook. You could sail in and tie your boat up at the pile that's now St Pierre Golf club, on the creek that led to Mathern Bishop's Palace, or at the quay that once existed at the back of Moynes Court.

I've come away from the coast for about a mile and am standing with William outside the gatehouse to Moynes Court. As

Coflein has it: "the court has its origins as the medieval castle of Moyns built by the Bishop of Llandaff, the moat and mound of which survives to the south west". Coflein is not a fanatical ley line detective (and there are any number of those out there on the web) but the Royal Commission on the Ancient and Historical Monuments of Wales's online database[7]. William doesn't agree with its description. We look out to where the mound and moat are supposed to be. That mound is in the wrong place, he tells me. There was no castle there. Moynes was built on a knoll which jutted out into the pill. William has done the research. He's also tracked just about every one of the many Court owners since Sir Bogo de Knovil founded the place in the thirteen century.

William Ayot is a poet, playwright, former croupier, a spokesman of the National Association for Children of Alcoholics, proponent par excellence of the oral tradition, and leadership guru of some standing. He reminds me more of a stand-up than a chief executive, although it's CEOs that he's been teaching. He's the Court's present owner, or at least that central part of Moynes that is currently known as Courtyard House. To great outcry the entire manor was partitioned in the 1950s by the then owner, Wing Commander Coombs. The Wing Commander created eight separate dwellings. The main building he split into three. The south western wing, including the grand staircase, became Knoville House. The north eastern section became Moat House. William owns the central part, Courtyard House, which retains the enclosed garden and the magnificent Elizabethan frontage. On his mortgage documents the property is described as a terrace. He also owns the fourteenth century gatehouse with its twin embattled towers. You can rent this from him as a holiday let.

It would have been easy enough, given the privations of centuries of neglect, the machinations of multiple owners, and the building's post-war, ad-hoc listing following an inspector's casual visit for Moynes to have simply fallen down and been allowed to re-enter the water meadow as hard-core. But Ayot was made of tougher stuff. He and his wife, Juliet, bought the place almost on a whim in 2003. Moynes being half-Welsh, half-English, simultaneously of the country and not, and a liminal place of myth and history, held huge attraction. Ayot made plans for regeneration. Out would come Coombs' inappropriate fifties-style modern intrusions. Damage and bugger up would be fixed. The narrative of the house's history would be adhered to. Ayot would engage in honest repair.

William is also the mastermind behind Chepstow's about to be established National Centre for the Oral Tradition (NaCOT), to be based in one of the town's disused schools. His personal history is certainly not that of a conventional litterateur. Nor is Ayot his original surname. Ayot is actually the place he was born in. Ayot St Peter, a Hertfordshire village now lost among the streets of new town Welwyn Garden City. William, from a doubled-barrelled and grand-sounding family, actually had a deeply dysfunctional upbringing at the village pub, the Red Lion. His father was the alcoholic landlord. He died when William was fifteen.

Feeling dispossessed and bent by the weight and grandiosity of his given surname, William changed it by deed poll. Ayot was much tighter and smarter. Fixed in place, William, stepped bravely into a new single-barrelled world, and became first a croupier and then a casino pit-boss. During the Arab Boom between the 1970s and the early 90s he made more than enough to stay afloat. His desire to be creative, however, would not lie down. He began writing plays. Not stuff that stayed in the drawer either. His one man show, *Bengal Lancer*, starring Tim Pigott-Smith, made it to the Lyric Theatre in Hammersmith.

But Ayot's earlier dysfunctional life eventually caught up with him. He scrapped his plans, such as they were, and looked around desperately for rehabilitation of his crippled inner-life. He discovered Robert Bly's seminal *Iron John*[8], hunted out the author, and then worked with him on the men's movement in the UK. What came out of all this was poetry. Mark Rylance commissioned him to write a poem for the four hundredth centenary of Julius Caesar at the Globe. Ayot read the piece before an audience of 1500 and something healed.

He got involved with Laurence Olivier's son, Richard, and formed the training company, Olivier Mythodrama. Mythodrama taught business management, leadership, personal impact and creative communication. The business was a runaway success. Things were rocking. Ayot wrote therapy poems, redemption poems, leadership poems, hero poems, boardroom poems, poems of truth and poems that got you through the agenda[9].

With his new wife, Juliet Grayson, a sex and relationship therapist (William never does things by halves), he moved to Moynes Court. Mythodrama had been abandoned now in favour of the itch of pure verse. He wanted to connect with poets but there was nothing going on locally. At Mathern Church he set up a charity reading starring himself and invited the literary world. No one in writing or publishing showed but ninety locals did. Poetry live, as engaging intellectual entertainment, seemed to work.

What grew out of this 2007 venture was 'On The Border'. High-end events at the Drill Hall, in nearby Chepstow, that paired Welsh poets with those from the wider world. Gillian Clarke, the National Poet of Wales, reading in the company of Carol Ann Duffy, the Poet Laureate, was the first event in 2009. Poets went back to Moynes Court, post reading, if not exactly to party in the Dylan Thomas sense, then to dine and relax. Many stayed in the lofty, fairy-tale rooms of the Gatehouse. Wendy Cope, Kathryn Gray, Rowan Williams, Kit Wright, James Fenton[10], Owen Sheers, and Don Patterson have all done this. My own event in the company of poet Kit Wright (as described on p.30) was the 'On The Border's' second outing.

William walks me around the village, its ancient heart to the south of the motorway and its newer development, known as Newton Green, to the north. The name *Mathern* derives from the earlier Welsh name, *Merthyr Tewdrig* (Tewdric the Martyr), a name that stands proudly again on local road signs. Mathern has five significant ancient buildings, William is keen to point out. They are all sited on the edges of what was once the port of St Pierre. Moynes Court, the Bishop's Palace, St Pierre Manor, Mathern House and the Tudor farmhouse of Innage. The Palace, now owned by Tata Steel, is used as an executive's retreat. There's one in action in white shirt and mobile on the manicured lawns. Innage is a working farm with caravans. Who'd holiday here? "Don't know," says William, "but they do."

Flanking St Tewdric's Church is the holy well of Tewdric

himself. It should be full of coins, thrown there in supplication and the bushes around it covered with fragments of cloth left by the cured. But in the dark water there's nothing. And there are no bushes growing anywhere in range. The cloth fragments were never offerings but pieces from the wound-dressings of the sick, symbolically left within the circle of the saint's power. "Do people come here now," I ask? "You don't see them," replies William. Saint's power on the wane.

Tewdric, history says, suffered mortal wounds in a battle against the Saxons at Tintern in 470 AD. His wounds were washed at this spring and he died and was buried on the nearby mound. The present church was built over his grave. Francis Godwin, divine, Bishop of Llandaff, one-time owner of Moynes Court, and author of the world's first science fiction book claims to have found Tewdric's stone coffin[11]. Back at Moynes Court, after a decent pub lunch at the Miller's Arms (originally the village mill, real ales, tug of war champions, 2010), William is talking up the history. There's a lot of it. "There were at least three Bogo de Knovils," he tells me. "I never realised that it was such a common name. The most significant Moynes owner was Bishop Francis Godwin himself who would have rebuilt the pre-existing house after moving on from Mathern Palace. It is his coat of arms as an heraldic plaque, dated 1609, that is over the Moynes Court door." In addition to his close association with god, Godwin was also an author of some significance. He wrote the *Annales of England*[12], a life story of half of the Tudor Monarchs. Francis Bacon wrote the other half. In 1620 he came up with that science fiction world first, *The Man in the Moone*[13]. This was a tale of escaping Earth's magnetic pull by using a specially trained bird called a gansas. The narrator, glory be to God, finds the moon inhabited by fervent Christians who live in pastoral paradise on the shores of its many seas. You can see them up there today. If you squint. Go out tonight and have a look.

Godwin would have worked with Bacon on the Tudor histories and its more than probable that Bacon stayed at Moynes Court. The missing Shakespeare plays that, in 1910, sent Dr Orville Ward Owen[14] excavating the bed of the River Wye looking for the lead box that contained them loom again. There's a persistent rumour that they are here, somewhere in Moynes Court. "I've looked in every void I could find," William tells me. He bangs some of the flagstones with his foot. "Hear that change in pitch? There's a space below. Turned out to be a Victorian heating duct." "Was anything in it when you looked?" "No."

Ayot's excavations, carried out as part of his Moynes Court 'honest repairs', did deliver quite a number of ancient objects. Examples hang in cases in the hall: a knight's spur, tile fragments, a sword belt buckle, pottery from many centuries, musket balls, and coins. He's most proud of the glass conservation he's achieved with the mullion and transom windows on the three-gabled front. 98% of the bubbly ancient glass retained. He's won an award from the Village Alive Trust for his, it has to be said, most tasteful restoration.

Moynes Court might be a mix of medieval castle and Elizabethan manor with Stuart roof beams and flagstones of even earlier vintage, but it has missed Georgian and Victorian addition simply by having a history of falling from favour. By being off the main trade routes Moynes has survived.

The Lave Fishing Grounds

The novelist and poet Richard Brautigan went trout fishing in America. There the fish were made of a precious and intelligent metal. Trout steel in the snow-filled rivers. Among them he found the dharma or the Buddha, or love or something. I'd never done any of that. I'd never really thought much about fishing anyway other than logging that lots of people did it. Blokes in wool hats sitting on piers, pond sides, river edges waiting and on their faces that distant look. It seemed all about waiting. And I couldn't be doing with that.

At the end of Black Rock Road, to the east of Sudbrook, is the small park the council has created facing Black Rock. In a corner is the Black Rock Lave Net Heritage Fishery's hut. Hand built in local stone. A salmon in wrought iron adorns the front. For most of the year the hut is closed and locked but today it's not. Martin Morgan, a fifty-year-old steelworker from Undy, is in action out front. Spread on the grass he has replicas of the fishtraps that have been used in these waters since medieval times. They've now been banned by the Environment Agency in an attempt to conserve fish stocks. "There used to be other methods of fish catching that are gone too," Martin tells me. "Stock boats, drift nets, tuck nets. Those ways are over."

The putt, a great ten-foot-long assemblage of bent willow in the shape of an open-mouthed giant cone, is the older method. The example Martin shows me is a replica made from an ancient original pulled from the river muds. These things go back to the eleventh century. The cone would be pegged to the river bed facing an ebb tide and once a salmon had swum in, it couldn't then get back out.

Also on show are replicas of putchers – smaller five-foot cones made originally of woven hazel or willow but from the 50s onwards of aluminium mesh. These would be assembled in racks known as engines with sometimes a hundred or more in a single array. These would be strung out across the river like radar sets. Salmon was the target but they also caught whitefish and eels and anything else that drifted in.

These were the fixed engines, the fish henges. In the sixteenth century, Rawlins White, the Cardiff martyr, operated something similar at the Rhymney River mouth. The remains of ancient putcher racks have been discovered by estuarial archaeologists in waders, stepping through the glutinous mud between the river's rapid tides. The largest, containing some fifteen hundred baskets swung out into the waters opposite Goldcliff.

The archaeologist J.R.L. Allen[15] has used aerial photographs of the Estuary to uncover a complex pattern of fish traps dating from Mesolithic times to virtually the present day. His shots show putcher lines running just off the river shores like the claw prints of giant birds. Further out are the remains of rod and wattle fencing, formed into complexes of stone and wood-posted weir. Fish dams, intertidal fish pools, fish gullies. Fish capture has gone on in these waters for thousands of years. But it's all banned now. Regarded as being as bad as fishing with dynamite. All that's left are the lave fishers. Eight of them. The Environment Agency refuses to issue any more licences.

Lave fishing uses large Y-shaped nets each individually made by the fisherman. The net has willow arms known as *rimes* hinged onto a stout handle called the *rock staff*, made of ash. Fishermen wade into an outgoing tide and wait. They can stand for hours with the Severn's tides falling around them. They call this cowering. Much more exciting is stalking, where the fisherman spots a fish moving over the sandbanks and gives chase.

Caught fish are dispatched with a short wooden baton known as a knocker. Weights are anything from five to seventeen pounds. The record was held by Martin's great grandfather. He landed a monster that weighed in at fifty-six pounds. There's a silver-coloured replica back at the hut. The net they also knit themselves. It was once made of hemp. Smacker Williams, in Sudbrook in the 1960s, could knit a single net in a day. That was going some. When he went, the practice died out, but Martin's fishermen have revived it. They use nylon cord today.

At the Heritage Fishery they are all lave fishermen, although as the season is so short they double up for the rest of the year with rod and line. They used to fish from February right through until October but the Environment Agency have now got them down to a mere three months. 1st June to the 31st August. They're allowed to catch an absolute total of fifteen fish, five a month, and that's it. Not much. Martin thinks the Agency would be happiest if it could close the lave fishermen down.

The Agency is at odds with the Heritage authorities who see the Black Rock fishermen as a relic of Wales' traditional past and something to be encouraged. Martin tells me that last week they had a camera team along from *Wedi Saith* who brought a Teifi coracle fisherman with them to compare traditions. We're out on the mud now, walking through the glutinous slime to get into the fishermen's tiny boat. "You take care," says Martin. "We've had camera crews slip here and go sprawling. They always somehow manage to save their equipment, though." In my Homebase green wellingtons I take it slow.

The fishing grounds all have names that don't appear on most maps. Grandstand, The Hole, The Monkey Tump, Lighthouse Vere, The Marl, The Looby and Gruggy. We row west of the Second Severn Crossing to anchor in waters that are moving at around five knots and are at least eight feet deep. "This new bridge was built right across our traditional fishing grounds," Martin tells me. We watch his brother Richard in the distance striding along the shoreline, net over his shoulder. "It's made the mudbanks shift and created new ones but we can still fish."

He and Tim Bevan, a tinplate printer from Sudbrook, are in the water now, chest deep, nets below the surface, that look of concentrated desire mixed with endless patience on their faces. Catching fish is all a matter of getting the wind in the right place and the spring tide flowing. "Are things right today?" I ask. "Could be." But in the end it turns out they're not.

During the two-hour window between tide ebb and flow I watch the water drop more than four feet. Fields of rocks emerge around me. Hundreds of boulders running in all directions like this was the Russian Steppes. The brown water slows from a rush to a drifting crawl. You can hear the muted traffic roar on the bridge high above. But the water itself is silent. The boat shifts on its anchor mooring then bumps against rocks below. Martin has walked off hundreds of yards into the distance. His brother, once separated from us by a river depth too great to navigate, now strides across, net over his shoulders, nothing caught where he was either.

Looking west the river runs off into a silver distance that points right out into the Atlantic. You'd think there'd be ship traffic but there is none. Nothing floats by. Just the ripples. "It would have been better if we'd caught something," says Martin. But half of fishing is the activity itself. Richard Fox and Rob Evans, two other Lave Fisherman in action today have been working the river east of the bridge. "They've not been with us that long," says Martin. "And they're the only two who haven't caught their first fish. We've two more days left. They'll be out tonight, 2.00 am, fishing in the dark, just to catch up."

We're back on shore now. The fishiest thing we'd seen all day was a tiny mullet about five inches long that Tim had in his net and then threw back. I missed that, too busy taking photos of English coast, power stations, or Sudbrook from the estuary distance, pumping station and the Seven Tunnel Great Spring outfall, still rushing fresh water into the river after all these years.

The EU control that limits catches is contained in Annex 11 of the EC Habitats Directive (council directive 92/43/EEC). It ripples off the tongue. But irrelevant today. Down the pub now, yes.

Sudbrook

The levels roll on west, here smeared with industry, or what was industry. Industry now lost in the greenness of this landscape, artificial, smokeless, hidden, gone. The distribution sheds of south Chepstow have given way to scattered farmsteads. Horses. Sheep. The fields regular, defined by reen and hedge. From the seawall path I can see them sinking slowly. Slumping down as they undulate back to the fen edge. The wall is still bund. Unadulterated, grass-covered mud, piled some five feet high, with a flat top supporting a beaten track.

Getting here from Mathern was easy. Park under a tree outside St Pierre's Leisure Centre. Watch the golfers laze across the course in their pastel colours, their mechanised golf carts festooned with bags and sun umbrellas. Track down to the seawall past fishermen working the pool at Pill Cottage. Cross the rail lines. Find the sea again. The sea that's a river. Water thick with dark deposit. The bringer of soil, the bringer of mud. The grey-blue Welsh Nile, its waters rich with salt.

The tide is up and St Pierre Pill is full of water. Yachts float in the lower basin as if this were the Welsh Med. In the creeks the underlying mud is barely visible. A man with his Volvo pulls up by the shack that is the shuttered clubhouse and threads rope into a buoy. A woman on the deck of her dingy drinks tea from a flask.

The Severn Estuary Research Committee[16] characterises this area as "a discrete parcel of coastal alluvium surrounded by bedrock on three sides". This means the land rises, slowly, hardly. If it's half a mile from here to Black Rock then I'd be surprised. It's not anything. You can tell we are near an urban centre. Sunday strollers are out. Perambulating the wall. Walk to St Pierre Pill. Walk back. Take the sun.

We ignore the pylons, all of them. The levels support these industrial intrusions in considerable numbers. When it needs it, the National Grid uses them to pull energy from the nuclear generators just over the water at Hinkley Point and at Oldbury. It powers up nuclear free Wales with joules of fission-bred power. The steel lattice towers and their copper and aluminium cables, suspension insulators, dampers, cross-arms, warning signs and integral ladders become somehow invisible the longer they stay in your sight. Their inherent greyness and buzzing silence blend them into the horizon. Their atoms seem to separate before our eyes. They meld with the sky. Elephants in the room. How long have they been here? No one can now remember their coming, the battles we fought then against their arrival, the arguments, the intrusion, the money that changed hands in back rooms. The eighty-foot-high deliverers of power marched across our landscapes unhindered. This between the wars, part of Britain's rush to join the modern world. We ended up welcoming them. We wanted what they had.

The British design goes back to 1928 when fervent anti-modernist, Sir Reginald Blomfield, chose the American Milliken Brothers' overtly modernist man-with-arms-outstretched pylon design to become the workhorse of the National Grid. If the power line came your way then you accepted it. If the Grid's foot strayed onto your land then you were paid a rental. When a pylon's footing ended up among the cabbages, householders welcomed the income this gave them. Landowners on the Levels delighted in the revenue this new, all-metal cash crop brought their way. In the 1990s studies showed that proximity to power transmission encouraged the development of human carcinogens. Down here that concern barely mattered. By 2011 it had gone away.

Sudbrook. Southbrook. The Welsh Beachley. It's an epicentre of transition. A border outpost where the leys, lines, trails, tracks and passageways all focus. It's up ahead with the glinting emerald of the second Severn Bridge's cable work pulling the eye towards it. This is Severnside now, the community website tells me. Magor, Undy, Rogiet, Caldicot, Portskewett and Sudbrook. The town names on their own are insufficient, Severnside moves the market up. My mother did this. Wherever we lived she adapted the given district name for her own purposes. And we lived in a lot of places. Every two or three years during my Cardiff childhood we moved house, my father endlessly wallpapering and panelling doors with hardboard. My mother following him around with a can of cream paint. Once the house settled and I'd discovered every nook and cranny they sold it. Moved on. I felt my gypsy blood rising. Finch wandering Jew.

Finch forever making new friends as the streets around him shifted.

When we lived in Roath, my mother instructed us to put Roath Park as part of our address. Our terrace by Roath Recreation ground was described as Cyncoed. She was adept at creating completely new parts of the city we lived in, my mother. Upper Victoria Park, Waterloo, Penylan Hill, Carisbrooke. When I told them in school that I lived in The Gardens, a district she'd invented on the basis that there was a park over the road from where we now resided, everyone laughed.

Black Rock sits east of the point at Sudbrook. Offshore is Charston Rock with its beacon. Between that and the English Stones are the Shoots, the Severn's deepest flow. Near what remains of the ferry landing there's a sign. This proudly retells the tale of Charles the First escaping Cromwell's pursuing soldiers by boat to New Passage on the English side. When the boatman returned, he was ordered at sword point to take the Parliamentarians to the place where he had landed the King. The boatman took the pursuers out to the English Stones, a great area of offshore rock that emerged from the river at low water. It looked, for all the world, like dry land. Left boatless the Parliamentarians found themselves stranded by the Severn's fast returning waters. Legend says many drowned.

New Passage on the English shore gives a clue to the ferry crossing that once operated here. During the eighteenth century, in competition with the service running from Beachley to Aust (of later *Severn Princess* fame, see p.31) the Lewis family of St Pierre began a boat from Black Rock to Chissell Pill in Somerset. The crossing took fifteen minutes. In the middle of the following century when the railways arrived, a wooden pier was constructed, a hotel built, a line laid by the Bristol and South Wales Union Railway and a steam ferry launched. Business flourished until, in 1881, the pier burned down. Its remains were demolished in 1886 when the Severn Tunnel opened. The Black Rock Hotel is now a private house. The track has been lifted, although the cutting along which it ran, guarded today by wire fence and fast overgrowing with scrub, remains unfilled.

Sudbrook is silent. The remains of industry girdle it. First the railway and its ferry crossings. Then the tunnel, the cottages for those who dug it, the shipyard that employed them when the tunnel was done, the pump house and the houses for the pump engine workers, the paper mill, the houses for the paper millers, the infirmary, and the place they all went to when industry cracked their ribs and bent their bones. The sound of all this, the smoke and thump of the beam engines, the sluice of water, the rocks dragged up from thirty feet below the deepest part of the Severn River. They used many of those to build the houses. The terraces at Sea View, The Villas, Marine Terrace. The Isolation Hospital now lost under the Wiggins Teape Paper Mill[17]. The Infirmary itself, which is now the Walker Flats. The Presbyterian Church.

The community council have produced a leaflet: 'Sudbrook – A Walk Back in Time'. To add historical gravitas, the name of the town is printed in bold Old English script. All the highspots are shown. Best of all it locates the first ever British houses to be built entirely of concrete. These are at the western end of Sea View. Under their Dulux covering, the walls bear the distinct marks of the wooden forms used to create them. This is of extreme anorak interest to those who spot traffic islands, collect diesel unit numbers and know the original number of every redesignated A road in the country. I take a photograph. A householder gives me a knowing smile.

The houses overlook the now deserted and grass-filled rail spur that runs down to the pump house at the Severn's edge. The tracks originally shipped in coal to power the Cornish beam engines used to pump out the rail tunnel. Occasionally they stabled the Royal Train, en route, always, to somewhere else. Now they are rich in Russian vine and cow parsley. The pump house working but silent. Not a speck of smoke anywhere in the summer air.

The Severn Tunnel is the Sudbrook centrepiece. It's the reason the town developed. Up the road is Portskewett. To Sudbrook much as Cardiff is to Penarth. Portskewett. Porth is Coed. The harbour below the wood. Porth Ysgewin y Gwent. In antiquity one of the three chief ports of the Island of Britain. Used in medieval Welsh poetry to denote one of the Island's extremities or measuring-points[18]. Site of Heston Brake, once chambered beaker tomb, now like so many, wrecked and unravelled. Unearthed, de-earthed, stones stolen for building, fragments of iron age pottery and burned bones discovered and taken clear by archaeologists. Grass grown back over the wreckage. But as you walk up to it[19], the site has a lingering power.

The larger town once housed King Harold's hunting lodge, referenced in Anglo-Saxon chronicles, built to the west of Portskewett Church. Harold of the arrow through the eye. Harold sworn enemy of Caradoc. Harold Godwinson. *Time Team* territory. When Channel 4's *Time Team* did actually come here in 2007[20] they found the remains of a medieval manor house with a fortified tower on the site of a late Saxon royal hunting lodge, itself built onto an early medieval Welsh *llys*. Some truth hung there in the rumour. The street above is called King Harold's View. All the locals believe. Harold's dead. Why not?

But it remains that Tunnel[21] that everyone recalls. A Victorian masterpiece excavated between 1873 and 1886. Thirteen years of digging, deprivation, disaster, and then eventual success for the two men responsible. Sir John Hawkshaw, GWR engineer and Thomas Walker, contractor. For its time this was a mega project of the order of flying to the moon. A four mile tunnel to be cut through the ooze below Britain's most virulently tidal river. Victorian enterprise par excellence overcame all obstacles. These included the 1879 discovery, when digging was almost done, of the Great Spring. This was a river below the river, and one that poured unimaginable quantities of water into the tunnel workings which were, at that point, right below the Severn's deepest channel, the Shoots. There were deaths and there were thoughts of abandonment. But the Victorians were made of stern stuff. Perseverance prevailed. Pumps were built. Great arrays of Cornish beam engine were installed. Rail tracks were laid. Pipelines and outlets were manufactured. Disaster did not triumph.

In the time since the tunnel opened, industries that use water have clustered at Sudbrook. Paper making, brewing. Water from the Great Spring has been fed into the public supply. And even this has not been enough. Surplus flows, still flows, out into the river from a cliff just to the west of Black Rock. Experiments using dyes and chemical trackers to locate the origins of the

Great Spring have shown nothing more than a rise in the flow some three weeks following rainfall on the Monmouthshire uplands. The Great Spring has a source but we haven't put our twenty-first century fingers on it quite yet.

Above us, bracketing our journey are the engineering marvels that are the twin Severn Crossings. The Severn Bridge, which opened in 1966 and, for a day trip, had my Dad drive out to it and cross to drink tea and eat sandwiches in the Aust Services on the Bristol side. And the Second Severn Crossing, which opened in 1996, and spanned the place where the river ceases and the Estuary begins. Dad never got to drive over that one. He died a few years before. But he did motor out along the M4 just to admire the wire bending, plate girder and reinforced concrete slab weave that, at one stroke, straightened the M4 and brought blue-green twinkling light and higher tolls to westbound traffic. Harri Webb's much quoted ode to financial politics: "Two lands at last connected/ Across the waters wide,/ And all the tolls collected/ On the English side"[22] is no longer relevant. Like the pylons (and in the future, maybe the wind farms too) the bridges are fast becoming invisible as intrusions. Instead they are now seen as eye-catchingly natural and as cliffs, tidal flats or railways with their signal gantries, tracks and cuttings.

The Shooting Range

I'm back on the wall. It feels strange, this being in a walled country. The sea defences marking the edge of the known Welsh universe. Like the plasterboard dome of the painted sky in the false world of *The Truman Show* finally pierced by the prow of Jim Carrey's boat. Could I put my arm through and find something beyond? The real world in all its commercial glory. Something that wasn't the fictional country it often feels that Wales is. I try it. Nothing. Air is all.

The second Severn crossing is behind me, glittering viridian even in today's dull light and incipient rain. Ahead the coast of Gwent bulges. This is the land of lapwing, snipe, redshank and curlew. Stillness and grey-green silence. And as if the landscape needed a boost, youths have taken the time and trouble to hack their way down here with their cans and bottles. The green of Grolsch and the grey aluminium shiver of Carling among the rushes. The flotsam of the cities seeping to the sea.

We've seen this arriving, slowly. First gangs of youths together on the urban streets necking cans under the sodium lights. Then lines of girls, shrieking, all wearing the same kit, plastic halos, sew-on wings, tees sloganed for Chantelle's Hen Weekend, hockey sticks, wands. Surging crowds bearing open Peroni Nastro Azzurro on high-wattage raids across the cities' centres. Gratification arriving like SMS. Instantly, constantly. Watching the morning football with your mouth round a bottle. One in hand at the cash machine. Clasped as if it were a smart-phone. The green of all this dirt cheap ubiquity granulated under city foot and now rolling here among the reens. Tramped into the clay. But only at the point where the access path reaches. Ten metres on down the sinuous seawall the city and its ways are forgotten.

Here it is still as much the Wye as it is the Severn. Sea with a riverine feel. Waters flowing along the littoral and not towards it. Waters passing, heading somewhere else. Ahead are the ranges. On the OS map this is marked as a Danger Area. Red chevrons delineating a slice of Rogiet Moor running from Ifton Reen to West Pill, more of it at sea than on land. There's a crack of gun fire in the distance and a red flag flying from a pole attached to a locked breeze-block hut. There's a notice on the wall bled to illegible letter fragments by the weather. But the surviving crossed red circle is plain enough.

There are two ranges here, cwtched up between the coast and the toll booths for the Second Severn Crossing. The Cardiff Small Arms Club manage the shorter Severn Tunnel Range. The MOD operate the Rogiet Moor facility. Through the long-distance lens on the camera, I can see lines of men dressed in combat jackets, blue jeans, and muffler caps. They are sprawled, guns in hand, on the grass. The boots of their cars are open behind them. Other men stand drinking tea from flasks. Everyone wears ear protectors. Next door the MOD range is empty. This is a weekend and the military relax. Today it's only the hobbyists who are shooting.

Beyond, the river is silent. I want it to sound something, make flow noises, a whoosh of water passing, a thrash of tide on rock, of wall eroding, soil bank collapsing. But there's nothing. Curlew warbles, rifle crack, a far distant vehicular thrum as the area's background radiation. These moorlands seem abandoned. A grid of green lane and rectangular field, crossed by power lines. No settlements. No monuments. Nothing to intrude. Ditch. Hedge. Drove way. Mud.

In the western distance the sky lightens. Comes up out of the riverscape filled with peace. I could be here with my player jammed in my ears (special earpieces of expanding, shape-memorising foam to stay fixed in my life-long headphone resisting ears), bass thrumming my fillings loose, the sound of my teeth echoing back up my jaw bone. I'd have Duffy Power[23] singing Sonny Boy Williamson's 'Help Me'. Power in his trans-formation from the Larry Parnes sub-standard British rock and roll front man to lethal blues interpreter I somehow managed to miss first time round. But I don't. That caterwauling sound-scape is back in the car. I stick with the curlew and the sound of the air.

Abergwaitha

If these were Vatican lands then you would see crosses, candles, prayers on scraps of paper, dead flowers, beads, shrines. At each turn there'd be great cathedrals celebrating. The roads would start here. The pilgrimages. All the way west to St David's, hamlet city, beacon of light. Welsh end to a Welsh Catholic universe. Three trips worth one to Rome. Five to get you on the clouds with St Peter. Eternity beckons. But that's not what the soil believes. Not here. The people have long gone. The coast is empty. Abergwaitha. Port of the lost. Vanished in a spray of salt, worn to dust by the endless tides.

Fantasy you might think, looking out west along the straight seawall in the glinting sun. Nothing moves. Habitation is scant. A sewage pumping station. The pylons looping off north. Two wind turbines turning slowly to prove, if it needs to be proved, that we can do renewable, even if it's token, in our car-crash economy of not cutting back and not letting go. Two turbines would give enough free power here to run a string of street lamps. Were there to be any. Or need for light.

Since I've left Caldicot Moor and hit the Porton Grounds the seawall has straightened and taken on signs of substantial rebuild against increasing tidal threat. Ocean rise and sea surge will be fought against with heavy concrete facing, hard core centre, outlying boulder, all capped with the backward S of a wave return, to dissipate the energy and send the rollers back. The wall's top is wide, the landward bank increasingly steep. Welsh Holland. Bristol's Zuider Zee. A West Anglia in the Cymric rain.

The seawalls run for some thirty-five kilometres. They have been constantly upgraded since the Romans first began their construction. Since the 1950s, modification has accelerated. Boulder and concrete frontings are common. But the past still exists. Around Collister Pill[24,] and on the levels between Newport and Cardiff at Rumney Great Wharf and Peterstone Gout, are relics of much earlier seawall construction. Rising tides could soon overwhelm them. Earth movers have been glimpsed in the Cardiff distance. Expect the walls of the world here to grow ever higher. Keep the waters back. Protect the rail links, the freight yards, the distribution depots, the power stations, the storage sheds. Watch the salt marsh fade as the rising, scouring seas erase them. South Wales as a set of island hill tops breaking the waters somewhere north of Merthyr. But not yet. God's still on our side.

The reens here have names you can engage with: Prat Reen, Pwll Uffern Reen, Petty Reen, Cold Harbour Reen, Cock Street Reen, Bareland Reen, Ynys Mead Reen, Windmill Reen, Cwrta Well Reen, Waundeilad Reen. I'm walking across them with my iPod in my ears. Half the country do this, traverse the world listening to something that is not the ambient sound of the landscape, that isn't birdsong, that is not nature chattering. Instead it's M People, Tori Amos, 12 Stones, Goo Goo Dolls, Lamb of God, Enter Shakari, Hannah Montana, Beach Boys, Gladys Knight, Mr Scruff, Moby, and all those other bands. I'd like to say that there are traces of this music in the landscape I walk, but other than inside the things I write, there's not a thing.

I pull the plugs out. Reduce the music to a scratchy squeak.

Magor Pill, up ahead, is actually St Brides Brook, canalized as Mill Reen, and then poured into the sea through a quite substantial creek. The tide is in, making the land look small. Two fishermen work the waters out at the sea's edge. Behind is Chapel Farm, the only habitation in a mile, sitting below the wall, protected by its stern notices which warn travellers that this is private land. No Shooting, No Fishing, Rod & Net. Bailiffs will be informed. Footpath to top of seawall only. Walk quietly. No singing. Head up. Hands out of pockets. This is ours, not yours. All the freedoms demanded since the Beats discovered the Buddha, gone in a flash.

On these foreshores, where the saltmarsh grass is shaded army green and the high tide glints in the cloudless sun, once stood Abergwaitha. The port lost to the sea in the fourteenth century. Boat tie ups, earth quays, warehousing, square-edged wood structures from the dark ages. Worked stone blocks, slices of roofing tile and window glass have been discovered deep within the palaeochannels[25]. Habitation folded into the encroaching mud lands as the river rose. The causeway from this once bustling Welsh place still runs back to inland to Magor village. Amid the landscape of reclaimed salt marsh, where horses now graze, there are Roman traces. This place meant something once.

Seawards archaeologists have found pottery fragments in their thousands, running from the Iron Age to modern times, twelfth century fishtraps made from hazel and oak, and the remains of two medieval boats deep in the river bottom. One seven metres long, a carrier of iron ore sourced from Llanharri, destined for the smelters working the Forest of Dean. The peats below the estuary mud are twelve metres deep here. Ancient landscapes in layers still extant. Rush out between tides and dig. It's what the archaeologists do.

At Cold Harbour Pill, creek itself reduced to a gouted outfall in the armourstone apron of the wall, sits the sewage station. Far enough from Chapel Farm for the odour not to drift. Cold Harbour. It sounds like something from an Appalachian songbook. Prehistoric trackways and preserved footprints, adult and child, have been found in the sliding mud. Take me back to ol Cold Harbour, ol Cold Harbour, place where I lost my wife. Banjo solo. High keening. Redwick Church now visible between the trees.

Redwick, Goldcliff and the Wetlands Reserve

The track up to the village is permitted. Makes Wales sound like Russia. Permission given to walk, but no real rights. Not if you want to stand on them, citizen, do that and you are lost. The track is slurry, a causeway between two reens, but in the sun hard and dry. It runs from the main sewer outfall at the Portland Grounds back up to the village. A palaeochannel of its own, wide enough for a car and these do pass along it. I count six in the short time it takes us to traverse one grid on the OS map. Dust cloud like Africa. Leisure travellers gawping at the countryside. Idle SUV drivers with a free Sunday and the kids screaming and making the windows sticky in the back. No one gets out. No one takes the air. They view the seawall and the flies and the Holocene estuarine peats with their Triassic mudrocks and Late Pleistocene ice-wedge casts then spin back up the ruin of a roadway to smother us once more in grey-brown smog.

In Redwick the weirdness of the levels lessen. This place is a classic English village – graveyard, church, pub, loop of roadway, the green, the great house – except it's in Wales. But there's no announcement of a local *ysgol feithrin* and no bi-lingual signage. South Row. Church Row. Green Street. The church, St Thomas the Apostle, goes back to the fifteenth century[26]. It has a list of Vicars of Magor & Redwick on a board inside that goes back to 1451. Behind a set of wooden gates that resemble the sort of thing that once fronted early British black and white television cabinets is a baptistry. A pool to enable full water submerged baptism. Now empty. Last used god knows when. There's a Victorian pipe organ and a very early font. Outside, in the shadow of a life-size, plinth-mounted stone angel with spread wings and beatific smile, is a marker showing the height reached by the Levels' Great Flood of 1607[27].

Between the Church and the Rose Inn is a village bus shelter which doubles as a museum. There are stocks, millstones, a cider press, agricultural bygones, historic warning signs created by the Commissioners of Sewers, gargoyles, slabs and crosses. A plaque shows that the shelter won a Prince of Wales Award in 1979 and was built by local history enthusiast Hubert Jones. From my time selling books I can recall seeing in a local guide a photograph of Hubert Jones, the man himself, locked in his own stocks, fake things that he'd built out the back. He sat there in black and white, all glasses and teeth, incongruously smiling.

Replete drinkers drift in the unseasonal sun. Like cats they fail to walk in straight lines. Nobody is pissed, you understand. This is the Gwent Sunday countryside. They are mellowed. King-sized shirts outside their trousers, trainers, flapping shorts. Large women in tights, flat shoes that would never cross a field, phones to their ears like muffs. Designer handbags. Rings on their thumbs. Cigarettes.

There's an ancient gravemarker inside the Church: "Yov Careless Yov the look well at me for as I am so shall yov be". Do they do that, the local youth? I doubt it.

Down the coast, over fields rich in ditch and vurrow, past half a mile of groynes, armoured wall apron and sunbathing conger eel fishermen, is Goldcliff. An island of limestone in a flat land of sedimentary dross. And was an actual island once too, back in the deep Mesolithic when the waters here flowed in a different place. In 2004, *Time Team* tried one of their urgent three days to do it archeological rescues out there in the sinking mud. They found microliths and footprints. Man back then built no buildings. The most you can hope to find, apparently, are bits of worked flint and burned stick. Goldcliff is also the site of a Benedictine priory[28] but now totally lost inside the recently constructed Hill Farm. The cliffs once glistened gold from the silica they contained. They did when Giraldus Cambrensis passed by in the thirteenth century[29]. Today all I can discern is mud.

The fisheries here used to be run by the Williams family who were the last on the Estuary to operate a putcher rack (see p.46). The posts in curving lines still dominate the foreshore. The Temperance Hotel at the end of Sea Wall Road operated until the late 1950s. In the village itself the Farmer's Arms, with its vast car park and comprehensive family open-air facilities, has just closed. Desperate signs outside offer young hopefuls the chance to run their own establishment. They'd be selling beer to a public that seemingly no longer want to drink it. Wine to those who prefer the grape at home. Lager in glasses to drinkers who like it better at a quarter of the price, on a park bench, straight out of the can.

At Goldcliff St Mary Magdalene Church there's a single bell in the tower. Back at Redwick there are five. Round here the Christian muezzins rock on a Sunday. Ring them bells. Did once. In my pocket is Iain Sinclair's excellent *Downriver*. Fiction as a device to portray fact. The author takes film crew down the Thames to trace the ruins of Margaret Thatcher's reign. He imagines her as still there, ever powerful, managing a one-party state in her fifth term. Sinclair bends fact to the narrative flow of his fiction. Makes fiction serve the reality of how things actually are. His river is nothing like my river. His Thames-side population is rich in poets, drinkers, men who burst into flames, doss house owners, makers of video nasties, booksellers, sailors, retired rent boys, actors, architectural advisors, laureates, swamp-field crazies, alternative comedians, property developers and the red-grey Dogs of Annwfn[30]. You'd never meet such people here. Never in a million years. I've the idea that in this place, among the lonely gulls and shelduck, I could create my own fiction. Take time, in the sun, and the air. Let the work distil. Let it move slowly under my eyes. Let it shore in stacks against my future ruin. But in the soft heat the idea fails to work. The bollocks of authorial fantasy. Can't do it. I'm no fictioneer. *Downriver*'s pages begin to thicken. In the Severnside air they are so hard to turn.

Sinclair, whom I've known distantly and sporadically since my days as a magazine editor and small publisher (*Second Aeon*, 1966 to 1974), has some sort of antipathy to Wales. He was born in Cardiff, and disowns his country of origin. Or used to. In recent times, he's been seen on platforms here, delivering talks and presenting lectures. Is he the man to turn to, following his chronicles in the Goldcliff light? I tap the book. Still in my pocket. Maybe not this time.

Across the lamb-filled field to the east of the golden outcrop is a fence marking out the edge of the recently established

Newport Wetlands Nature Reserve. Established in 2000 to mitigate the loss of habitat for wading birds following the opening of the Cardiff Bay Barrage, the reserve runs for more than a thousand acres. A mix of farmland and power station fuel ash disposal site this western end of the Caldicot levels have been part reflooded. They provide pool, reed bed and marsh for lapwing, oystercatcher, redwing and plover.

The route to the Visitor Centre runs through the village of Nash (pub, church, another flood marker) and on down what was once Perry Lane. This was named after the Perry family of West Nash Farm who worked here until their land was requisitioned by the Usk Mouth Power station for use as an ash tip in the 1970s. The Centre has the expected café, RSPB shop, binocular hire and interpretation panels. The manager tells me that mortality of dunlin, redshank and shelduck from the Cardiff Bay mudflat impoundment in 1999 has been as high as 70%. "Didn't they come here?" "Why would they. These are not mudflats." Bird death on a considerable scale. Just as the barrage critics predicted.

But these new wetlands are not without their attractions. The day board shows sightings of everything from grey heron to little grebe and from grey plover to marsh harrier. Down by the East Usk lighthouse, a white cone at water's edge, the seawall has gone from the Pill's aggressive concrete to soil bank and hedge. Here the warblers, finches, tits, thrush, duck and gull flock. A youth takes snaps through a giant telephoto lens. There's a woman with a pushchair and a toddling child. A man in a Marks and Spencer cardigan smokes. A pensioner on sticks eats an ice cream.

But beyond the fences at the Reserve's end, this gentle world finishes. Fence. Danger. Keep Back. Dim Mynediad. Industry returns.

Newport

The Mouth of the Usk

In the 1950s the future was a threat. There was the menace of the reds, the dread of the bomb, the fear of a world made desolate by science. In Britain the paranoia seeped. On Venus, Dan Dare might have been winning his war against the Treens, but in the cinema the British space scientist Quatermass[1] was up against terrors that were harder to beat. The insidious forces of extra-terrestrial invasion. There were things out there, beyond understanding and beyond reason. They would come from the skies and we would be stuffed.

The Quatermass films showed a middle-aged man in a tweed overcoat fighting off alien forces from the skies with British space rocketry, British ingenuity and British grit. As the alien meteorites fall from above, guards dressed like puppet versions of the Cybermen chase them with detectors on sticks. In post-war darkness Quatermass ponders the future. He has Jodrell Bank at his disposal and the might of British science. He presses the button for lift-off. British Blue Streak power launches and destroys the aliens' asteroid in an instant. The world, in glorious black and British white, is once again safe.

The backdrop against which this and other Quatermass fictions play out is always industrial. Full of rusted pipes of large dimension, containment buildings, smoke stacks, cooling towers, storage tanks and relays. For secrecy, it is always deep in the country. Guarded by men in uniform. Operated by workers wearing breathing apparatus and protective clothing. Helmets. Gloves. Space-age boots.

At the end of the wetlands nature reserve, where the ground rises towards the eastern salient at the Usk's entry into the Severn, stands such a fifty-year-old space-age vista. Uskmouth.

This is Newport's outrider, a giant dual-power generation facility. Scottish and Southern Electricity's coal-fired station (Uskmouth B), and DONG Energy's sparkling gas turbine (Severn Power). Industry back with a rocking whack. Coal in banks the size of Penarth Headland. Covered transporter belts. Generator housing as big as the Millennium Stadium. Towers. Masts. Pylons. Pylons by the dozen, tall and ever taller, their arms full of endless wire.

Reaching the entrance to the site is easy. It's less than a hundred metres down from the Wetlands car park. Gaining access, however, turns out to be a totally different matter. I approach the gate and although everything is polite, the answer is you can't. On the phone I try the press office. I get Scottish and Southern first. I tell them I'm at work on an important book. I need to place their operation in historical and geographical context. I'll paint a professional picture. We welcome enquiries from professional journalists, reads their website. I should be in but I'm not. A soft Scottish voice, answering from their office in Perth, is as polite as the gatehouse guards. "I'm sorry but visits are not possible. Ever. No."

DONG, the second electricity generating company on the same site, could not be more different. DONG Energy. The name sounds like Wang, or Chung, or Shinco. Far Eastern hi-tech. But it's actually an acronym for Danish Oil & Natural Gas, Denmark's national operator, 60% owned by the Danish state. Their plant[2], a silver and green gas turbine, is the newest in the

UK. It was commissioned at the end of 2010 and stands like the Madonna against a backdrop of river mouth decrepitude, stacked coal, third-hand steel strip mills and assorted industrial squalor.

DONG has welcomed my visit and is laying on a tour. With me I've John Briggs, my partner in creativity and fellow admirer of the wreckage of industry. John is festooned with cameras and cases. I've rarely seen him not. We drive across site from the gate to the DONG entrance and slow down to pass behind Scottish and Southern's coal-fired monster, Uskmouth B. *DIVERSION WHEN FOGGY* reads a traffic sign. I roll down the window and John takes a shot. We can't have travelled more than a further hundred metres before a uniformed security guard roars up in a 4x4. "You can't take any pictures here," he says. "It's not allowed." He's shaking his head in the way that determined men do. I'm fearful that he might get out of his vehicle, throw us to the floor, and rip the film from John's Nikon. Just like you see them do in the cinema. John is apologising furiously. Smiling pathetically I agree, unreservedly, that we will not, under any circumstances, photograph anything unsanctioned, not another unauthorised thing.

In the conference room – video facilities, white boards, tea in DONG mugs, views of the National Grid sub-station and then the Usk beyond – Ian gives us a history of power generation. This features the vicissitudes of Thatcher privatisation, the imagination of Welsh-enterprise and the credit crunch that nearly wrecked us all. This is Ian Crummack, External Affairs manager for the site. He's ex-Army but has been in power generation ever since he realised that it was electricity that made the modern world turn. He reminds me of Jeremy Paxman but without the vicious streak.

In the aftermath of World War Two the country was an infra-structure disaster zone. The cities had been bombed to the edge of unsustainability. The power grid, such as it was, barely worked. Generation was weak and cuts were a fact of life. The CEGB, the Central Electricity Generating Board, Britain's state-owned, Soviet-styled monolith began a programme of power station build. They chose sites along rivers – the Trent, the Thames, the Humber, the Severn, the Usk – places where water could be used as a coolant and where coal was easy to deliver. At the place where the Usk met the Severn they built two stations – Uskmouth A and Uskmouth B. These were fossil-fuel burning monsters in a landscape of industrial decline. Their architect was the same man who put up the iconic brick cathedral at Battersea, celebrated on the cover of Pink Floyd's *Animals*. Pigs high over the four chimneys. Smoke in the sky. At Uskmouth there's a family resemblance, half of one, as Uskmouth A is no more and only the twin stacks of Uskmouth B remain.

Uskmouth A was closed as inefficient in 1981. For a time the site was used for emergency services and other training before it was eventually demolished in 2002. Under Thatcher, everything was sold. The State was to wither. Electricity generation and distribution were to fly away, driven by late twentieth century capitalist winds. In the event, the free market became a car boot sale. National Power bought both sites at knock-down prices and then sold them on to a company called AES (Applied Energy Services) in 1998. AES showed willing and refurbished Uskmouth B before stumbling into receivership in 2003. Power generation was turning out not to be a golden goose game. A new operator, WPG (Welsh Power Group Ltd)[3], bought what was left from the receiver. They began redevelopment of the Uskmouth A site in preparation for the construction of a new and cleaner generator, a gas turbine.

By now the state of the planet was beginning to impinge on even the most fervid of capitalist enterprises. Steadily increasing restriction and regulation were making industrial activities difficult things from which to spin an easy buck. The Uskmouth A site was bulldozed and remediated, asbestos removed, coal ash resited and the cavernous basements filled. Then the gas-fired power station build began, using extensive finance from the banks. When conditions became difficult in 2008, WPG were forced to sell. The gas-fired power station (on the old 'A' site) was sold to DONG first, then a few months later on Scottish and Southern Energy purchased the 'B' coal fired plant.

Severn Power, as the new power station was named, is a twin steam and gas-powered turbine generator. Through its copper bars the size of car engines it can kick out 3% of the UK's energy needs – enough to power every house in Wales. Gas comes in through a thirty-metre deep, six-mile pipeline connecting to the natural gas transmission system at Marshfield. The place may throb, and in the turbine house can throb loud enough to require you to wear ear protectors, but compared to Britain's coal-fired past, this is wide-screen, HD television. Big, efficient, beautiful.

Brian Miller, the construction engineer in charge of the build, shows us round. This is a full hard-hat, steel toe-cap job, John with plugs in his ears instead of his hearing aids, and me looking like the horny-handed workman my mother had always insisted I would never be. The plant is as controlled as a nuclear sub and as clean as an operating theatre. Beyond the giant overhead air-cooled condenser with its windwalls and massive rotors, everything is clad, coated and labelled. The turbine is hydrogen cooled. Its insides are ceramic lined. Like the space shuttle. Outside a pair of workers roller-paint a recently delivered portakabin marshy green. "That's to fit our colour profile," says Ian. Colour decided by the local authority so the plant won't frighten migrating birds.

At the river end of the plant is a bund, 'the wild flower meadow' Ian calls it; a mound of top-soiled fuel ash and waste dug out of the plant's foundations. In spring it's nothing but a mass of flowers. It fits DONG's image.

DONG is 58% efficient[4] compared to the Scottish and Southern plant next door which only manages 24%. As regulation increases, Uskmouth B may slowly be allowed to rust out. The EU's Large Combustion Plant Directive, an incoming regulation that deals with acidification, ground level ozone and particle emission, may well see it off.

DONG's Danish parentage is obvious. The operation is environmentally aware, engages with the local community and does what it can to mitigate ecological damage. They tell me this in the conference room before we leave. "Tak[5]," I say. I've watched all twenty episodes of *Forbrydelsen*[6] but to judge from the blank looks nobody else has. "Thank you," I say. Just to be sure.

Newport Docklands

John Briggs and I are sitting on a bench outside St Stephen's Church in the heart of Pill[7]. According to Gwent Police, priorities for this district are: tackling drug use, anti-social behaviour, and on-street prostitution. The poet W.H. Davies was born in Portland Street, not far from here. The ethnicity is dense, mujahideen clothing, shawls, African mumu, celtic interlacing tattooed behind the ears, hair cut to a point at the nape, nose rings, pointed shoes, seen better days. Between us we have polystyrene-cupped coffees and fat slices of bread pudding bought for almost nothing at the Cornerstone Bakery. John is talking about Gary Winogrand's 35mm Leica photos of mid-twentieth century America, the shots he took so that he could see what the world looked like in photographs. Pictures of the Bronx Zoo, museum parties, protesters beaten by cops, women getting into cars, marching in parades, skinny-dipping in ponds, snapshot immediacy on speed, Cartier-Bresson bent through the eye of John Updike, the fast world caught but never slowed. When he died in 1984, he left more than two and a half thousand rolls of undeveloped film, six and a half thousand developed but not proofed, and a further three thousand proofed but not examined. A third of a million unedited exposures. Obsessive compulsive genius. He'd leave his film undeveloped for a year so that he could get beyond the emotion prevailing at the moment when he took the picture. "I could never do that," John tells me. Briggs, of course, is famous for never carrying enough film. Witness the Roath Dock railway debacle[8] where lack of rolls reduced the record to twelve shots and a few snaps taken on my Instamatic. But that was then and the world now is instant, all-digital, including John, garrulously taking shots of anything that moves, and most things that don't, 24/7.

Heading for the port, we've come here from the power stations on foot, walking the south of Newport's diamond-shape, crossing the mouth of the Usk in about as much time as it takes to catch a Cardiff bus into town. This is entirely Briggs territory although, as an American originally from Minneapolis-St Pauls (the frozen Minnesotan twin cities), his claim has been earned rather than given. "I knows that," he tells me, laying on the local twang. "But I lives in Newport now." The accent, even the Briggs' version, has less buzz saw to it than Frank Hennessey's Cardiffian.

Inland from St. Julian's Pill, base for the Uskmouth sailing Club, we skirt the former Alphasteel rolling mill, now operated as Mir Steel by the Russians. To the east are the two giant wind generators installed at Solutia UK's chemical works. Ahead is an overgrown but designated path that runs along the side of the river from Bird Port, APB[9]'s small-scale shipping rival built onto the site of the Channel Dry Docks[10]. The route takes us over what Google Maps calls a Ferry Terminal but is actually part of Hanson's Felnex Sand Wharf aggregate operation at the end of East Bank Road. We eventually emerge beyond Coronation Park at Stephenson Street. Here an artic, directed by sat nav, is attempting to get onto the six-car platform of the restored Newport Transporter Bridge. Not a chance. Light Vehicles £1, reads the sign, Pedestrians and Cyclists Free. "You'll be hanging off the edge mate," shouts the operator, laughing.

The Transporter Bridge[11] is one of the great Newport landmarks and is visible from miles off to anyone approaching the city on the M4 from the west. It was built in the early years of the twentieth century as an innovative alternative to swing-bridges, tunnels, and crossing mechanisms that could be raised. Access was needed from the west bank of the Usk to reach British Mannesmann's tube works (and later Orb Steel) on the river's east. Upriver from the crossing point was the original Newport Town Dock – now filled in – and the river wharfs. Beyond them was the Castle. In 1906, when Lord Tredegar opened it, this was a busy spot.

The Bridge is a cable-drenched, blue-painted monument to how things were when coal was king and money flowed in the industrial Edwardian age. It's still a working crossing, although now a tourist luxury given the existence of the updated Sydney Harbour bow string arches of the new City Bridge that goes over the Usk just to the north[12]. We cross along with five smoking teenagers, a fat-bellied man in cycling gear and a couple down from Porthcawl in their Honda, here just for the excitement of having their car swung out over the waters on a platform held by wire.

The structure may well be operated by industrial-booted council employees but it's looked after by FONT B. This acronym had me hunting my Letraset memory for a while until I worked out that it stood for *Friends Of Newport Transporter Bridge.* The Friends are volunteers who manage bridge celebrations, run fundraising events, and hand out certificates for those who are "brave enough to walk across the top on open days". I'm up for this but the next opportunity won't be for ten weeks. In the small interpretation centre there are toilets and a stall selling coasters, fridge magnets and large print histories. The dead have had their ashes scattered from the gondola. In 1968 the *South Wales Argus* ran a campaign to have the bridge taken down and sold for scrap. In a fit of uncharacteristic concern the Council said no. Some years later, a local businessman tried to sell the structure to the Americans. His plan was to re-erect it either at Niagara Falls or Hollywood. The attempt failed.

At the port gates we're met by Chris Green, the ABP Sales and Marketing Manager who is facilitating our access. The core of Newport's seafaring now lies in ABP's Alexandra Docks, North and South, set in a water-filled L between Crow Point and the mouth of the Ebbw on the west banks of the Usk. Chris takes us down the conifer-lined port office access road, which has all the feel of the rail line between Moscow and St Petersburg. Nothing visible other than the way on, the surrounding country entirely hidden by green. Chris, a marine geographer from Kingston-on-Thames, is responsible for all five of the south Wales ports, Cardiff and Barry, Port Talbot and Swansea, and Newport. Newport is on its own. It has the deepest dock and the widest gates. Only Avonmouth is bigger.

Unlike any of the other ports this one has the feel of activity. There may not be gouts of steam and smoke filling the air, nor, it has to be said, that much actual industrial noise, but there is movement. Ships are berthed, cranes are swinging, artics prowl the roads, trains wait to be loaded. Newport is a centre for coal, animal feeds, timber, metal coil and bulks. We pass a dark mound on the South Dock's northside. "That's biomass," Chris says, "olive pulp." Next to it are white stacks of pumice, here to be formed into breeze blocks. Beyond are acres of horizontal telegraph poles. These are from the Baltic and in the process of being treated. Even I, with my poor olfactory sense, can smell the chemicals.

We are in hard hats, high vis vests and wearing life savers. Safety is high on the tree. John has the added difficulty of wearing two cameras and an equipment case on the top of this gear. He's constantly drifting off to shoot moving cranes or coils of steel being discharged from the cargo holds of waiting ships, and has to be pulled back. Chris, it turns out, is a pretty fair photographer himself. He's taken some of the pics that adorn ABP's brochures. The light down here is a gift. The skies are huge. The sun bounces off the concrete quayside. It radiates across the flat massif of the empounded water.

What is it with industry that makes it so psychogeograpically attractive? John has disappeared among the mountains of Russian coal that rise from the quayside. This black gold is bound for the power stations at Aberthaw and dark-age Uskmouth B just back down river. Is this how the south Wales world once was? I've got small coal in my boots and black marks on the bottoms of my trousers. Maybe. But if I turn around I see Chris in his business suit, a neat row of clean, parked cars and not a sign of smoke anywhere.

Chris is talking up the cruise trade. Visits by cruise liners are something high on the WAG[13] (now WG)'s agenda. In their glittering size and with their well-heeled passengers by the hundred, these vessels are the jewels of the high seas. They drift the world's waterways, and in recent years have begun to find their ways into the drizzle-drenched reaches of the Severn. There have been twelve or so landings, spread out between here and Milford, over the past decade. Holland America's 800 passenger *Prinsendam*, visiting last year, was a local triumph. It was beaten only by The World's 2007 squat in the waters off Swansea. "There's no need for great embarkation sheds," says Chris, as we stand among the dockside industrial detritus. "All you need is a set of coaches to take them off to wherever they want." Where did the *Prinsendam*'s passengers go? Cardiff.

What else happens here? "We recycle metals. Break cars. Remove the dangerous components from fridges, vacuum cleaners, televisions and computers. We import animal feed. Sometimes we import and export the same product at the same time using two ships berthed next to each other. It has happened. Steel arrives, gets loaded onto waggons and sent to the Midlands. Steel manufactured locally is trucked in, put on ships and then exported. It's all twenty-first century, late capitalist economics."

Above us towers the bulk of the 41,000-tonne Liberian-registered *Wanderlust*. A single stevedore is fixing bar codes to its cargo of metal coil. John catches the shot in all its crisp light and precise shadow. After a while you discover that this is the core of what a photograph actually is. Not people. Not landscapes. Not things. But that which you use to see them all. Light.

In the hunt for a drink that follows our Port amble, we try the first pub we come to outside the dock gates – the somewhat inappropriately named West of England Tavern. The barmaids are on the street outside, smoking. "Can we get coffee here?" They shake their heads, stubbing their fags and smiling. "We only does alcohol." This is a Newport thing, I'm sure. "When you're in Newport, chips, cheese, curry makes you feel brand new. Washed down with a Special Brew. Repeat the word Newport, Newport, Newport."[14] Yes, Newport, that's so true.

Caerleon

The band have just kicked into 'The End of the Vision', and we've got the audience listening. It's been a story of my life, this one. Getting the audience to pay attention. Do little and they'll go their own ways, talking, scratching, examining the contents of their pockets, checking who has just arrived and who is leaving. If there's a noise off then you're done. As if they were a single creature the whole mass will turn. You've got to catch them, engage their eyes, hold them with a line they just want to follow.

The Second Aeon Travelling Circus[15], for that's who we are, have drums, bass, two guitars, me on assorted things you shake and blow, and a microphone. 'The End of the Vision' lies somewhere between Eugene's Pink Floyd axe and Adrian Henri's The Liverpool Scene science fiction. It's going well, it usually does. We're at Caerleon College of Further Education, where they make the product that Wales today is best known for: teachers. The kids are enthralled. Poetry and rock music, how can you mix such things? But in 1970, in this mystical corner of a myth-filled country we do just that.

Caerleon. I hardly knew it then. The Circus, who'd done this gig for the rapacious students at least half a dozen times, arrived with no thought for the history or the landscape through which they were passing. Got in, did the show, then got back out. Today, decades on, it's all so different. Caerleon town of things and places, stones and marks, floors and walls, fields dug over and poked at endlessly, an epicentre of what was.

I've come up the tidal river so far that there's barely any trace of the Estuary's salt sea left. This is the Usk now, the Isca as the Romans called it. It meanders on its flood plain in bows and bends, shaped like a snake of rope, a different one now from the Roman version of two thousand years ago. Rivers move, change their courses. If you want to fix a landmark then a river won't hack it. I'm standing at the site of the Roman Quay, just south of Arthur Machen's watering hole, the Hanbury Arms. It was here, or it might have been. But two years ago they excavated a whole Roman port of considerable size and significance downriver to the east. Perhaps it was there after all.

Caerleon in 2012 has a population a little over eight and a half thousand and manages to keep its identity as a village, despite nudging Newport so hard that it really ought to be called a suburb. It's one of those places Wales is famous for, where history mixes with myth and the ley lines cross and clash enough to make it a spot that's hot in the firmament of the alternative. Caerleon – it's a Laugharne or a Cardigan – a place where Celtic wannabes and Arthurian revivalists meet full-time historians and unflappable academia.

I've walked back up here from the Estuary coast simply to admire the Romans' ingenuity in making this place their Western home. A key base of some significance for the Second Legion Augusta and a port taking triremes and ships bringing supplies all the way up the Sabrina. Caerleon was a fine example of the Roman technique for subduing difficult regions[16]. Build a base right in the centre of your opponent's territory and then supply it by sea. Being this far up river made Caerleon safe from Estuary-born attackers. It's hard to imagine that now as I stand outside the Post Office that also does dry cleaning and shoe repair. Just a little back down High Street is a shop selling scented candles, crystals on strings and packeted incense; the world smouldering on peacefully after all these years.

Despite a literary presence (birthplace of Arthur Machen, home of Sam Adams and workplace for poet Alan Barrow) and with history strewn around the place like this was still part of the ancient world Caerleon is an incredibly noisy place. Overhead there's a helicopter hovering. On Cold Bath Road the boombox boys rev their racers. Around the one-way system, traffic roars. I retreat to the Village Bakery on Backhall Street where I drink tea next to a far-from-silent Fanta-filled refrigerated cabinet and a bread slicing machine that would give most power stone cutters a run for their money. The woman behind the counter carries on a shouted one-sided conversation with someone unseen out the back. "Tomorrow night, love, yeah, drink a load, be sure you do, I would." The peace of the green amphitheatre, when I get there, is palpable.

Caerleon is known for its Roman remains and, along with the footings for the enormous barracks that run right under the local comprehensive school's fields, this half grass-covered lion-killing enclosure is one of the best. According to Geoffrey of Monmouth, it's also the site of the Court of King Arthur and the place where he set his Round Table. Fantasy, yes, and fantasy even when the good Geoffrey first came up with the idea in the twelfth century[17,] but this hasn't stopped the Arthurian war bands from making Caerleon their base and filling it full of bardic poetry, carvings of Guinevere, and quests for the sword, chair, crown and last resting place of Arthur at various sites in the locale.

The town is home to a thriving college, now a branch of UWCN (University Wales College Newport) and no doubt on the verge of being merged into something larger as the Education Minister, Leighton Andrews, follows through on his intended course. All this means extant pubs. Loads of them. Open and making money from drink rather than sizzling steaks. Mostly. Although I was rather disappointed to find the ancient Drovers Arms on the edge of Goldcroft Common now converted into a take-away peddling fish and chips, kebabs and something called sf chicken. Science fiction chicken. That's a prospect worth considering.

The sixteenth century Hanbury Arms, where I began my circular tour, is famous not only for being old and for having the horror-writer Arthur Machen among its regulars, but for renting rooms to Alfred Lord Tennyson. He came here in 1856 searching for atmos to help with the writing of his Arthurian masterpiece, the *Idylls of the King*. Tennyson, by all accounts, was a moody and reticent man who slept soundly and alone in the pub's wooden bed. For years after, the landlord made a bit on the side showing this piece of inspirational furniture off to visiting fans who'd come to see where the great Poet Laureate had once worked. The bed eventually fell to bits, riddled with woodworm, and had to be burned. The bay windows to Tennyson's Magistrates' Room, however, still overlook the river. Below them, smokers gather.

In the Roman bathhouse, CADW has done a splendid job of restoring the virtually unrestorable. This two-thousand-year-old leisure facility now actually looks like somewhere you might want to spend time. Hot water, steam, facilities for scraping olive oil off your skin and a place for a swim. Pool bottom incorporates a clever film showing two Roman swimmers doing incessant lengths. There's a soundtrack of splashes and drips to add to the realism, but it is marred a bit by the incorporation of something that sounds a little like Aled Jones's 'Walking In the Air' rolled on top. No Arthur here, no snowmen either. Just members of the legions (afternoons) plus Roman women and children (morning only).

The Museum[18,] behind its neo-Greek classical columns, houses a great mass of Roman finds including coins, grave markers, tablets, bottles, cups, jewellery and armaments. As a vehicle for the interpretation of the sunny Roman way of life here in this part of dismal Wales, it's unbeatable. Not only does it have on show more Roman coinage than I've ever seen in one place, but the grave stone, recovered from nearby Great Bulmore where it had been reused as part of a house, of one Julius Valens, veteran of the Augustan Legion. Julius managed to live to a hundred. Tonight, a sign on the four-columned entrance proclaims, is a once in a lifetime opportunity to hear a talk on the Military Role of Eunuchs in the Late Roman Empire. £3.50. Pre-booking required. They are clearly expecting a rush.

Outside, amid Caerleon's rich mix of the real Roman with the faux Arthurian, there are sculptures. Dozens of them. Mostly wood, more than life-size, and reminiscent of the sort of things that might have been used on the prows of sailing ships or to guard the entrances to magic caves in many of the fantasy world's variants on Tolkien. Quests are rich here in Caerleon, the gap between the actual and the imagined not that great. The annual arts festival with its re-enactments at the Amphitheatre, its plays and performances, and its art work trails invites sculptors from across the world to spend time here hacking live tree trunks. Their works stay on behind them.

In the eighteenth century walled garden of Caerleon House, built on top of what was once the Porta Praetoria, the Roman main gate to the fort, is the Ffwrwm Arts Centre – a ramshackle mix of craft shop, bardic centre and sculpture overload. Here, Arthurian legend mixes with tree-sized love spoons, snakes, and serpents, and creations drawn from the Mabinogion. If anything, it feels as if I am in Ubud, in Bali, where carving wood is a city-wide occupation. Or, more likely, Glastonbury, where the ley lines erupt from the sacred ground and the spirit staggers or soars, depending on your persuasion.

My Caerleon Heritage Trail[19] (twenty-four sites from all periods) took two miles and two hours to walk, not counting the bread pudding diversion to the bakery. At the Museum they've told me that the Roman Quay can't actually be accessed as it's on private land, but that it will feature soon on *Time Team*. I buy the book and pay an extra 5p for a bag. What sort of bag is it? It's a lovely bag, says the woman. It is too.

Uskmouth West

After the industrial overbuild of the docks and the city noise on this trip I'd completely forgotten about the silent coast, a welcome contrast. Access this time is via three false starts from the Duffryn housing estate, all Radburn curving streets, child buggies, kids on bikes, men in jeans, and zigzag-linked terraces where the front door is at the back. The not-yet-built-on fields beyond the housing are a waste of builder's fly-tipped rubble, discarded flat-pack furniture and *Boys from the Blackstuff* bitumen scrap. The route in is Heol Pont y Cwcw, Cuckoo Bridge Road. It's full of bends and US prairie-like dust. Cuckoos long gone, if they were ever here. It hits the coast where the Ebbw and the Usk join at New Gout. The Ebbw was straightened in 1904 to facilitate dock build, the old pill subsumed and a new one formed. You'd expect water fury but instead the rivers move like tea slops. Here are Newport's proud South Dock gates. The West Pier. The East Pier. No history in those names. The Port fallen from grace but still New. It'll be like that forever.

In the distance there's St Brides Banger Racing, £6 a car. You can hear them roaring in their figure eights. Numbers on the roof. Bouncy castles, burger vans, fries, scream and dust. Stuff that only happens in places where one thing ends and another begins. Liminal. Edge. Interzone. Fringe.

There are other things down here that I have no interest in. Dinghies, hunting for flat-fish in the ooze, keeping cattle, botanising, ship spotting, leaving wrecks of rusting cars in hedge rows, dumping scrap in ragged lines across the saltmarsh, rabbit trapping, shooting at things that move. The shooting is endemic along the entire levels. These summer days are punctuated by the sound of men in combat gear firing shotguns, peppering tree-trunks, wounding squirrels, showering the sky to miss slow moving mallard and out of range gull, defacing the signs everywhere that ban them. Private. No Guns. No Shooting. Bugger that, carry on.

The path runs straight now, heading for a white-painted Martello half hidden by greenery, a lantern room protruding above. West Usk Lighthouse. Built on a river mouth island by James Walker, Scottish architect, in 1821. It took until 1856 for the land to be drained and an access road put in. The lighthouse was eventually decommissioned in 1922 and, after a ragged history of use as a private residence, dereliction, and subsequent service as a World War Two lookout post, it was eventually refurbished for use as a hotel by the present owners, Frank and Danielle Sheehan, in 1987.

There's no one about as I pass, lights off, silence. Caravans half-obscured by bushes, mildew, a yurt in a low yard, a closed ticket booth at the head of the rough track that leads here from St Brides. West Usk is celebrated on Trip Advisor as the most expensive b&b at which anyone has ever stayed. It has been featured as 'eccentric hotel of the week' by everyone from the *Daily Telegraph* to Channel 5's *The Hotel Inspector.* Their website calls it "a personal workshop and paranormal laboratory... subjected to Frank's quirky brand of DIY, with miniature light-houses and ships glued to the ceilings". From the outside, there is a definite air of the handmade repair.

In its wind-swept, light-filled fastness, West Usk offers an alternative universe: Mongolian yurt culture, waterbeds, Psych-K workshops, infra-red saunas, floatation tank therapy, reconnective healing, thought-pattern management, rejuvaslim, Columbian healing lights, DNA theta therapy, Indian head massage, self-hypnosis and reiki kinesiology. "Only in loving states does God's energy become available to mortals to work divine magic upon them." There's a restored full-size Dalek in the hall. In the lamp room is an experimental device for contacting the spirits of dead scientists. Outside the white benches weather. Inside five rentable rooms wait. Extra space offered in the vans and the yurt. Outside jacuzzi. Candles. More light.

It's fifteen minutes steady walk on to the Light House Inn – coast edge, steak and ale, bandits, beer garden, upstairs restaurant. The pub is set in a trailer village, hedges, flowers in pots, white fencing out beyond the car park. Newport's outriders. Where you go to drink with the kids around you, let the dog sniff the sea. Peanuts. Crisps. Watch the world.

Wentlooge

St Brides turns to Wentlooge. Medieval Llansanffraid Gwynllwg. These are the peat lands after which the whole levels substrata is named. The seawall grows in size and strength. Seawards, the Estuary takes on a deeper, more distant feel. Colours slide down the spectrum, outcrops grow less grass. There is a sense of designed sea rise protection, built from stone and concrete, in place of slung-together hopeful mud banking.

Away from the coast are trees, scrub hedging and a sense of expansive flatness not encountered before. Bigger country. This is a Roman landscape, first drained by legionnaires based at Caerleon (see p.72). Where they have not through the centuries been amalgamated, fields remain long, narrow, and trapezoid. There is much evidence of early fen banks, and set back and abandoned sea walling. Over the centuries, this place has seen waters advance and recede as seawalls have been built, failed, become derelict and then rebuilt once more.

This is still Newport, just. The village of Peterstone with its clustered houses, beer garden pub and St Peter's Church. Held services in Welsh in 1851. Allegedly built in the twelfth century with money from Norman conqueror Robert Fitzhamon's daughter, Maud. "Indeed the noblest and most beautiful Perpendicular church in the whole county," says John Newman in *Pevsner's Buildings of Wales*[63]. Grade One listed. External plaque showing the line of the Great Flood. Sold by the Church in Wales in 2002. Now a private house. Kitchen and bedrooms added. Toys in the churchyard. Kids playing out the back.

Landscaped between the seawall and the Wentlooge Road are golf tees, coarse fishing ponds, club houses and manicured lawns. This is the location for Philip Hayes' film *The Way It Grows*[21], a Finch poem performed by the author wearing a rust-red, fish patterned shirt, squatting at the edge of the rapidly filling Peterstone Gout. The film was made in 2006 after the Arts Council of England, fearful that it might get left behind by the advance of technology, threw a shed of cash at Paul Beasley's 57 Productions, one of the UK's more enterprising and non-centralist poetry outfits. Paul was moving into web film and iPoem – verse to be experienced on your portable device, although that name had yet to catch on. Then you signed up and paid to view. Today it's all free on YouTube.

We'd done early lunch and beer at the golf clubhouse and then slogged across the tees carrying cameras, tripods and sound equipment. Took all day. The tide rushing in to fill the gout and then belting back out again. You can see it, speeded up, although it hardly needs that, on the resultant film. Philip rushing off across the flatland salt marsh to film peat hags (as the outcrops are called), drainage channels, spinning rocks, and abandoned waste.

The film crew, all three of them, had stayed on my – on reflection – dubious recommendation, at the wonderful (and now closed) Blue Dragon on Cardiff's Newport Road. The signs outside should have given it away. Function Suite's. One extra greengrocer's apostrophe. Cheap and, according to the much quoted Trip Advisor not really that cheerful. "My wife caught impetigo from the pillow." "Used condom found on floor at reception." "Two of our party slept in our minivan rather than put up with the room." "Mould found in the bottom of the kettle and pubic hair in the shower." "A dump." The Blue Dragon is, as I write, for sale. A developer's future. Back then Paul said they were glad to leave.

The poem[22] layered landscape descriptors in tottering piles, building them into a merging stack of salt marsh and waste places, wayside barrenness and green overgrowth, cliff edges and damp scrublands, and then, just at the point where the listener was about to give up, bored, overprovided, on the edge of drifting elsewhere, the piece changes gear. Real life intrudes. It hits you with marshy foreshores of misogynist sex and tears and rage and endless duplicity. How it is, how it once was. Written to expunge, to cast the all too real experience into outer darkness. To move on. Now, here it is, rolling across the Peterstone foreshore, back again.

When we'd finished the crew got into their limo and headed back to the smoke, moment captured in the distant principality, poet exercised, fees in the post. I went home and wondered a bit about how the world is. How it's all too often impure and hates itself. How it makes those who live in it feel cheated. But it was a fleeting wonder.

Anything left of that poem today, hanging on in the ether, at the outfall? Here there's a sign that reads *USK RIVERBOARD PETERSTONE GOUT These sluices were opened on the 25th July, 1960 by the Chairman of the Board Councillor Clifford Williams B.E.M. J.P.* Does my verse still hover here? Certainly not.

Cardiff

Tower

There's wind in my face, but, given how it can blow down here, that's nothing remarkable. There's a faint shift in the roadside scrub and a shimmering in the cow parsley. Then up ahead you can see it. The grey tower, skyscraping. The slowly turning rotors of the second highest wind turbine in Europe. Silent, almost, in its circular dance. Grey bladed, like the sky.

This is the future, I suppose. A thing to hate at first and then a thing to love. Like the arrival of the railways in the nineteenth century, and the canals before them. The workers' terraces. The Bath stone town halls. The roaring works of steel. The docks. The smoke and the dust. The whole industrial infrastructure. Hated with huge intensity by anyone not involved in squeezing a pound from their arriving. Hated by hardly anyone at all.

The locals are up in arms. Lack of consultation by the builders. Intrusive monstrosity. "It's an eyesore. I just think it's bloody ugly." "It's in your face wherever you go." At 120 metres the turbine is higher than Capital Tower, Cardiff's tallest building. Did anyone complain when they built The Pearl, as Capital Tower was formerly known? No. In the 1960 Cardiff we wanted the future. By the 2010s we've had so much of it we no longer care. Instead it's down to not in my back yard. We don't need this. I like things as they are.

Technically we are only just in Cardiff here, heart of the Wentlooge levels, west of the Shirenewton Gypsy & Travellers site, east of Maerdy Farm. The 'Welcome to Cardiff' signs face off those of Newport. Newport's win hands down on size. But it's a changing landscape. It's full of below sea-level industrial units, self-storage facilities, cladding operators, logistics parks, laminators, and rail freight forwarders. Everyone is dry on their concrete floors and safe behind their extruded metal walls. It's a land of white vans and horses standing in fields. The Netherland Levels. Welsh Holland. Risk of inundation – greater than 1 in 200. Rely on the seawall. Believe it will hold.

G24i – the company that lease the turbine (£2.3 million, erected in early 2011[1]) – are named after Prof Michael Graetzel, Ecole Polytecnic Fédérale de Lausanne, man of the future, inventor of the dye-sensitised, nano-structured solar cell, the innovation that inspires this operation. That's the 'i' in their name. 'Innovation'. The cell comes in strips like print. It generates current from ambient, indoor light. Hold it under the table and the thing still glows.

The factory has been here for six years and occupies the site that Acer were due to move into before the bubble burst. There's a council road sign marking the place as a Computer Centre. But it's hardly that. On the gate it says 'Wentloog Environmental Centre'. Fences, cameras, guards. You can't just arrive. This is the security conscious, hi-tech future. A wetlands silicon valley. Blue-roofed industrial units, green-framed glass, landscaped car park, scrub plantings, water features, snaking paths. Graetzel's G24i sunburst logo surmounts a sign reading 'Personalising Solar Power'. What will happen tomorrow, today.

But they don't make wind turbines, solar panels, biomass briquettes, composting toilets, pellet-powered Agas or sheep-wool insulation panels. They make third generation, thin film, photovoltaic modules known as DSSCs: dye-sensitized solar cells. These power anything that runs on standby. 7% of UK generated electricity is currently lost by leaving equipment on standby, red eyes lit, waiting. DSSCs may not save the entire world, but at a time when all counts they can help save a bit.

I'm checked, signed-in, badged, asked to sign a unilateral non-disclosure agreement and then met by the company chief, Richard Costello. He introduces me to his team of senior officers who'll show me round. Everyone's wearing open-necked, company-branded polos, soft shoes and chinos. The corridors are lined with large, block-mounted colour photographs of the company's supporters – shots of Graetzel talking, Director Robert Hertzberg addressing the staff, and Advisory Board member Robert Swann walking to the north pole and sailing his green energy boat around the world. Out back is a wildlife reserve, a drainage pond on which swans have been encouraged to nest, and a bird-spotting board much the same as those I'd seen earlier at the Newport Wetlands. This one lists greylag geese, great tit, green woodpecker, fox, and "a grey bird like a heron but without feathers sticking out from the top of its head". Nearby is a photo of helpers from Swan Rescue assisting a bird attacked by a fox while defending its signets.

"We're installing charge points for company electric cars soon," Daryl Sindle tells me. He's the company Environmental Health Officer. Food is grown on site and then consumed in the canteen. He gestures towards a set of polytunnels. All waste is recycled. You expect to see tie-dyed tees, dreadlocks and tepees. But this is real business. Not a hippy in sight.

Secrecy is high. I'm rushed passed closed doors behind which white polypropylene suit-clad workers tend production lines and test products under extremes of heat and light. Everything in this plant is commercially sensitive and that sensitivity is peaking. It feels vaguely like something out of science fiction. I'm shown into an enormous hanger-like space which is entirely empty save for a single and unmoving production line along one wall. Can I take a photo? "We'd rather you did not." We're at the pre-volume manufacture stage. Full operation will begin in Q4. We're on the verge. It'll all start rolling soon.

Currently the plant uses around 18% of the electricity generated by the turbine outside. The rest goes back to the grid. Use will rise to 57% as production ramps up but that will still leave a substantial surplus. There's something poetically appealing about an operation that gives rather than takes, that saves rather than squanders, and that despite its furious secrecy, tries to smile. Daryl, Paul Rebhan and Martyn Clark – my interlocutors, my guides, my minders – all certainly do.

The demonstration room is kitted out by IKEA. It shows off cells in use, powering TV remotes, LED lamps, fans, computer keyboards, mice, cycle lights, clocks, modems and phone chargers. There's a coffee table with a surface made entirely of DSSCs. Enough to power a computer? Not yet.

We enter another door and find ourselves in a supermarket. Shopping trolleys, a checkout, shelves stacked with cans and packets, boxes of Kellogg's, cake mix, Tate and Lyle, Sugar Puffs. "This is the future," says Paul. There's a sign above, directing us to Melysion / Confectionery and Bisgedi / Biscuits. We're still in Wales. Sainsbury's are a strategic partner for G24i. Their centrally-managed shelf stickers will spot who you are by scanning your Nectar Card as you pass. They'll flash you messages appropriate to your buying history. Buy me. I like you. I'm reducing my price. You bought these beans last time you were here, want more? It's a brave new world. The rooster on the corn flakes looks at you and winks.

Outside, the turbine continues to spin. If the wind blows too strongly then it stops, I'm told. Safety is paramount. The blades are as long as articulated lorries. Erecting it was no easy matter. G24i had looked at and abandoned geo-thermal energy, but still felt they had a responsibility to the environment. Installing it required newt surveys, bat surveys, a check on bird migration patterns, a testing of wind stratification by erecting a pilot tower, and then the construction itself. Giant cranes. Engineering skill of aircraft carrier-building proportion. "You can climb up inside and emerge on the top to view the world," Paul says. Takes courage. "Have you done this yet?" He shakes his head.

Back on the Wentloog Road, there's a rush of lorries. Business park users. Dust and fume. The trains roll down the south Wales main line. London up ahead. You can hear them, still diesel, burning the planet. The arguments about main line electrification continue. G24i we've a way to go yet.

[Following a long period of overstretching itself, G24i ran out of development money in December 2012 and was put into administration. Jobs hung in the balance for around a fortnight before a consortium of private investors bought the company in what is known as pre-pack deal and immediately resumed production on the same site. Jobs fixed. Solar cell future still golden.]

Flood

It's morning. The window in my study shows the grey sky. Flat colour fields like Rothko. Watch them and they move. Watch further and they don't. They fill the panes, wash my room with unending quiet. Dull unending light. No rain yet, but it'll come. Then there'll be the hammer and the windblown thrash. The water coming in round the seams, leaking through the vents. I look southwest into the heart of it, from where, in this part of the world, it all arrives. The stream of rain-thick lows, moving up channel. On target. Settling landward like collapsing lungs.

In my pocket is a notebook. Mostly empty. Where scrawl exists, it's pretty illegible. There's a stack of similar books on the shelf beside me. More in a box. By mistake I've sometimes left notebooks in my shirt pockets when those garments go into the wash. The books return, ink run, twisted, paper pulped, and bent into snail shapes the consistency of wall filler. Their words mashed. They have a unity now – of the kind they never would have achieved on their own. Proust obsessively wrote longhand, working through the night in his cork-lined room. The same endless novel of time and space that kept him on track through-out his life. I rise at the time he would have collapsed, his energy exhausted, rain an irrelevance. The darkness held it back.

His notebooks held jumbled, crossed-out, chaotic drafts for his novels. Stabs at passages, sections of dialogue, descriptions, rehashes, rewrites. He named them, the notebooks: Fridolin, Babouche, Dux, Gros Cahier Rouge. They had a life. Mine do not. They are tiny, full of flickers, scratchings, jottings, overheards, findings, spotted, seen. They are micro-particles of the books they may one day lead to. Although they never do.

They are anonymous, indistinguishable from each other, like the lows, the latest of which is now arriving. Soft drizzle starting on the panes. Sky like the sea. Deeper. Blue. Grey. Then slate again.

I open a notebook at random. *Memo Pad Small* it says on its tea-stained, dog-eared cover. No date. There's a list of what I recall are suggested section titles for an earlier work in the Cardiff series. Prison. Sophia Gardens Pav with Animals. Cyncoed. Rolling Mill. Brendan Burns. Heath Hospital Cardiac. Tide. John Tripp Footprint. Written while sitting in the Vulcan, I think, waiting for Ifor Thomas to show. He's the one who'd told me about the last footprint of the poet John Tripp, unmarked, fixed forever in the concrete of someone's path in Heol Penyfai, Whitchurch. Full of rain and street detritus. We were going to hunt for it. Fix the rumour. We never did.

A few pages on and there's the word *flood*. Isolated on its own six-by-ten centimetre page. Scrawled while out walking. Description of the churchyard lights. Start of a poem about water. Reminder to check on house defences now that the former mill leat run of Roath Brook in Waterloo Gardens has burst its banks and come right up to the doorway of the Teahouse, threatened the hallways of the terraces and filled the car park of the flats. But most likely a prompt to check on just what did happen round here in 1607. The Great Flood. The great ouerflowing of waters in the saide Countrye. That was it.

Out on the Levels you keep finding them, the markers. Plaques preserved in churches, flood-height commemorations engraved into the walls outside. It's the same both sides of the Estuary. They're at Goldcliff, Nash, Peterstone, Kingston Seymour, St Brides. In the church at Redwick, the marker on the porch wall records the waters as having reached almost two metres. *Great Flood AD 1606*. In Peterstone Wentlooge the tablet shows *The Great Flood Jan 20, 1606*.

These dates employed the Julian Calendar which had been in use since 45 BC. It had a year of 365.25 days. New Year's Day was the 25th of March. The dates for Easter and Christmas were moving ever further apart. In 1582, Pope Gregory XIII published a decree of correction. The calendar would be altered. British suspicion of anything emanating from Rome, however, kept the Pope's changes from these shores until as late as 1752.

Under the Gregorian calendar, the Julian successor and the one we use today, 20.01.1606 became 30.1.1607. Times change.

The Great Flood, when it stormed in more than four hundred years ago, inundated the Severn estuary coast on both sides, from Gloucester to Barnstaple and from Chepstow to Laugharne. There are stories of inundated cellars and ruined stock at Bristol, and washed away farms at Llanstephan. The levels in both Somerset and Monmouthshire were the most seriously affected. Two thousand people drowned. For the population of those times that was a serious number. The waters rose to higher than two metres.

Where they existed, seawalls were overtopped, fields swamped, cattle washed out to sea, buildings flattened, hedges uprooted, boats smashed, bodies left stranded in trees. The flood came in a tumultuous rush, unexpected, unforeseen, on a bright Tuesday morning. Like a tsunami. In fact a number of eminent men, notably Professor Simon Haslett from the University of Wales and Dr Ted Bryant from the University of Wollongong, Australia, have postulated that the flood was, in fact, the direct result of such a tsunami. Their paper, published in 2002, suggests that there was an undersea earthquake, a tectonic plate shift, and submarine volcanic eruption somewhere in the deeps to the southwest of Ireland[2]. In the wake of the Indian Ocean tsunami of 2004, their findings were the subject of a 2005 BBC TV programme that caught the popular imagination. Local history societies celebrating the 400th anniversary of the Great Flood took up tsunami as the cause. Plausible as this may be, there are doubters.

The report of Risk Management Solutions, Inc. into the floods suggests that the combination of a wind-driven storm surge with an extreme spring tide is a far more likely explanation. They point to the lack of contemporary flooding in other places where a tsunami might have hit. Nothing in Ireland. Nothing on the south coast of England. Nothing in France. They query the likelihood of tectonic plate shift of sufficient size in the suggested latitudes[3]. They analyse the written evidence of the period – and this is extensive – and find little to support the idea of tsunami.

The report looks at increasing sea levels (2 mm annually over more than four hundred years), the likelihood of some sinking of foundations as a result of the draining of the levels for churches on which flood markers exist, and the height of sea defences in 1607, where they existed. It compares these with today and then calculates that if such a flood recurred the present-day cost would top £32 billion. Our own Fukushima nuclear plants at Hinkley Point and Oldbury would be at risk. Barrages would be topped. Far more than the 1607's two thousand would drown.

The early seventeenth century was a time of Christianity, where God loomed large in daily life and nothing happened without His intervention. All acts were acts of God. Rising from bed in the morning. The size of the harvest. Death of a neighbour. The arrival of the outrageous waters. The flood was delivered by the Almighty. He was the cause, He was the outcome, He was the reason. The sins of men were being paid for. "Wee see that Almighty God being mooved unto wrath by their enormus vices, sent a flood upon them, and swept them away from the face of the earth like dung and excrements[4]."

Contemporary accounts[5] such as *Lamentable newes out of Monmouthshire, God's warning to his people of England, and Newes out of Summerset Shire*, composed in full King James Bible English, were privately published and sold by printers operating out of places such as the churchyard of St Paul's in London. These were days when newspapers did not exist and colourful tales of war and disaster were produced for popular consumption. The accounts paint a picture replete with the wrath of God and the scourging of his Kingdom.

"Many men that were rich in the morning when they rose out of their beds, were made poore before noone the same day."

"So violent and swift were the outragious waves, that pursued one an other, with such vehemencie, and the Waters multiplying so much in so short a time, that in lesse than five houres space, most part of those countreys (and especially the places which lay lowe) were all overflowen."

The accounts describe a four-year-old hanging onto the roof beams of a house with nothing but the warmth of a chicken to keep her alive. A child set afloat in a cradle steered to shore by a cat. Gentlewomen escaping to the roofs of their houses only to be swept away as the floods rose further. "Mighty Hilles of water, tumbling over one another. Fruitful valleys everwhelmed and drowned. The furie of the waves driven ever forwardes. All bridges in the area collapsed, broken, carted off. Ferries sunk. Wild beasts destroyed. Great harme done."

The poet, John Stradling, acting as the John Simpson of his day, was caught by the rising waters while using the Aust ferry, trying to return to London. He survived. "I have seen fish and men hanging from trees, while the cow, sheep, and horse swam in the sea. Where wagons used to roll, there the skiff flies along with sails unfurled, and goes and returns by unaccustomed routes[6]."

In Cardiff, where the Taff at high tide had long been nibbling away at the edges of St Mary's Churchyard, the Great Flood brought the whole building down. Walls, alter, crosses, grave-yard headstones, coffins and bones were all washed to sea. The church as a church ceased to function. The graveyard, what remained of it, continued in sporadic use. It was enclosed on its three landward sides, the fourth being the Taff bank[7]. By the beginning of the nineteenth century, however, even these remains had been lost. In 1849, Brunel diverted the Taff into its new cut, and tram sheds were built on the site. Today, Great Western Lane crosses the spot, running at the back of Weatherspoons' Prince of Wales pub. Stand with your back to the flower seller. On the rear building wall there's a fake church outline, an architectural conceit. Of St Mary's, save for the name of the capital's most famous street, it's all that remains.

Outside my window, the rain is still arriving. Sheet on sheet. The garden pools, even in places where I've installed a soakaway. Didn't do this twenty years back. Risk Management Solutions have a map showing the likely penetration of flood waters should the 1607 event return. Dry land in white. Cardiff, to the bottom of the northern hills, is entirely black. I check the garden again. Wet, yes, but flood, not yet.

Lambies

Who am I today? One-meal-a-day Henry Miller in a Paris café compiling a list of books you must read before you die.

Dostoevsky, Hamsun, Balzac, Blaise Cendrars, D.H. Lawrence, Lawrence Durrell. I could be him. He expounds all the right values. The search for truth. The hunt for personal, social and artistic freedom. The need to see. I'd be him, coming along this seawall with a cigarette going, in my baggy trousers and my tweed coat. They'd be after me, the world who couldn't cope – those who accused me of being a sexist and an anti-Semite – those who saw art as a sort of decoration to obscure their epic failure. There were hoards of these guys when I started out. People who wouldn't know a vision of glory if it came up behind them and grabbed them by the throat.

But this could all be too much. Maybe I'm not Miller. His *Tropic of Cancer*, where sexual liberty blossoms like an internet blog, begins: "A year ago, six months ago, I thought I was an artist. I no longer think about it. I am. Everything that was literature has fallen from me. There are no more books to be written, thank God". No more books, such a state of grace. But for me, some hope.

The city is ahead like an anti-rural king. Steel works, heliport, towers, cranes, storage tanks, docks. Not the city the Cardiff Bay developers have suggested exists. Instead, this is the real one, the poor city, the labour city, Socialist Worker, buggies, benefits, all that stuff. The liberals and their yellow orange compromise have been left up there in the outer suburbs. This city is full of tattoos, terraces, hard-edges to the voice, boots, fags. The only Miller this city knows is one that's Lite.

As I move west, the wall has steadily risen. The earth-movers have done their work. Ancient stones banked up with landslips of soil. The city land protected. The waters, no matter what the cost, to be forever held back. If you are a local you can get coast access here down a bright, crushed limestone topped path that sides the sinuously turning mitigation reen, the recently dug double-sized drainage ditch installed as part of the vast Lamby Way landfill site's eastern expansion. It runs from the new Tredelerch Park to breach the seawall through an industrial-sized gout next to main sewer outfall. They've named it *Cors Crychydd Reen*. Bog of the Heron. Herons in sight when I pass? What do you expect?

The Lamby Moors, as this place is called, are not moors in

the accepted sense but for centuries were tidefields bordering the River Rhymney. They were fronted by the Rumney Great Wharf and, nearer the river mouth, the Little Wharf. Lamby in 1401 was *Langby*. Long Village. A Viking name. The snaking Rhymney with its shifting oxbows embraced two further slots of land, both now lost to shopping mall development and housing – The Luggs and Kesja (seen on later maps as keyscroft). These are two further Viking names. *Luggs* means marshland. *Kesja* means spear. The Vikings were here in their longboats and the town of Cardiff, tiny behind its wooden walls, trembled. The invaders got in. Womanby Street, oldest thoroughfare in the new city, is also a Viking name.

The Wharfs I'm crossing are not docks. Wharf here comes from *Warth*, derived from the Anglo-Saxon *warath*, which means seashore, or from an old Danish word meaning untilled land. On the phones I'm listening to Moby. *Play*. Richard Melville Hall's ambient, chill-out reworking of blues melodies and Afro-American voices. Moby is his stage name[8]. *Play* is the perfect antidote to the Lambies, a place that has been reworked to death since I first discovered it forty years ago. As landscape, it's as ambient as a smack in the face. With their domed hills, vertical gas extraction pipes, leachate drains and outfalls, the Lamby Way landfills are going through a process of geo-textile membrane and sub-soil capping prior to the sewing of grass. From trash to reserve. These cells, as the filled sections of the dump are known, will become nature reserves, public walking areas, golf courses. They told me that when I was here in 2001[9] but the transformation is still to arrive.

The Lamby Way site covers some fifty hectares and is fast running out of space. It is built largely on abandoned Rhymney River oxbows and the pits dug into the clay for use in nearby potteries and brickworks. At the south eastern corner of the site is a trig point, cracked, slightly leaning. It's a starting point for psychogeographic runners who spend weekends cross-country-ing the twenty-seven miles around the Capital's four other trigs at Lisvane, Rhiwbina Hill, The Garth and Ty Bronna in the City's west.

From here, the city does not resemble the city I know. The tide is out a million miles and the acres of pock-marked mud glisten in the new sun. There are beaches, small things with sand, squashed between the alluvial deposits and the smashed brick and concrete discard that lies below the seawalls. Celsa's Tremorfa smelting works sits like a nuclear power station with its arms in the water. The Rover Way Gypsy site is a seaside holiday camp. Beyond are the capped ash bunds protecting the ferrous scrap metal yards and then, looking like an island of green trees rising from the flat marsh of the muddy Bay, the plantings that back onto Cardiff's heliport.

The path tracks the outer edge of the landfill, separated by scrawls of undergrowth and a razor-wire topped mesh fence. It's barely a path, descending to sludge overgrown with reed grass, and pitted with pools that would be full if the season had not been so consistently dry. Moby is out of my ears. Against a backdrop blazed with space and light and crossed by low looping National Grid power lines, I try to phone home. Vodafone says full four bars but the pylons say no.

Rubbish flows everywhere here, escaped from the dump, washed back by the tides. Certain items predominate, repeat themselves among the sun-seared, mud-worn spread. Fridges with their doors off, crates, blue-topped plastic bottles, footballs, dented, deflated, lost. There's a complete child's plastic horse, galloping on, yellow-maned, blue-green rockered, in the long grass.

I'm opposite the Rhymney River Motor Boat Sailing and Fishing Club on its tight river salient. Its name these days has been made more comprehensive, and a clubhouse and yellow pontoon added since I last passed. The river here keeps trying to shift, self-eroding one bank to push itself into a new cut further on. It is held back by the dumping of hard-core. This is river orthodontics, braces to make the water course flow against its essential nature. For now, it does what it's told.

Above me, although I can't see it for the overgrowth, is Jeroen Van Westen's never completed CBAT[10] public artwork, 'Breathing In, Time Out'. My poem, 'Ysbwriel'[11], a blend of Welsh and English which processes various words associated with rubbish much as the landfill does with the real stuff, still runs in metre-high lettering along the side of a structure Van Westen had built. You can read it from Rover Way, from the

Yacht club, from boats on the river. GRASS.GASH. FFLWCS.BGS it stutters, in severe Bauhaus Univers upper case.

The path dumps me through a thicket of nettle and bush onto the main road near the Lamby Way site main entrance. The start of Cardiff Council's Wentloog Business Area – financial sweeteners available if your business relocates. The nomenclature proliferates: Waterside Business Park, Capital Business Park, Eastgate Business Park, Springmeadow Business Park, Lamby Industrial Park, Wentloog Corporate Park, Lamby Way Workshops. Fiefdoms, city states, semi-autonomous regions with their own traffic laws and their own business rates.

It's a short walk to get myself out of this traffic zoom and onto what the Council have designated as the mitigation reen path. I'm walking this section in a great circle. My car is parked on wasteland in sight of the seawall near Maerdy Farm. Despite the presence of the Lamby Way site, the atmosphere here is country. Swans on the reen guarding their signets. Mallard. Banks of reed. Dragonfly. I'm followed down the track by two Poles in three-quarter drop-crotch pants, flip-flops, shaved heads, cigs, fierce dog off its lead. Reminder of how near we must be to places where people live rather than work. Another fiefdom. This one in the shadow of the wind turbine at G24i. You can see the blades turning, beyond the trees.

There are fields here, full of buttercup and pony. Lungs of green air. But it's an illusion. Behind the thick hedges are acre-wide car dismantlers, motors in lines, stacks of car doors, retrieved windscreens, engine parts. Despite the signs stuck on poles and lost in hedges announcing turf and horses, this is now an industrial belt. Farming is a thing of the past.

Near Sea Bank Farm I meet Ken and Tim, two pensioners unfolding a plastic caravan cover in a field. They identify me by my camera as an ornithologist and start telling me about the head of a great auk that was dug out of the foreshore. I'm more an historian, I correct them. Starting on the psychogeographer tack will get me nowhere. "This was an army camp in the war," Ken tells me. "Gun emplacements on the seawall, armaments store in that building over there." He points at the car dismantlers workshop. The officer's quarters they've turned into a house at the end of the lane. We get to talking about the dump and the receding sea. "Cardiff's mostly ash-tip," says Tim. "At Leckwith and Maindy. And all round here. The boats used to bring in rocks as ballast and we've used them as hard-core." The world keeps changing. That it does.

In wartime, bombs destined for the docks often fell short and exploded here. Upper Newton Farm took a hit as did the Pottery. Cows in fields died and the sewer outfall was wrecked. The Americans built supply warehouses on land now occupied by the Freight Liner depot at Wentloog Business Park. Their vast sheds held military stores as well as the bodies of US Servicemen killed in action, kept there before onward transport home.

I return to the car again, still there, not towed for dismantling nor stolen. Beyond is Maerdy Farm. The entrance lane is lined with beech. For a moment, rurality returns. But beyond are acres of land with their surfaces scraped, ready for development. The rural a myth. Cardiff flatlands, the empire expanding, on and on.

Crossing the City

At Trusty Bite I drink sweet tea. Things have come on a million miles since food hygiene regs started to interfere with this sector. Counter tops are wiped, the mugs are new, sugar comes in individual servings, you get plastic spoons and serviettes, and there's a set of outdoor chairs to rest in while you sip, unused, rain splattered, but there. Tea is the only thing that will make the day work. Start it right, then cross the city.

I'm here because of this conceit that I've adopted, that's got me this far along the route, which says that I should stay as near to coast as is reasonable and travel all of it. Walking, mostly. I'm outside one of the great American-style out-of-town super stores that line Newport Road. A car-friendly homeland of bathroom fittings, safe storage, DIY, flat-pack, ten pin bowling, pet requisites, computers and beds. The site is huge and you can only walk it if you believe you can defy death. Some do. You see them, couples in trainers and sweats, carrier bags in hands, ever hopeful. They stand, stranded on the central reservation with artics booming past and no gaps in the four-lane stream, stuck for the duration.

The city is big despite it being small. Cardiff's great inbuilt contradiction. I'm going to cross it more than once. I've got my Brompton, a highly-prized and exceptionally rideable cycle, folded into something similar to the size of a triple gatefold-sleeve lp set of albums by Yes. It's the next best thing we have on the planet to a Harry Potter Invisibility cloak. Ride and you vanish. You can go anywhere. You are rarely challenged. No one looks. I've got it standing on the floor at my feet. This small-wheeled cycle, which can get through city traffic faster than a Smart Car, can be collapsed in less time than it takes to find your cash card and can be carried with you into paper shops and up lifts. It only ever let me down in Lower Splott. Here, cycling in light snow and with my woollen hat pulled tightly over my ears, I passed a school bus queue and was pelted with snowballs for allegedly looking stupid. Conformity is clearly an issue south of the rail tracks.

Rather than walk it – the traffic-thick slog across the lozenge-shaped city east to west – I intend to use the cycle lanes. Cardiff's pride and joy. Red-tarmacked road slivers, delineated by white boundaries and ideograms of bicycles, these lanes of safety and green speed start, stop, thin and vanish with all the vagaries of a southern Italian election campaign. Everything blocks them, from skips to wheelie bins, from beer lorries to builders' merchants, from bendy buses to police patrol cars. If you are delivering anything and need temporary storage, then stick it in the cycle lane. No one uses them, least of all the cyclists themselves. They mostly ride on the pavements. On the Tyndall Street half cycle lane/half pavement section that goes over the railtracks beyond the Magic Roundabout, the peril is the drifting pedestrian. Head glued to a mobile or ear-phones in, feline approach to straight lines and a tendency to never give hand-signals the right of these death-defiers to walk anywhere in the world they want to without let or hindrance, is absolute.

On Newport Road, heading west, there's no bike provision. Official advice is to use the bus lane. However, anyone who'd ever stood next to a low-rider, passing inches from the kerb and at speed, would recognise that air dynamics don't favour this.

I'm on the pavement, a thing I never do, of course. Slow rider. Passed by hoards of immigrants, mostly on bikes too small for them. Not one cycle helmet, no hi-vis vests and not one rider keeping to a direct path.

I'm beyond the petrol station at the place where, for decades, a thin, dark-haired man in shirt sleeves would spend hours making karate blocks at passing traffic. Gone now. Taken away or died. Today, instead, there's a mad woman with a thick gold necklace and a face like Granny Clampett dancing up the pavement, transistor radio clamped to her head like this was 1958. Newport Road, land of the stretched and the challenged. I dodge her in a flurry of jangly dance music and accelerating buses to brake again, just in time, to avoid the next obstacle. This time it's a family of head-to-foot, black-clad Afghani tribal-heartland immigrants with double buggy, regulation shopper-on-wheels, assorted kids and multiple packages of industrial-strength, giga-sized, Super Dry Huggies.

North of the Feeder on the path, sunk into the green below Boulevard de Nantes, things are easier. Shady cool. Tree roots. Woman using a wheeled Zimmer. Man with a NHS aluminium, clump-ended, adjustable stick. Should I be cycling here? Who knows.

Along Castle Street, among the never-ending roadworks, the Cardiff population surges. Locals mix with tourists photo-graphing the Castle, scavenging seabirds, and Dragon taxis returning to the Central Station where they'll queue again for a rare fare, twenty-four deep. Crossing Canton Bridge, the path resumes to run, more or less consistently, all the way into the heart of the city's bohemian, Cymric and most Cardiffian of suburbs. Canton. St Canna's Town. Named after the sixth century female saint and not a Chinese-sounding creation of the Far-east obsessed Third Marquis of Bute.

I'm heading up the curved and consistently non-uniform terraces of the Canton heartlands to visit Des. Des Barry: writer, Buddhist, world traveller, Jesse James expert, filmmaker, graphic novelist and Gurnos-born renaissance man. He's about as tall as Rhondda-born historian Dai Smith but rather less determined in his world approach. In his book-lined study he serves coffee and cake.

Unaccountably, my image has been lifted by Des to become Gerardo Fischer, the missing playwright and director of the Argentinian Compañía de Teatro Real y Presente. This is the fictional (or maybe not) Real and Present Theatre Company[12]. According to the quite convincing website, Fischer disappeared on 9th January, 2006. There's a film showing me fleetingly glimpsed among the shelves of a Buenos Aires antiquarian book retailer. This was actually filmed in the basement of Castle Arcade's Trout Mask Books. But it looks convincing. There's also a poster, my face taken in the 80s, dark, thin hair, Italianate skin. *Have You Seen This Man? If You Have Any Idea As To His Whereabouts Please Contact Clara Luz Weizzman.* Weizzman is the present company director and coordinator of the Far South Collective and is leading the search for Fischer. David Enrique Spellman provides written context and news updates.

In Montevideo, photographer Diego Vidart updates the web presence[13]. He posts shots of Fischer sightings, photographs of Fischer possessions, interviews with those who knew him. He compiles reports from others. There's a filmed response to Fischer's theatre productions at Chapter Arts Centre, and an offer to include responses from other creative individuals who may have known Fischer or imagined they did. Reality and fiction begin to merge. There's a photograph of the age-worn cover of Fischer's *Los Delincuentes*, published in Buenos Aires in 1968. It could be my own *End of the Vision* published in Cardiff, 1971.

On the Fischer biog section of the web site you get a photo of me taken by the *South Wales Echo* in 1966. Young. Hopeful. Cord jacket. Typewriter. At the Harrogate Crime Festival, Spellman's publisher, Serpent's Tail, will distribute a handbill – *Missing: Gerardo Fischer*. My 1980s face again, the ghost back from the past.

"Why me," I ask? "You don't look Welsh," says Des. "You seem more, well, Spanish, or Italian." Like my Uncle Eric, in that photo of him standing in some lost back garden in 1937 with his accordion, looking completely Hispanic. Or my father's parents, their countries of origin removed from his army paybook in a fit of denial by my censorious mother. Information now lost as there's no one on his side of the family still alive to ask. No memory, no written records. He always talked about Naples, my father. A place that meant a lot. But who knows, that might have just been the War. His father, my grandfather, worked on the Taff Vale railway. Signalman. Maybe it's just a dark-skinned strain returned to the surface. You are what you think you are. I think I'm Cardiffian.

Des is explaining how he works. The way text springs from physical objects, and the way Quick Response Codes[14] spin the reader from word to image, throwing them from one reality into another. Des Barry, Cardiff's Beat Generation William Burroughs. If he were that, then Lloyd Robson would be Gregory Corso, and John Williams, Allen Ginsberg. In this reality mash he has created, he's Des Barry as well as David Enrique Spellman. His co-conspirator Diego Vidart is Esko Tikanmäki Portogales. Portogales, a fellow Fischer spotter, is currently bound for Finland to engage in Des's next project, tentatively called *Far North*. But that's just a working title. Things will shift again before too long.

He shows me a copy of Julio Cortázar's *Hop Scotch*[15], the first ever hyper-link novel, actually written at a time when the internet had not been invented. Cortázar has been a great influence on Des. Reality and fiction once again merging. Like they did when on the sea-front at Aberavon watching Michael Sheen in Theatre Wales' production of *The Passion*. In this, the Mayor – chain, suit, microphone in hand – delivered public order announcements and advice to the crowd on where the buses were and which steps to use to reach them. Real information the audience needed. He thanked the theatre company and then called for order, holding up his arms. He began to sound just that bit too fluid for an elected man of the people. Reality slid. He was an actor on the company payroll. The real Port Talbot Mayor, Councillor Llella James, must have been sitting in the audience, watching. The rest of us didn't notice. We got on the buses as directed and moved on to the next piece of action.

We talk about 9/11. Des was there, on the Jersey City shore ,watching the collapsing towers and the plume of smoke and dust obscuring Manhattan. He was there, returning home from four years in Tibet where he'd studied meditation. You can still hear Merthyr in his voice, but only just. "Was Burroughs really an influence?" "Yes, but not in the way you'd think. Try Barry's most famous work, his Jesse James reworking, *The Chivalry of Crime*[16]. Not a cut-up in sight." Outside the sun beats the Canton streets. I unfold my bike and set off for a traffic-snarled return trip. An episode of cut-up after cut-up, all real, none of them textual at all.

The Zone – Pengam to the Bay

Cycling is, of course, not walking. And I haven't made my mind up yet, given the parameters of the whole Chepstow to Worm's Head transit, as to how much I am going to allow myself to do. But today it's once again feet. I've winkled Des from his study and we're outside TGI Fridays – a leisure eatery bolted into one of those great edge territories of our sprawling world – half shunting yard, half retail park, half allotments, half place of rough ground, grown over with bramble, that no one wants. We're heading for the Millennium Centre and we've got three hours.

The road we are on, which crosses the main railway, up from the main Newport Road and over to the Lamby Way Rhymney River Bridge, is known as Rover Way. It was named after the British Leyland plant that once made Rover cars on the site of Cardiff's former Airport on Pengam Moors. All in the past now – the tidefields and open moors of Pengam, the farms that were built onto them, the airport and the wartime RAF base built after that, the factory that made cars, the Ocean Club, the flatlands of the growing city, pulling in the wind from the Severn Sea. Today it's housing – the apartments of Roath Brook, the semis of Pengam Green. Estate Agents' names: Brook, Green, Close, Court.

We reach the river by crossing more liminal territory, the waste green spaces that surround the roadways and the traffic island housing, the twin-towered cross bars of Eillis O'Connell's *Secret Station*[17]. In weathered bronze, and when working full of steam and light, these towers mark the gateway to a city that's already stepped at least six further miles to the east. Des, wearing a flat cap on backwards and with videocam on tripod, stops to take a shot. He's the urban filmmaker among roaring artics and highsided vans. No one looks. No one stops.

From the river's edge, we are now directly opposite 'Ysbwriel'[18], last glimpsed as I fought my way through the overgrowth surrounding the landfill site. Des is impressed and films furiously. The council have done much here for the route of the All Wales Footpath, offering a hard-topped walk right the way down the side of the river. What was once a stumble through muddy revetement and over hastily-piled river defence is now an easy stroll. Ten minutes to the Estuary, the place where the rapidly snaking Rhymney reaches the slow moving Severn. A flat shading of grass, to mud, to foreshore stone, to slopping, earth-coloured sea.

Standing here you can imagine what Cardiff might have looked like when the Romans came. A flat and almost treeless river delta of tall grass and tidal detritus. No buildings. No encampments. A fisherman, perhaps, with his henge of nets. A few primitive boats pulled up onto the shoreline's sinking mud. To get the full effect you need to mentally block out the tanker you might see out there on the Severn and the power lines that loop along from Newport. You also have to ignore the shambles of hard-core, bits of brick wall, smashed concrete, sea-worn stone and lumps of mortar, broken furniture and rusted car parts that litter the entire foreshore. But you can do it. I tell Des. He's unconvinced.

Ahead, behind a low retaining wall, is the Cardiff Traveller Camp, a prefab fort housing eighty in breeze block accommodation made to look like an embryonic 70s housing estate. If you allow, that is, for the lack of greenery and the addition of scrap metal and old tyres in heaps in the yards. A resident, out walking an aged greyhound, who imagines, laden as we are with cameras and notebooks, that we work for the Council, tells us that the gash of wrecked furniture and mashed metal dumped among the bushes here is the work of others. "Terrible," he says. "The site manager turns a blind eye, you know." So who does dump the stuff?" asks Des. The static traveller points vaguely out towards houses in the distance, bottom end of Pengam Green. "Dunno," he says.

"Where do you come from?" I ask. "I was born here," he

says, "I like it." Smoke drifts over from the Celsa plant just up the road. In the air is a mix of slushing sea, passing artic and squawking gull. Edge territory again.

The path goes up behind the camp and the Water Treatment Plant next door to climb over the piles of earth-topped blast furnace ash that front the shoreline. Travellers are in hot dispute with the council about the path's precise route. They need their privacy and object to it being placed within a few feet of their rear walls. The council argue that their privacy is no more invaded by the path than it would be by the building of a public pavement. Pavements in this part of the city are notable by their absence. Walk the road and you walk with trucks.

From the top of the capped slag the views of the sludgy sea are the best since Goldcliff, and the highest until you get to Penarth Head. Below are sea defences, ragged groynes, breakwaters fashioned from rock, and the inevitable mix of crushed stone and rusted, abandoned car. Behind us are the dipping tracks of Council's off-road motorcycle training and practice facility and, beyond that, the still operating ash mounds from Celsa's Castle Works.

This is Cardiff's Zone. Des is drawing parallels with Tarkovsky's film *Stalker*[19], filmed amid the wreckage of Russia's industrial might, broken walls, destroyed pipelines, half-flooded chambers, boilers and furnaces rusted shut. It's where the Zone is, a place of fulfilment of innermost desire, a place where everything is ordinary but of course is not. The stalker is the guide, the client is the guided. We, Des and I, clients both, are here, crossing Cardiff's Zone. We are looking for something. We pay great attention and do so with presence and awareness. We are unsure, though, just what it is we seek. Nirvana, understanding, path's end. Path's end would do. Des stops to shoot more film. Panoramas of the Estuary, the local Zone, and then of me stalking my way along the roughly descending track.

This is a post-industrial landscape shaped by the waste of the vanished East Moors Steelworks. Clinker and slag are in heaps at the water's edge, rising in mounds and now topped with grass. "I used to visit such places in Merthyr, as a child," Des tells me. "The huge heaps of iron dross there were in great lava shapes, rent with fissures and caves. We gave them names, these industrial hills: Whitey at Penydarren, The Eagle, The Radle and the Five Fingers nearer to home. I'd clamber and be in awe."

"As a Cardiff child I'd come here," I say. Eight years old on a bike, cycling for a dare into the steel works roar and spuming dust.

We emerge at the roundabout bottom of Ocean Way. Ocean Park: an estate of post-industrial units selling hairdresser supplies, lighting, ceramic tiles, car parts, flooring, bioscience, fitness, and office furniture. The traffic noise is as bad as anything the GKN Steelworks ever kicked out. Lingering at the roadside is 'Atlantic Echo'[20], a public art work, a series of oxidised doorways welded to the ground with slabs of rock. A bus shelter with no roof, entrance to a wormhole, the fractured ends of a locomotive, the unravelling bridge of a tanker, a rusted gateway from here back to then, and from then back to now.

Cardiff Bay is ahead, the route rolling to the flyover by Pierre Vivant's magic roundabout, over the wall at Tyndall Street and then along the side of the now empounded but still extant Bute East Dock. "Swansea Bay is nothing like this. I went there with my brother as a child. We stayed in a b&b right over the road from the water," Des says. "Glorious. When we came here, to Cardiff, I always thought of the place as being black and white. We only visited when my mother wanted to buy something. For people from the valleys in those days, Cardiff was no place of hedonistic desire and alcohol like it is now."

Dock maintenance, a rare sight, is in action as we pass. Two men in stained tracksuits throwing great hooks into the water and then dragging them back out. On the quayside are some of the treasures they've recovered – rusted railings, steel mesh, car panels and a fire-black mangled bike, already gone most of the way back to dust.

Before us is the Millennium Centre with its great opera stage, its theatres, its cafes and bars. It almost touches the water of Cardiff Bay, the empounded lake held in place by the barrage. A return to the Estuary. Freshwater and tideless. Here the Estuary is a place that is no longer quite river and not really sea. A place of frontier and borders, where change ebbs and flows. An unpredictable place.

Leaving Des with his bowl of soup at Bar One, I walk on to

the eastern end of the Cardiff Bay Barrage. The Dr Who Experience, a new Cardiff money-spinner, is going up inside a black slug-like tensile structure of membrane stretched over steel frame. Cheap, quick, set to last about as long as it has taken me to walk here from Chepstow. Although ascribing time to anything involving the good Doctor is usually superfluous.

Next the Barrage itself. Although maybe not quite yet. I need to go back and cross the city proper first, and take in a little of that.

Cardiff South

It's big enough, this city. It's the biggest thing on the whole walk and hangs its eastern side right at the sea's edge. I've just crossed it with Des and now I'm doing it again with John Williams, just to be sure I've covered it all. In the large and mostly empty car park of Tesco Pengam Green, down at the bottom of where the runways once were when this moorland doubled as Cardiff Airport, we're discussing who the clientele of this south Cardiff superstore might precisely be. Tremorfa, the Cardiff district this technically is, barely seems large enough. The gypsy camp I tracked around the back of a couple of hundred yards further on would hardly tip the balance. Celsa Steel Mill workers at the end of their shifts buying four-packs to quench their thirsts. Leisure sailors walking in from the Rhymney River Motor Boat Sailing and Fishing Club. Maybe there's an expansion to Cardiff that we don't yet know about. Tesco in place, ready to serve the new apartment blocks being built among the scrap metal yards and the car breakers, on piles sunk into the foreshore and on piers cantilevered out over the river. If this were still 2003, when anything was possible, then maybe.

For my third scramble across the capital, I'm with John Williams, master of *Cardiff Dead* and biographer of Shirley Bassey[21], who has just told me that he's thinking of changing his name. Ten books down the road and he's just discovered that the one he's been using is hopeless.

John Williams guitarist
John Williams composer
John Williams New Zealand horse breeder
John Williams football sociologist
John Williams Welsh historian
John Williams Welsh artist
John Williams user interface designer
John Williams Blackburn Rovers chairman
John Williams BBC reporter[22]
John Williams philosopher
John Williams Texan novelist
John Williams Brooklyn blogger
John Williams Detective Chief Superintendent

It's this last one that rankles. Detective Chief Superintendent John Williams, head of the 1980s investigation into the Lynette White murder. That murder, in a flat in James Street, Butetown, Cardiff, in 1988, became the obsession of the John Williams I am with. The murder changed his career direction from chronicler of detective fiction and novelist of the noir to Cardiff fictioneer par excellence. He's the man against whom all other narratives set in the capital are now measured.

So, if you were not John Williams, then who might you be? John reflects. "Johnny Highnote, maybe. I got that one from a dream. On the other hand I quite like Johnny 'Nightlife' Williams. There was a Bertie 'Nightlife' Jarrett who was one of Shirley Bassey's early co-stars. My wife thinks I'm insane."

Our plan is to walk from here to the Barrage, right through the centre of the city's southern half. The working class suburbs, the office units built where heavy industry once was, the playing fields, the lines of shops. We go up through the Pengam Green private new build, along Hind Close, De Havilland Road, Handley Road and Hawker Close, the names of the planes that once flew from here now celebrated in orange brick. Tremorfa Park, in full socialist fashion and untroubled by herbaceous plantings, is large, flat and dense with football pitches. A notice at the entrance still announces last November's firework display. At the western end, St Alban's School sports, sack races, penalty shoot outs, team relay and slam dunk is in full end of term swing.

John, described by the Independent as bald and stocky and with "the air of Donald Pleasance" (which is a little unfair, I'd say it's more the air of Peter Sallis or, if he were white, Willie Dixon) finds a hole in the park fence and we emerge on Runway Road in the heart of the council house territory that Tremorfa always was. Sunset gates, half-rendered pebbledash semis, badly cut hedges, notices warning of dogs and against junk mail, NO MENUS. There's no sense anywhere of the sea that you could virtually touch if you stood on stilts. These are post-war homes for heroes, housing for East Moors Steelworkers when that place filled the local skyline with smog, an eastern Splott beyond the Roath Dock rail link. Hardly any of these things are relevant now. A train a day to the rolling mill comes down the link. The steelworks closed in 1979. The space is now a business park.

We cross the bottom of Splott Park, going under the South Park Road railway bridges, to emerge by the now boarded-up Grosvenor. These south Cardiff workers' pubs are closing as fast as the industry that once supported them. John is talking about his latest enterprise – touring the capital's social clubs in the company of novelist Rob Lewis. They've already tracked City Road, starting at the Conservative Club, taking in the New Park Liberal Club, the Cardiff and General Municipal Works Club and Institute, and then ending in Charles Street's Cardiff Ex-Serviceman's Club. These places, once all-male bastions of working-class exclusivity, are now pleased to hear from anyone pressing their buzzers. Obtaining temporary membership is no longer the problem it once was.

In Splott proper, where we are now, the nineteenth century terraces are a familiar sight. John lived here in the early eighties. We walk along Splott Road to the refurbished Star Centre. Here at night, when I regularly came twenty years back to learn martial arts, they'd steal the wheels off your car if you didn't pay the local kids a pound to guard it. In the centre's window are adverts for Zumba Dance Fitness and Flash-mob meditation. It's a changing world.

Railway Street, running past both writer Susie Wild's place and the now closed Cardiff Arms, eventually reaches the New Fleurs, Skittles & Darts, Function Room, Bar Food, on Walker

Road. "A place of great significance in the history of Cardiff punk," John says. For a late-70s guitarist who couldn't really play, the arrival of punk was a gift. "I regarded it as mass conceptual art movement," he tells me. "The music business was promoting bands like ELP and Yes and you couldn't just have a bash at being them. But with punk, anyone could join in. I was living in London and running a punk fanzine called *After Hours*[23]. I got it printed, appropriately after hours, by a friend who worked at Communist Party HQ. The whole thing was very socialist. On a visit back home to Cardiff to see my folks, I put copies on sale in Spillers. Cardiff band Reptile Ranch, who'd recorded a do-it-yourself 7-inch single[24], bought one and wrote to me. They lived at 1 Walker Road and invited me down. I ended up staying."

Z. Block Records, Reptile Ranch's label, operating out of the Grass Roots Coffee Bar in Charles Street, but using Walker Road as a business address, then released *Is The War Over*. This was Cardiff punk's trailblazer compilation album. In addition to Beaver, Mad Dog, The New Form, Addiction, Test to Destruction, and The Riotous Brothers, the album had two cuts by probably the only Cardiff band from this period that the world will remember, Young Marble Giants.

Outside the Fleurs was once a red phone box. John and I stare at the empty space it occupied. "We gave out the number of that box for Z. Block," says John. "Rough Trade rang us there to offer a contract for the Young Marble Giants." The future was bright. For a time.

John's own band, The Puritan Guitars, then fell apart when his inability to actually play started to become apparent. Instead, he formed a band in which you sang. This was a nine-piece doo-wop with added David Bowie outfit called the Skeleteens. "The band practised over there." John is pointing at the Maltings Warehouse, a little to the west of The Fleurs. "We went to Paris to busk. I was there more for my ability to speak a bit of French and pass the hat round than my ability as a singer." Music, despite considerable desire, wasn't to be John's future.

Beyond the magic roundabout[25] lies the now enclosed East Dock, full of water, weed and sometimes fish. It's a sanitised reminder of how this area once was. Warehouses demolished to be replaced by apartment blocks resembling warehouses. A single preserved dock crane. Metal loading buckets cemented to the walkways. The dockside itself railed for safety. No ships bar the preserved and rotting barge, the *Eben Haezer*[26], moored outside the Wharf pub. Diving ducks in action. Floating bags and half-submerged cans.

Access is officially via Schooner Way, but Atlantic Wharf, as the top end of the dock is known, can be reached by climbing a low wall on Tyndall Street. John is telling me about how Cardiff ended up being the place that defined him as an author. If doo wop wasn't going to get him there then crime would. The printed version, anyway. Beyond music his abiding interest was the novel noir – crime made literature, crime written down. He'd completed *Into the Badlands*[27], a book about American crime writers, and, along with the black London crime novelist Mike Phillips, had decided to research a book on the event that, as we've heard, changed his own career direction, the killing of Cardiff prostitute, Lynette White.

On Valentine's Day, 1988, in a flat above the Kingsport Betting Shop in Cardiff's James Street, White had been brutally stabbed more than fifty times. The police, floundering around for a suspect, selected three locals as perpetrators, massaged the evidence, and got their conviction. Stephen Miller, Yusef Abdullahi and Anthony Paris, the Cardiff Three, were sent down in 1990. Local indignation was considerable and a campaign to prove their innocence was launched.

John, who'd parted from Phillips at this stage, found himself in Canal Park at the annual mix of dope, Clark's pies, curried goat, Haile Selassie and dub that is the Butetown Carnival. Here he met Abdullahi's wife, Alex, working a fundraising stall. Perceived, correctly as it turned out, to be on the side of the innocents, John was invited back to the family house in Alice Street. In the tiny terrace he was confronted with boxes and boxes of prosecution evidence, formally released to the defence. There were interviews with almost every drug user, pimp, sex worker, petty criminal, streetwalker, layabout, alcoholic, and low-lifer at large in greater Butetown on the night of the 14th February, 1988. Five thousand reports. A sociological document without equal.

As the book progressed, John found himself sitting in Butetown's now closed Paddle Steamer pub surrounded by known criminals and drug-dealers getting the news straight from those who made it. Around him spun an outrage of incredulity and barely repressed rage. People who would normally never speak to a middle-class boy sitting there with a notebook were induced to tell him just how their world worked. The cause was everything. Williams was fighting for them.

John was inspired. His *Bloody Valentine*, the true tale of justice appallingly being miscarried, came out in 1993. The Court of Appeal had ruled that a gross miscarriage of justice had taken place and the Three had been released. It then took until 2000 for the Police to reopen their investigations and a further three years for the real killer, Jeffrey Gafoor, to be convicted using DNA evidence. In 2011, eight more years down the line, ten of those involved in the original Cardiff Three conviction were finally put on trial. In the way of things this trial then collapsed. The judge ruled that eight of the defendants were not guilty of perverting the course of justice and two more as unable to get a fair trial. The truth recedes and the mist returns.

I'm getting all this as we cross Dock bottom to wend our way through West Close, where the Taff Vale Railway once built steam engines. We go along the side of the old Slipper Baths and enter Canal Park, the grasslands that run south from Cardiff Central Station almost to the sea. This was once the basin of the Glamorgan Canal – the Sea Lock Pound. The place where the barges carrying coal and iron all the way from Merthyr met the sea. The Pound stayed full of water until the steam dredger *Catherine Ethel* ripped the sea lock gates off in 1951 and the waterway was abandoned.

We sit on a bench pretty much from where the famous 1950s Bert Hardy *Picture Post* photo of the Canal Basin that currently adorns John's study wall would have been shot. John is talking about the *Cardiff Trilogy*[28] that made his name, linked stories of low-life grit and humour set in the city of his birth. He'd written a short story about a prostitute ripping off a sailor and sent it, along with the manuscript of a spy novel he'd finished, to his agent. "The novel is okay but it's the short story we like," was the reply. "Do more." With the Lynette White evidence to hand

and the prospect of publication up ahead, the idea for what eventually became the first book of that trilogy, *Five Pubs, Two Bars and a Nightclub*, was born.

Beyond the park is Dumballs Road. To the north, this leads to Curran Road and off that, to Williams Way. This was once site of the Williams steel stockholding and, later, aluminium window family business. Famous enough now to be marked on the map. We forgo the chance to take a photo of John standing by a road sign that bears his name, to walk instead past South Wales' Police's new fortress-like HQ and over the bridge into Grangetown. The sea, or at least Cardiff Bay's fresh-water empounded replacement, is in full view. The sun is glinting, aeration pumps are pushing up their bubbles and, officially, there's not a leak in anyone's basement for miles around. Prior to the building of the Barrage, this was the district's fear: ground water would rise, sewage would back up and roads would be deluged. Didn't happen.

The birds that once dined on the flats here have gone, to be replaced with swan and duck. On the Taff's western bank, Channel View Leisure Centre looks out at serried rows of moored yachts. If you live in Butetown, then Grangetown is another country. But Henry Bassey, Shirley's brother, lived here, says John. So did Lynette White, once. We pass the Marl, drained playing fields now but once tidal flats, to reach the blue and yellow bulk of IKEA.

IKEA is a Cardiff magnet. Built on the site of the gasworks at the top of Ferry Road, it's been a destination for the upwardly mobile, the wannabe, the hunter for cheapskate shelving, the newly-wed and the working class kitchen replacer for most of the past decade. It's seen off Maskrey's and Habitat and wrecked the profitability of BHS's lighting section. There's pretty much no one under thirty who does not possess an IKEA cutlery drainer or one of those battery coffee frothers that cost a pound.

John, it turns out, carries an IKEA Family Card. We are here for a traditional lunch and since we're too early for the much advertised IKEA Swedish Crayfish Season – *be a part of the largest crayfish party in the UK & Ireland* – which is a pity, we stick with what they've got. Mash, gravy and Swedish meatballs with lingonberry sauce followed by jelly that looks like Swarfega but tastes like Sunny Delight. What else?

Leaving John, I trek back through the Grangetown streets, over the much celebrated Clarence Road Bridge, to side-cut through the residential docks south of James Street. If it were not for the liner-styled buildings that line Mermaid Quay ahead, this could be Cardiff's past hanging on. Thin terraces, gulls, sense of the sea beyond.

I pass the waterside conglomeration of restaurants on which the Bay centres, thick with customers in slow shoes and Marks & Spencer coats. Ahead is the white spire of the wooden Norwegian Church, moved, rebuilt, everything cleaned and replaced so that virtually nothing of the original remains, yet authentic to the last nail. South of it is the Barrage. The coast. Back on track again.

The Cardiff Bay Barrage to Penarth

All week I've been plagued by god. The door-knocking Jehovahs handing out *The Watchtower*. The street-walking Mormons in their crisp-white US shirts. The American evangelicals from Alabama, here on a mission trying to change the world. I tell them all that I live at an epicentre of crossing leys, a place of great belief and huge power. St Margaret's Church in its once circular yard is at one street end. Parkminster United Reformed Church, the Congregationalists and the Presbyterians in a fluid mix, is at the other. Marking the point of the triangle drawn by these two Christian altars is the Minster Gospel Hall, two streets away. In this place, God won't let us escape. The Americans from Alabama smile. Have you let the truth into your life?

Suzuki taught me. Before him there was Christmas Humphreys. Jack Kerouac in all his Tathagata Seat of Purity hunt for the pure land helped point the way. "In the ethereal perfume, mysteriously ancient, the bliss of the Buddha-fields, I saw that my life was a vast glowing empty page and I could do anything I wanted[29]." I wanted some of that. "I bless you, all living things, I bless you in the endless past, I bless you in the endless present, I bless you in the endless future, amen.[30]" What you did was you made yourself empty and then life began.

Humphreys said that Zen was "the apotheosis of Buddhism". It was a "direct assault upon the citadel of Truth". It had no reliance on "concepts [of god or soul or salvation] or the use of scripture, ritual or vow[31]". It was unique. This was white light clarity that even the Pilgrim fathers, the lucid Congregationalists and the austere Presbyterians could never achieve. Should I tell the Alabama evangelicals? My god is the same as your god. Same power. Same ghost in the machine. But he's there in the nothingness of being. He's in the space beyond the emptiness. He needs no apparatus. Just light. He's easy to find. But I'm still looking. That's the dichotomy and the story of my life, I guess. Allahu Akbar. God is great, I tell them. My father told me that at the end of his.

Is it all the same? Feels like it as I walk the street, the churches bending their belief around me, like a warm cocoon. The dust of my thoughts settling on the land. Head empty, trying to be so. "What did I care about the squawk of the very little self, which wanders everywhere?[32]" That's what it was all about. The squawk. Stop it, bend it, control it, make it shine.

I'm on the folding bike again, Penarth Headland in front of me as the complete denial of anything alluvial, moor-like or drowned in water. Penarth Headland, the fist protruding out into the Cardiff Bay waters, the Penarth coeval strata, interspersed layers of limestone and pink alabaster. A crumbling, forever-eroding salient into the tides of the Severn Estuary. It feels sometimes as if I have spent my life gazing on this reclining Buddha, with its broken teeth that are the remains of the Billy Bank flats (now under private development, but oh so slowly), and its great Christian monument, St Augustine's Church. It's there, 200 feet above the river delta, gazing down on the Capital city of the Welsh empire. Cardiff – still resented by anyone and everyone living north of Merthyr, west of Cowbridge and east of St Mellons. Do they know that the city gives 40% of its business rates to the rest of Wales? St Augustine's dates back to 1240 and has a nineteenth century tower designed for the admiralty as an aid for shipping. Joseph Parry (1841-1903), composer of 'Myfanwy', is buried in the churchyard.

I've looked at it from the Cardiff streets on which I've lived, from the top of Penylan Hill, climbed almost daily as a child. I've gazed at it from my round, porthole windows in my Academi office at Mount Stuart Square. Now here it is ahead again as I cycle towards it. It's an empty god casting his Buddha eye over a very impure land.

Where the barrage begins, construction workers are in enormous evidence. They are employed on the dockland south of Roath Basin. This is the latest slice of Bay territory to get a shining upgrade. It has been redesignated, with barely a thought for veracity, as Porth Teigr[33]. Its thirty-eight acres of commercial, retail and residential space being developed as a joint venture between Igloo and the Welsh Assembly Government[34]. There'll be a new 40,000 square feet digital media centre with controversial projecting timber boxes at its ends built to recall, as the developers have it, an irregular stack of large baulks of timber. A specially made origami access bridge[35] known as Porth Teigr Outer Lock Crossing is already in place. Between earth diggers and lines of men in hard hats I can see the repeating motifs and Burges-inspired three-hundred-metre frontage of the BBC's new drama village, Roath Lock. The Corporation is moving a significant amount of its TV production facilities here. New studios for *Dr Who, Pobl y Cwm, Torchwood* and *Casualty*. More Tardis sightings for the streets of the capital. More marching Cybermen across Mount Stuart Square[36].

Beyond, there's still evidence of boat building in what remains of the Port of Cardiff. Two yachts on stands, hull build in progress. But no workmen in sight.

The centre of the barrage, out where the onshore winds whip at their strongest, there's a comprehensive new BMX and skateboard park[37] along with a whole raft of outdoor exercise machines. Jog here, do a set of lifts and crunches, jog back. Great idea. There are plenty of runners in action. But I see no skateboarders and the exercise stations all lie vacant.

At the Penarth end, locks negotiated and foreshore reached, there is no option but to climb the steep incline of Dock Road. The promised round-headland cantilevered walkway is yet to materialise. I could, I guess, fold the bike and lug it around the Dardanelles as the 500-plus yards of fallen rock headland foreshore are known. The Brompton catalogue suggests that a folded bike can be carried but that distance might be just a little too far. I wheel myself up the hill. Past the end of Paget Terrace, home of IWA Director John Osmond[38] and up to the Victorian hotel that became writer Phil Carradice's Headlands Special School.

On the promontory's far side, the long-hated, water's edge concrete car park has gone. The Grade II listed Pier still points out into the water, a hang-on from a previous age. The wood decking has been replaced by public subscription. Pay your money, say what you will. JOHN SLEIGH PROPOSED TO KATHY BAINS HERE 9-11-07 SHE SAID YES. MR AND MRS JEWITT GOLDEN ANNIVERSARY 20/08/10 LOVE ALWAYS. Now the Pier's Pavilion will also get an upgrade. As a 'multi-use leisure facility', the local council has agreed operating costs to match Heritage Lottery money, which will pay for the capital works. It's all promised. But not yet in the bank account. I wheel myself around the building in the increasing drizzle. Today everything is still boarded up.

Opposite me is the Edwardian seafront building, Beachcliff, which once housed Rabaiotti's and Chandler's restaurants: long Sunday afternoon destinations for visiting families, and in the process of demolition. Developers Richard Haywood Properties have pledged to retain as much as possible of the original façade. From what I can see, most of that venerated frontage already seems to have be removed. In the local papers there's been a fuss. Plans to include a three-storey flat and gym complex in the main building, six more flats next door and a restaurant "mooted" for the ground floor have not yet materialised as actual build. The council have served an *Untidy Land and Building Notice* and are threatening legal action. The developers have promised that, given an "uninterrupted construction period" the work will be completed by the end of 2013. It's on slow to stop as I pass. Wye Valley demolition are still labelled as being on site but there's no movement I can see beyond the flapping of tarpaulin and the gliding of gulls.

That's how Penarth usually is. Quiet. Slow. This is not Cardiff, never so. The docks where the marina now sits were Davies the Ocean's rival operation to Bute's Cardiffian world beater. The railways that served the two places were managed by different companies. The buildings used different stone. Same today. Cardiff's local government sits in Cardiff Bay. Penarth's is in the Vale at Barry.

Out at sea the tide is returning in its usual array of muted colour. I may be getting a different view from this east-facing frontage but the water, that's the same.

The Beaches Everyone Visits:
Lavernock to Fontygary

Lavernock

The Sunday morning zip out through south Cardiff is a dream. The link road, Bute Tunnel, Cogan Spur, Windsor Road, all empty and clear. At Penarth clifftop, I take tea at Cafiero Cioni's Bistro and Pizzeria. Sun arriving by the gallon. Diners around me knocking back cheap red like the world might end soon. The world on holiday.

The park here runs due south over layered and crumbling cliffs made up of Jurassic and Triassic mudstones, rich in fossils. The bone beds hold the remains of ichthyosaurs, plesiosaurs, belemnites and ammonites. They are chased after by hunters with special hammers and collecting bags. The council have done a fair job of making the route accessible to just about anyone, on wheels or not. The path, which runs for a good mile and a quarter, is flat enough to be driven down on a castered arm-chair. It sinks slowly past Roundbush Rocks and Ranny

Point, paralleling the old Taff Vale Railway line to Lavernock and Sully. That track bed is still walkable, in part. Enthusiasts have set up a website which shows pictures of all extant bridges and sections of track bed and has notes on which bits have now been fenced off[1]. Householders in the streets around Cosmeston Drive report sightings of enthusiasts tracking the former rail route through their gardens.

Towards Lavernock Point path overgrowth increases. Striking off-piste to a gap on the clifftop, I look back up the Estuary towards the cities. Beyond the shifting shapes of its brown-grey seas, the whole waterway is empty. One idling tanker, two pleasure craft. The trading ports of Bristol, Newport and Cardiff stand waiting. What's out there today is not going to keep them satisfied for long. In the distance the green glint of the Second Severn Crossing's suspension mesh is on the edge of visibility. The wind turbines at Newport and the giant at Wentlooge slowly turn. You can see the cities clearly with their storage tanks and their white, high buildings. You can imagine mariners, back in the days of coal rush, sailing up this decep- tively treacherous waterway and facing the choices before them. Left for Cardiff, through waters as rough as roaring tigers, eye fixed on Guest's Glassworks towers[2], or right for Newport, line up with the lighthouses that mark the Usk's glutinous sides.

Lavernock itself, with its leaking sewage outfall pipe and its scratchy sands at St Mary's Well Bay, is a ghost of what it once was. Visitor numbers are in free-fall, the sands themselves have been washed southwest as the mid-Severn dredgers do their work, and all seaside facilities are gone. In the 1950s, before Beeching wielded his axe, things were very different. Trippers from the big city and the valleys that served it made the trip here using the railway that looped to Barry Island from Cardiff Queen Street via Penarth and Lavernock.

There were two cafes, the Golden Hind pub, stalls selling beach gear, an ice cream parlour and the three-star Lavernock Bay Hotel. I came here. Sat with dad, him smoking and reading the paper, me eating fish-paste sandwiches. I dug ineffectually in the sand for Australia, and then paddled with the turds in the sea. When the trains stopped arriving so did the trippers. Only the Lavernock Point Holiday Estate with its rentable, self-catering chalets and on-site pub (breakfast served 8-12, seven days a week, open to non-residents) remains. It is sign-boarded in the olde English script often seen on the vans of builders: The Marconi Inn.

Guglielmo Marconi's visit here in 1897 is Lavernock's historical placemarker. On the 13th May that year he sat on the clifftop with his assembly of batteries and aerials. His assistant, George Kemp, and helper, William Preece from the Post Office, sent him signals from nearby Flatholm Island. The message was in dot dot dash dash Morse. ARE YOU READY. Marconi, failing to pick up a thing, decided he might try shortening the distance between him and the broadcaster on the island. He took himself down from the point itself and onto the rocks of the foreshore. In so doing he inadvertently lengthened his aerial enough for it to pick up Kemp's long wave signal. Radiotelegraphy was born.

Marconi, son of a rich Irish-Italian family from Bologna, womaniser, fascist sympathiser (Mussolini was his best man) and scientist, sold his ideas for wireless messaging to the British Post Office after the Italian government had turned him down. The Flatholm to Lavernock's three and a half miles was the ideal distance to test Marconi's new system over water. CAN YOU HEAR ME. YES LOUD AND CLEAR.

At St Lawrence's Church[3], a tiny and now redundant Church in Wales outpost right on the headland, there's a memorial plaque to Marconi's achievement set in the churchyard wall. It was made of bronze and installed in 1947 by the Rotary Club of Cardiff. It lasted until 1996 when a local drinker stole it along with a couple of metal fleur-de-lys grave markers. I'm getting this story from Glyn Jones, ebullient chairman of BARS, the Barry Amateur Radio Society. Glyn looks a little like Captain Birdseye and has a salty dog Devon accent, although he insists he's a Gog with a five-hundred-year family history at Holyhead on Ynys Môn, the island of Anglesey. Lucky for us, Glyn tells me, an enthusiast had taken a plaster cast of the original inscription. That's the sort of thing you do if you are a Marconi fan. In 2000 BARS had a replacement made. They epoxy-cemented it back onto the wall. "That bugger'll have trouble getting it off if he tries again." Glyn smiles.

Glyn is in action at the back of the church where a flower

festival with attendant *Marconi and his Legacy* exhibition is in progress. Admission free, including orange juice. The vicar, the Rev Margaret Stark, is conducting tours around the exhibits. There are replicas of Marconi's equipment set up on top of the organ, a plastic and turf model of Flat Holm complete with lighthouse and radio tower, along with a papier-mâché version of the headland (made by the vicar). Flowers are in vases and have been strapped to pew ends.

Glyn is retelling the Marconi story non-stop to anyone who'll listen. He's told us about where Marconi's hut once stood and how you can still detect its rust in the mud. He's now moved onto a description of the great man's womanising. Behind him, sitting in front of two computer screens covered with initials, sits a headphoned BARS member speaking into a microphone. This is Golf Charlie Four Bravo Romeo Sierra, he intones. The air is thick with call signs. It's a secret language. It all feels vaguely like citizen band radio, fretwork, and steam modelling. A worthy activity of the past and, despite the arrival of portable device instant messaging, still valiantly hanging on.

Outside, in a churchyard, wound about with aluminium pole and metres of cable, Glyn pulls his YAESU radio ham cap on for me to take a photograph. "We can contact the whole world from here," he says. A woman emerges from the church clutching her mobile. "Barely a signal, I can only get one bar," she complains. Reminds me of how it is trying to speak on my mobile at home. I have to lean against the front door to get anything. We clearly haven't solved that technological glitch just yet.

Behind us, near the cliff path I've just walked along, are the remains of a Royal Observer Core nuclear bunker. Built in 1962 and in use during the Cuban missile crisis, it was closed and abandoned in 1975. Vandals took control, as they usually do with deserted structures. There's an entrance hatch and ventilation tower allegedly still extant near Lower Cosmeston Farm but I couldn't find them.

Ahead, up beyond the Lavernock Point Holiday Estate static caravans and the far side of the Wildlife Trust's Lavernock Point Nature Reserve (purple hairstreak butterfly, ash wood, cowslip, devil's-bit scabious, whitethroat, bullfinch and chiffchaff), are the remains of the listed monument that is the Lavernock

Battery. This is a concrete complex of what started in 1870 as a gun housing to defend against the French[4] and had, by World War Two, developed into a network of anti-aircraft and bofors gun emplacements, searchlights, ammunition magazines and bomb shelters. Today it is empty save for encroaching grass. It's less graffitied than I might have expected it to be, large and rusted. The War and its remains. As a 40s born baby boomer, it is the background to my childhood.

When we fought as kids, we were always the Allies and we fought against the Germans. We haunted the wreckage of the real fighting that lay right across the city, the downed planes at Pengam, the bomb sites on Marlborough Road, the bunkers on the hill. When we did this I wore a salvaged motor-cycle helmet that looked vaguely like US Infantry headgear. "Why don't you use British helmets," my father asked. He pointed at genuine examples of the wide-brimmed Brodie Home Guard, ARP, and brought back from the real fighting hats that we had stacked in the shed out back. "They look old," I said. That was that.

Swanbridge

The moral panics have always been with us. The skinheads, the razor-wielding neo-Nazis, the knife gangs, the garrotters, the Bloods, the Ninerz, the Gripset, the Scuttlers, the Billy Boys, the Latinos Callejeros Cartel, the Shanavests, the Hawkubites, the Yiddishers and the Yardies. The rising underground foam that puts middle Britain into a spin. The world as we know it is over. Can this be the country we fought for? The slide from restraint to unregulated self-indulgence is unceasing. The rules go out the window. Honesty, charity, passivity, consideration, regulation, quietude, pointing one way not vacillating, turning right when you should. Order. Order. How we try to make it and how it can never be.

As the 50s turned to the 60s, the Teddy Boys with their drape jackets, drain trousers, folded razors in their pockets, began to fade. What you looking at me for? Repeated *ad nauseam*, that phrase no longer quite hacked it. The Mods were the successors. Smart kids in Sta-Press trousers, button-down shirts and slim ties. Italian suits. Hush puppies. Parka jackets. Bombers to keep you going. Dexies to stay the course. In south London they held sway. The hippest thing on the planet. Listening to ska, Hammond-driven r&b, The Kingsmen's 'Louie Louie', Marvin Gaye, James Brown, The Yardbirds, Brian Auger, Georgie Fame, The High Numbers, The Who[5].

In 1964, along the south coast of England, a good three years before the summer of love, and well before music finished off changing the world, the mods ran running battles with the rockers. These were their life-long opponents, the black helmeted, leather jacketed motorcycle biker gangs. Moral panic swelled. Youth, what could be done, these people, not good enough, how dare they, I am locking my door. The *Mail* exasperated. The *Daily Telegraph* trumpeted. The BBC showed black and white grainy films of parka-clad youth in their hoards, swarming across the shingle of Brighton beach. Hippest thing I'd ever seen.

They had their scooters parked up on Marine Parade. Vespas, Lambrettas. Wing-mirrors in fans like Aztec jewellery. There was a style about all this that the beat bohemians never had and the Teds, love 'em, just couldn't match. In the big south Wales city, the only one we had, where 'big' wasn't a word we often used, down in Charles Street's Cellar Grill and in High Street's Barracuda, we considered this.

The gang was up and off, half a dozen Vespas, someone with a minivan and a few others who said they'd get there by bus, or somehow, but never did. The destination was the nearest place that anyone could think of that might have rockers hiding out on its seafront, drinking beer from Party Sevens. Not Penarth, which could have made it as a reasonable replica for Brighton. But Swanbridge. Where? Down there just beyond Lavernock. Beach – pebble and dumped rock. Facilities – non-existent.

I've seen the mod films that glory the battles. 1979's *Quadrophenia* with Sting overdressed as the über-Mod, his Vespa with more lights on the front than an ocean deep-trench submersible. And 2010's *Brighton Rock* where the mods in rampage across the shingle are a backdrop rather than a central action. They're all the more realistic as a result. Frank Roddam's *Quadrophenia* with its Who soundtrack and retro-*Trainspotting* evocative mid-60s recreation is the easier on the eye. Rowan Joffe's *Brighton Rock* is a remake of John Boulting's 1946 original take on the Grahame Green novel. It pushes the action forward two decades and loses none of its intense British gangland battle of good vs. evil, love, sin, violence by the bucket and dark acid-burned redemption. There's no period music here, just Martin Phipps choral and orchestral score full of malevolence and dread. The High Numbers might have been the ace of 1964 authenticity but they could never have gone to the macabre, dirty, difficult places Phipps' music does.

Neither of these two films has anything near the Welsh mod experience that unfolded on the front at Swanbridge. Swanbridge – named after Sweyn Forkbeard, the Viking Jarl who made his stronghold Sully Island. That island is linked to the coast by a solid causeway that gets drowned twice a day by the tides. The causeway would have been known in Old Norse as a *brygga*, a bridge. Sweyn's Brygga, Swanbridge. Up the coast the same marauder gave his name to Swansea. Sweyn's Ey.

The Welsh mods reach Swanbridge, the farm and the winding road that led to it, at dusk. There were no rockers. Music came from a portable Dansette that someone had been clever enough to carry. It banged on for a while, spinning singles which all featured blokes blowing harmonicas over the top of British beat music masquerading as r&b. There were a bunch of twist records and then the Gary Edwards Combo on the Oriole label doing 'The Method'[6]. After that the batteries died. There was no drink, but then again Mods didn't major on alcohol. A few parka-clad youths, tired of the darkness and the lack of anything either real or imaginary to actually do, climbed into a field and began to raid the crop. Onions. Rumour then went round that the disgruntled farmer, his quiet darkness broken, had called the police. The Vespas were started and we beat it back to the twinkling lights of the Capital's Queen Street. Brighton, Margate, Broadstairs, Hastings, Cardiff. Marks in the mod annals.

From Lavernock Point to Swanbridge is a slide through woodland, caravans in all directions as if this were a south English coast holiday destination. Families come here for weeks at a stretch. Don't they know it rains? Swanbridge itself was once a harbour importing butter, skins, wine and cheese and delivering them to the market at Canton Cross. There was a string of fishing boats. But among the surfboarders and the jet skiers in action in the bay and the couples sitting with their cans on the pebble beach today, there is no sign of seafaring. Mooring rings were rumoured to have been visible here as late as the 70s but I never saw them.

In the car park, the vast and seemingly never-ending car park that fronts the Captain's Wife pub, there is not a sign of anything remotely cool. On the hot Sunday afternoon when I arrive, families sprawl. There are chips, crisps, shandy, coke and spritzers on the outdoor tables before them. It's the expected mix of kids, men in vests, women in on-the-razzle high-rise high heels, tights and bulging fatness, walking the seawall like it was what they always did when they dressed like this.

The pub was once Sully House and its outbuildings the cottages of the fishermen. Behind rises wooded Hopkin Mount. In front is the eroded sandstone outcrop of the Island. It is the possessor of both an Iron Age fort and a Bronze Age barrow. Both are almost lost now to erosion. Through the years, Sully Island has seen beached ships, wrecked steamers, smugglers, been in use as a base for pirates[7], a home for renegades, and a venue for sea fishermen hunting cod, whiting, poulting, dogfish, conger eel and bass. The tides wash it. Over the past decade its fourteen acres have been put on the market at least twice. Starting price £1.25 million, dropping rapidly to less than £100K. Planning permission to build – unlikely. The 1990s proposal to construct an underground health centre and spa failed to attract enough investors. The onion fields have been built on. Swanbridge Farm is a mansion. The mods are a memory. Louise Louie is on the player right now. Still incomprehensible and incoherent. Still magnificent.

Bendrick

Beyond the Captain's Wife the moral panics subside. This is, after all, a fine day out for all the family. Walking by the sea's edge, throwing pebbles, dawdling among the drifts from beach barbeques. It's a landscape of rock shelf and shingle. Here occasional tattooed men with their tops off burn burgers and pour lager down their throats. The hordes rarely reach this place because the attractions don't warrant it – no shops, distance from the car park to the coast more than five minutes' walk, one pub and that full to overflowing. But today, adjacent to the sea, the entire expanse of Barry Plastics' Sports Fields is given over to a car boot sale. Serried rows of Hondas, Fords and Nissans with their boots gaping, overflowing with the sort of junk knick-knackery you normally bin or, if you can be bothered, stuff into a charity plastic sack and leave out in the street for the night rains to drown. Spider plants, clocks, broken toy cars, soft bears, rap CDs from the 90s, cups, vases, Dan Brown fiction, Titanic DVDs, phone rechargers, plastic dinosaurs. It's our collective, recent past, the one we've shed like a reptile skin and rather than flaking down to dust it's all back, here, to haunt us.

This boot sale is a local world beater and has been in action for more than a decade. Stalls are the expected mix of discarded life spilling out of crates or thrown onto the grass with barely a thought for display. Books upside down, clothing in jumble heaps, DVDs backwards in sprawling stacks. There are tables manned by dabblers, further heaps of unmatching cutlery, bottles, jigsaws, table mats. The professional touch, if was ever present, has now flown. At the far end I do find a guy selling crockery, dark glasses, fags, who tells me that trading, as we once might have known it, is on the edge of extinction. The internet has made everyone their own seller. Who needs experts? His plates go for pounds rather than pence like every-one else's. Or rather, in this heat, they don't.

The coast path, south of the sports ground, runs the margin between the beach's pebble expanse and the gardens of Sully's upmarket, sea-view bungalows. Down here you should be able see how the other half live. It's a weekend, hottest of the year, Wimbledon fortnight, clear blue sky. But the gardens are largely deserted. Swimming pools are covered over. Fountains are off. Water is drained. It's a landscape from the near future where want has been satisfied and the landscape left to fill with dust. The owners are elsewhere on health farms or in casinos, engag-ing in recreational violence or seeing through tontine[8] contractual futures where they'll emerge at some point owning the moon but haven't quite got there yet.

Beyond, amid the thickening shoreline trees, are the bright colours of Ty Hafan, the children's hospice. It's a place where death moves amid shining lights, where darkness is banished and love endures. Its architecture is all sloping slate, white walls, round windows. Its calm warmth touches you as you pass.

Sully Hospital, William Pite, Son and Fairweather's 1936 white goddess of a sanatorium for tuberculosis sufferers, never ended-up being used as accommodation for Britain's burgeoning mass of asylum seekers, as the council once planned. Vocal local opposition saw to that. The building stands to the west of Sully itself, on from the hospice, and in its original form is one of the last great Modernist landmarks in Wales. In the mid-2000s property developers Galliard turned this masterpiece into 235 apartments and renamed the site as Hayes Point. They added tennis courts, saunas, a swimming pool, a cricket pitch and a gym and then laid a claim to the privacy of the foreshore. But to judge by the scattering of vests and barbeques in action today that exclusivity is not enforced. Behind the trees, the spirit of British Art Deco just about hangs on, but of its white liner at sea detail little now remains.

Sully took its name from the Norman Baron, Reginald de Sully, one of the twelve knights of Glamorgan, who was awarded the manor at the time of the conquest. De Sully's name has been variously recorded as *Sulie, Sulye, Silly, Scille, Sulia,* and *Sylye* although never, from what I can tell, as its present Welsh form *Sili.* There's a fair amount of justified local opposition to having this on bilingual road signs. A ballot in early 2011 voted for a change to the nothing-like-as-funny-sounding *Abersili*[9]. Map-makers have yet to respond.

Beyond the Hospital and the rocks of Hayes Point the Barry East Breakwater and Nell's Point come into view. Despite the manicured presence behind razor wire of *HMS Cambria*[10], the Royal Navy's reservist shore-station, this is now largely Barry's Atlantic Trading Estate territory. The coast roughs up with evidence of erosion, revetement and vandalism in equal measure. Ahead the trickle that is the man-made estuary of the Cadoxton River[11] slides into the sea at Black Rocks. To the south, revealed in all its glory by a tide that has retreated to near invisibility, is Bendrick Rock.

Bendrick, carboniferous limestone eastern outrider of Barry Town, site of dinosaur footprints. And we're big on dinosaurs around here. In the early Triassic period bay the footprints were made in the silt at the shoreline of a shallow sea. There are twenty or more examples and they show the distinctive three-toed imprint of the small coelophysis dinosaur that made them. Being famous, these imprints have been subject to any number of vandalistic attacks, official and unofficial. Examples have been cut up for display in the National Museum, others have been hacked-off, taken home, and offered for sale in the fossil supermarkets of Lyme Regis. One, famously, was put on e-bay. E-bay. The unregulated world market for everything from nuclear triggers to the bones of saints. So it sometimes seems.

The prints are not quite where most people think they are. They do not lie in the red marls which outcrop the path just beyond *HMS Cambria*, as the internet suggests. Nor are they at the water's edge where the fishermen stand. They're out there, somewhere, in the heart of Bendrick Rock, outlined in crayon, marked with paint, their million-year-old continuity gone to buggery.

On the headland the path peters, as these things often do in the places between country and town. This is where the docks begin in an industrial scrapland of breakers yards, aggregate supply, scaffolding and the council waste recycling centre. The trading estate is built on top of what the Glamorgan Gwent archeological Trust have identified as the site of a Bronze-Age village[12] with visible post holes and the remains of hut circles. An invaluable resource. An irreplaceable part of our heritage. Worn flat by official indifference. Overrun by bikers, truck drivers, waster dumpers and marauding youth.

Unaccountably there is a uniformed waste-picker in action here among the broken concrete and curling scrap. "Can you get to the Dock this way?" I ask. Ahead, among the rampant undergrowth, are the impenetrable fences that protect the rock bulwark of the breakwater. "Nah, you'll have to go round." So we will.

Across Barry

Access. This is a big Welsh Government word. It's what they came up with when the Welsh Assembly was established back in 1998 and it has been high on the promotion agenda ever since. Access to the countryside, the coastline, the riverbank, the highway, the railtrack, the cycle path, water, gas, electricity, broadband, Wi-Fi, news information, swimming, sunlight, education, health, loaves of bread, agendum, population statistics, plenary proceedings, background reports, scoping documents, meeting minutes, action plans, financial analyses, forward strategies, legislative consultations, pre-planning regulations, policies, policy clarifications, proposals for policies, statistical policy reviews, comparative policies, indices of policies, future policies, and ministerial policy agenda rendered by geographical district, economic strata, material effectiveness, political leaning and linguistic drive. English equals one point, Welsh equals two. *Dwi'n dysgu Cymraeg oherwydd y bobol.* Watch me fly.

This machine and its whirrings are completely transparent. They've told us they are. They take place in a glass debating pit inside a glass room within a Crystal Palace of a building that has won awards for its energy efficiency, use of renewables and out and out style. They are heated by sustainable biomass and cooled by recirculated ambient air. Turn up and you can come in. Ask for it and it's yours. But not the route here, at the bottom of the Vale, from the end of Bendrick Road to the start of Barry's glorious southern highway, Ffordd y Mileniwm. This is the road that soars into the heart of old Barry. It does it on bright new tarmac, with cycleway and waymarked pedestrian path adjacent. It heads straight for the statue of David Davies, the man who made this town.

Bendrick Road, with its working class housing stock and kids in the street with bikes and skateboards, seemed ordinary enough. The Atlantic Café, at the end of it, a sort of brick roadside bunker selling breakfasts all day (takeaways also available) offered one outside table which I took. In the sun with lorries and white vans passing me in volume it was only the mug of tea in my hand that convinced me that I was not sitting at a

US roadside diner. Opposite was the premises of Rock'n'Critters. Down the way greenery made grey-brown by vehicular detritus. Signboarding said no, you can't. No Access for Pedestrians. Speed Limits in Operation. Unauthorised Entry Forbidden. Safety Signs and Procedures Must Be Complied With at All Times. Could I imagine myself going against any of this? I could.

This is Wimborne Road, a permitted access route across the end of ABP's Barry Number Two Dock. Using it allows me not to have to take an inland diversion of several miles up pollution-drenched Hayes Road. Here sits the huge Dow Corning Chemical Plant and its fellow travellers Cabot Carbon, Borden, Zeon Chemicals, and Vopak. Coal might have made Barry but it's chemicals that keep it alive. On Vopak land, trapped behind wire mesh and unrestricted overgrowth and just in front of the company's bulk storage tanks, is the totally inaccessible Vale of Glamorgan Registered Treasure[13] no 840. Barry Windmill. "Circular rubble tower containing original wooden machinery including three of four mill stones in situ." In an admission of history's use as a marketing tool, Vopak have called their twelve tank 42,000 cbm terminal by the same name. Windmill. But if you want to walk up and see the original then you can't.

I set off along Wimbourne, ignoring the signs and the thundering vehicles, Nikon slung around my neck, tracked, no doubt, by every security camera on site. I comprehensively shoot the vast and empty expanses of blue water that is Barry Port. Liquid bulks in tanks, stacks of timber, piles of aggregate. As it turns out nothing happens. The road is a throwback to the 50s past. It's uneven, repaired by patch, full of hump and turn, crossed by rail tracks, guarded by gates and mesh and further notices that demand identification and warn against trespass, rabies, and deep water. It's a world desperate to be regulated, ordered and secure.

Barry is *Y Bari* in Welsh, one of the few places with its own definite article. The place might have been founded by a saint, had its fair share of Roman invaders, Norman castle builders, pirates and Welsh-speaking farmers, but in the end it was coal that made it. David Davies, Llandinam, the arch-rival of the Marquis of Bute and with the advantage of being self-made and

Welsh as opposed to hereditarily rich and Scots, chose Barry as his coal-exporting route to the world. It was a whammo of a choice. Not only did the port he built have permanent access to deep waters (thus avoiding the Severn's notorious and ferocious tidal fall) but he managed to beat Cardiff at its own game. In 1913 it was Barry that topped the world league as a coal exporter.

The Dock Offices, at which Ffordd y Milenium points, has been polished, depolluted and repointed to make it the polar opposite of the Windmill. This is Vale of Glamorgan County Treasure number 992: a neo-Baroque/Renaissance structure[14] with a dominant clock tower, 365 windows and a reassuringly solid construction in red brick. Block work cleaned. Front doors open. Interpretation board outside.

On a plinth stands Alfred Gilbert's[15] statue of Davies the Ocean in boots, long jacket and waistcoat, bareheaded, studying the unfurled plans to Barry Dock. A duplicate of this statue, identical in every detail, stands by the A470 in Llandinam itself. Davies: man made good.

To his west are the Quays, Barry's answer to the apartment within sight of water boom. They cluster around what was originally Barry's Number One Dock and is now an empty sheet of water bigger than anything at Cardiff or Newport, glinting blue, fishermen on its shores, the Island rising beyond. And you can see Barry Island as that from here – the island that was, in the days of the saints and the monks, but no longer.

The Quays, Barry Waterfront's £230m Taylor Wimpey / Persimmon / Barratt Homes development, was half way there when the crash came. Like the rest of the world, it's limping now. The promised waterfront café quarter, functioning innovation district, hotel, new primary school and much-pledged public art have been slow to arrive[16]. A supermarket, however, has. Morrison's trades just up the slope from the Quay's pastel-painted apartment towers. Last week they managed the world record for shopping purchased by a single customer. "Pandemonium at Barry supermarket as shopper fills 22 trolleys" ran the *Barry & District News* headline. Turns out the buyer's credit card failed at first swipe. Staff had to put three thousand pounds worth of crisps, wine, beer and spirits back themselves. The customer has now been banned, reports say. Maybe they should have checked out the size of his car boot first.

Between dock end and the Old Harbour, the land once occupied by the Woodham Brothers rail engine scrapyard is fenced off ready for the Quays Phase Two. Two thousand more homes. The Start of a New Journey. Register your interest now.

The sun beats. There's not a ship anywhere. Nothing loading at ABP, not a single pleasure craft on the Quay's empounded waters. A parked taxi with its driver reading the paper. A woman walking a pair of terriers. A fisherman given up, taking his rods home. Silence pushes, especially now that the enthusiast-run Vale of Glamorgan Railway Company, who once operated a preserved steam railway here, has lost its Council funding. Its replacement, the Barry Tourist Railway operated by Cambrian Transport, have profit in mind and use a restored diesel called Iris[17] to pull their few trains. The fake and frothy tourist creation, Waterfront Station, is empty. Its car park is deserted. In the bushes behind Barry Station proper stand the wrecks of three steam locos, renovation now unlikely. There's talk out there in trainspotter land of them being broken for parts.

I could take the shortcut to my destination along the pedestrians-only Powell Duffryn Way, past the one-time oil storage terminal and up the steps to enter Barry Island's Clive Road. Instead I take the long route, trying to keep the sea in sight. I duck below the rail link and emerge where Broad Street becomes Harbour Road. Today this is a rundown mixture of estate agents, chop suey bars, kebab houses, a tattoo parlour, a dry cleaner, the burned-out shell of Buffs Club (lunches and bar snacks a speciality), a Masonic Hall and a last-hope, hang-on Brains Pub, complete with exclamation mark, The Gordon Bennett! Bennett was born in Scotland. His son, of the same name, was a balloonist. Connection with Barry? Slight.

But I'm allowed to walk here. Industrial no admittance notices are a thing of the past. I've got unrestrained access all the way to White's Cosy Corner, outlier of the funfair. Teashops and stalls once, now a place to park your car.

The Island

I'm here now, on that famed Island. The one that's shaped like
a fish. That's what it looks like, the smiling white-hair with the
stick and the fleur de lys in his button-hole tells me. I'd been
poking my camera down Clive Road trying to get a shot of the
Quays, where I'd just come from, when he struck up a conversation, as pensioners do, filling their time with whatever comes
to hand. "If it's the shape of a fish, where would we be now?" I
ask. "Half way down a fin." This is Michael Banks who once
worked for Dow Corning, manufacturer of polyolefins,
polythenes, polypropylenes, polystyrenes, styrofoam, epoxies,
epichlorohydrins, acrylates, polyvinylidenes, plutonium triggers
for hydrogen bombs, napalm, Agent Orange, and breast
implants made from silicone. They didn't do all that list at Barry
but they did some.

Michael is talking non-stop telling me about how they once
tried to barrage the bay here (a long time before they thought
of doing that at Cardiff) how they almost built the docks at
Ogmore, and how they finally decided that they had to build
them here. "Quite a place," I say. Michael smiles and I take his
photo.

Below me is the perfect sand of Jackson's Bay, the beach most
visitors never reach. It is named after Sir John Jackson who built
the harbour breakwater at the Dock entrance. The bay started
life as Breakwater Cove but local usage turned that swiftly to
Jackson's Bay. It's too long a walk from the train station and
nowhere near the car park. There isn't a chip shop, carnival ride
or café for miles. The Marine Hotel on Plymouth Road, up for
sale as I pass, a sure sign of imminent closure, is about the only
place within walking distance you'll get anything.

By sheer chance I'm standing on Redbrink Terrace outside
Dai Smith's[18] house when I meet Tony Curtis[19]. Dai's not in,
otherwise this piece would be more about lack of height than
striding across the Island. Dai is the shortest historian I've ever
met. This fact he uses regularly in his on-stage patter before
introducing whoever he's up there to welcome, or delivering a
lecture. His three-story house once belonged to a sea captain.
It's high on the Island with views right across the Channel. The

artist Jack Crabtree had it before Dai. It was here that he created his seminal mining paintings of the industry in its last gasp. Crabtree was here when Tony Curtis arrived in the early 1970s.

Tony had stumbled on Barry somewhat accidentally, coming to work at the Training College because the one at Cardiff, under the poet John Stuart Williams, turned him down. We talk about the Barry famous. Tony lists them. Margaret Lindsay Williams, the painter. Robert Thomas, the sculptor. Grace Williams, composer. Authors Gwyn Thomas, Dai Smith and maybe himself. He laughs. When we started out as writers his name and mine went into Amstrad's Locoscript spell-checker and came out as Peddle Fish and Tiny Curses. John Tripp reckoned we were both movie stars. As Emeritus Professor of Poetry at the University of Glamorgan, Tony is now beyond all this.

The Island, the one we are on, was only connected to the mainland when the docks were built in the 1880s. Transport came in 1896 when the rail link, using a 250 yard long pier, arrived at what's now Breaksea Drive. The island was once a base for the Vikings, and in the eighteenth century for pirates. This is a fact not lost on the Council who in their desperate redevelopment of the aging resort have built a fully-featured pirate golf course on the front, complete with flags, cannons, barrels of rum and female buccaneers strapped to masts. Has Tony, an expert golfer, ever played these links? Not yet. St Baruc, after whom Barry is named, came here in 700 AD. The ruins of his holy well and chapel are fenced off on the top of Nell's Point. You can see the footings of walls. The well, long ago, was let into the sewers.

The whole of Nell's Point, the island's dominant feature to anyone approaching by sea, was leased to Butlins in 1966 who built their last camp here, and their smallest. Barry Butlins, salmonella city as its was known by local GPs, was a mere forty-five acres. That didn't stop the owners cramming in more than eight hundred chalets, a chairlift, rides, dance hall, restaurant and the Beachcomber Bar, the biggest in Europe. South Wales Hi Di Hi lasted until the mid-1990s when changing fashions and aging huts forced closure. The site was cleared and, against considerable local opposition, half of it was given over to new-build housing. We go past, on the cliff path, housing stock behind us, as unobtrusive as two hundred and fifty orange brick homes situated on a headland can be. The remainder of the promontory was recently considered as a potential site for fulfilment of the Council's dream of establishing a university here[20], but in these times of financial collapse the plan was abandoned as fantasy. More housing is the likely outcome. But there are no signs of groundwork on site just yet.

Below the Point is the place almost everyone from south Wales over fifty will know intimately. The resort of Whitmore Bay – the endless golden sands of Barry Island. In the early years visitor numbers were huge. 250,000 were recorded attempting to arrive on Bank Holiday Monday in 1938. In the 1950s I can recall in miner's fortnight the entire beach being a mass of bodies. Today the place's heyday may be over but it is still a draw. The sands are swept daily, there's a no public alcohol ruling, and money has been spent on repaving, upgrading the public gardens and adding street furniture.

We cross the front, pass the shelters that, when I was young, were where you ate your fish-paste sandwiches when it rained. At the eastern end where the gates to Butlins once stood are the remains of the public toilets and the collection point for lost children. There was a stall outside that sold buckets, spades, beach-balls and inflatable water-wings. Parents pacifying their wandering offspring would spend heavily to assuage their guilt. Run away get a spade. I had a great collection.

The talk is about verse. Those in the business do this. Tony is telling me about his Barry poems. There are a few. One about the American Dough Boys reaching Barry during World War One and parading through the town. His verse radio play about the island. His poems about the home front in Barry during World War Two. Tony has this ability to turn historical fact into tight impressive verse. He can also contextualise the entire poetry world without notes. It's how you are if you are a Professor of Poetry, and he's Wales' first. But it's painters that really interest him.

His house on Colcot Road has almost as many paintings on the wall as does the new gallery at the National Museum. David Tress, Henry Moore, Barbara Hepworth, Shani Rhys-James, Brendan Burns, Will Roberts, Charlie Burton, Eric Malthouse,

Felicity Charlton, Evan Charlton, John Selway, Terry Setch, Rae Howard Jones, Robert Thomas, Frank Brangwyn, Leslie Moore, Merlyn Evans, Augustus John, Ernest Zobole. In a pastel by Martin Bloch from 1930s Berlin, Hitler is shown playing the banjo. Hanging over the fireplace is a Gyrth Russell painting of a church entitled 'Cowbridge in the Snow'. The red dot of its graveyard visitor is like the red dot moving through the black and white ghetto in the film *Schindler's List*. Why waste time on poetasters when the visual world can do that sort of thing with a flick of the brush.

The funfair, long the only reason for many to visit Barry Island in the first place, is a sad, jerry-built hangover from what it once was[21]. Half the rides don't work. The scenic railway is long demolished and the log flume abandoned, unable to get through the rigours imposed by health and safety. Health and safety, makes us live longer but in such a pasteurised, disabled world. The dodgems and the waltzer are operating, just. There are a few roundabouts and attempts by youths with cigarettes behind their ears to sell you balls to throw in buckets in the hope of winning a soft toy you'd never want, but little else. Evolution, the high-g swirler stands silent. The House of Fun has run out of jokes. The ghost train is itself a ghost.

The fair was started by the White family in 1897, gazumped by the showman Pat Collins in 1930, bought out by Hypervalue owner Ken Rogers in the 1990s, and is now in the hands of his son Ian. There's been much talk of restoration but as I cross there's little actual sign. In 2012 the Council approved redevelopment plans which, so long as the finance can be raised, will see the 4.7 acre site turned into a mix of restaurants and cafes with cinema and bowling alley added, and of course, 124 new sea-edging flats. Meanwhile out front, on Friars Road, the chip shops bracketing a giant branch of Hypervalue still trade. The fair's cut-price character endures.

At the eastern end, near the *Gavin and Stacey* made-famous Codfather of Sole eatery, a local junior school has been let onto the sands as an end of term treat. Buckets of the stuff are being hauled about by six-year-olds as if this were a construction site. There's cricket and there's football, but the donkey rides have gone. So, too, the deck chairs and the rentable windbreaks you hired if you were well-off enough. But the joy is still here. You can hear it in the shrieking.

We cross Friar's Point with its visitor-worn Bronze Age cairns, bio-diverse hay meadow[22], and pretty t9red-looking Friars Point House[23] to circle Barry's Old Harbour. This is a much-silted remnant of how things were before the docks came and the sea surged through here with ease. Abandoned boats with their hulls fractured picturesquely sit on sinking silt. If they were cars they would have been long ago empounded, suggests Tony. But here they've just been left to rot.

On the far side, where the island ends and the mainland begins, past the lime kilns and the 1864 watchtower that once doubled as a lifeboat station, is Cold Knap Point. The Knap. The tea-less place of pebbles that only the rich and the childless ever visited. This place was always windswept and grey, never warm and yellow like Whitmore Bay. These days it's been considerably upgraded. The lido with its paddling pools and changing rooms has been grassed over. The harp-shaped boating lake smartened. An upmarket development of desirable sea-view properties (the sight of water always improves the value) known as Whitehouse sits in the pale sun as if this were the Mediterranean.

The pebble expanse of Cold Knap itself stretches all the way to Porthkerry. We pass what's now known as Glan-y-môr, the excavated remains of a substantial third-century Roman villa, to climb Bull Cliff and access the woods that surround the country park.

"Urien Wiliam lived here," says Tony, pointing at Trem y Don, which joins exclusive Marine Drive on the clifftops. Urien, creator of *Wil Cwac Cwac*, the Welsh-medium children's staple and co-conspirator with TC on a rival to *Superted* that never took off. Things that might have been, there's a world of that.

Ahead are the golden stairs that lead down through the wood to Porthkerry beyond. Under each step is buried a golden coin. Placed there carefully by local authority park maintenance. This it suggests in my local authority-funded handbook. It also says that as the steps have been restored many times so any chance of such treasure remaining is slight. But you are welcome to look.

The Far South – Rhoose Point

There are people out there who have no time for maps. I know. I've seen them. They are the ones who stop you along Newport Road, shouting out from the driver's seats of Ford Fiestas and asking if you know where Toys R Us has moved to, how to get to the Divorce Courts and for precise directions to Ocean Way. Nobody on earth knows the location of Ocean Way. It's the most frequently demanded and totally under-signposted destination in the entire city. And, yes, I do know where all these places are but explaining how to reach them in terms of turning left and then right and left again at the fifth set of traffic lights after that always causes eyes to glaze. You can see the information I impart draining into the ground never to rise again.

And why ask me? I suppose I'm now old enough to look either knowledgeable or safe or even both. I've been thinking of having a business card made that reads *YOU HAVE BEEN SAFELY DIRECTED TO YOUR DESTINATION BY THE AUTHOR OF REAL CARDIFF. BUY YOUR COPY NOW.* I might as well get something out of the deal.

Printed maps in the twenty-first century are unaccountably in decline. They are missing from guide books, rarely used by newspapers, not there in leaflets that describe country walks. Today I've hauled up Google mapping on the PC screen. Key in anything, zip code, postcode, fragment of name, and the system will locate your destination. Porthkerry Park gets me ten or so red pins, which identify everything from the Porthkerry Hair Salon to Porthkerry's Parish Church of St Curig. In the middle of the list is the park.

These maps are instant, enormously wide-ranging, but totally lacking in any topographical detail other than the road network with flat blocks of green to indicate open ground. No paths, no contours, no lines showing the routes of the national grid or marks indicating the sites of ancient tombs. OS this is not. You can't spend an evening reading Google Maps like you can an Ordinance Survey Explorer with its rich mix of quarry (dis), sink hole, Church (rems of), sprs, brooks, bridle-ways, paths, national walking routes, abandoned railways, disused mine shafts, and blue marks the shape of beer mugs identifying country inns.

But on Google Earth everything changes. This is the company's attempt at world domination. They've blended world-wide satellite imagery, visible down to the level of identifying a back garden barbecue, with street level photographs of just about everywhere. Press that button and the world arrives in full colour. Toggle the paddle and you'll get a version of the world you're illicitly viewing in sort of 3D. The effect of all this can be dramatic. On the path I've been following, fields behind hedges and spaces beyond buildings can turn from the vacant lots I imagined them to be instead acres of abandoned vehicles, yards filled with containers, mountains of aggregate, or massed machinery. The countryside, the neat rurality we imagine to surround our towns and cities – Newport, Cardiff, Barry – turns out to be nothing like it seemed.

The local green world is not full of cattle and wheat, rape and turnip, corn and sheep. It grows as well sheds, outbuildings, bunkers, prefabs, vehicle parts, storage tanks, stacked pallets, wood pulp, bunds of topsoil, sand, hard-core, peat, compost, abandoned televisions, lampposts, broken breeze blocks and heaped clinker. Beyond the hedges lie worlds you just did not know were there.

On the eastern outskirts of Cardiff the badly-fixed sign stuck on a zinc topped post and pointing to Maerdy Farm, reads CARAVAN PARK. Amid the rust there were stylised swirls which suggested an old-fashioned two-bed van of the sort retired couples might rent. Sitting in a field, deck chair, tea on tap, rural splendour. Google Earth reality could not have been more different. Running back from the farmhouse this revealed acres of storage yard in which hundreds of vans were parked, cheek by jowl. Not a pensioner's deckchair in sight[24].

I'm up on the Bulwarks to the west of Porthkerry Park. An Iron Age hillfort with extant ditches but mostly crumbled into the sea. Excavations here in 1968 uncovered three buildings, one Iron Age and two Roman. But today the green is unsullied by history. It's overflown by landings at Rhoose Airport which lies directly to the north. Flybe, British Airways, BMI Baby. Cut-price credit card surcharge charter mostly. They come back laden with 200-cig packs of Bensons, Turkish rugs, Tunisian pottery, find the word puzzle mags and matching sets of shot glasses. Most of this dross ends up in the car boot sale, another of which is in action today on the Bulwarks itself. The whole operation is pretty indistinguishable from that at Sully[25], other than in size. The car boot is clearly a Vale of Glamorgan predilection.

Porthkerry itself is a gem. Acres of country park which run between Barry Brook and Knockmandown Wood hitting the coast to the west of Barry. So sinuous and close-cropped green is the place that you imagine it to be private rather than local authority public. It's an absolute triumph. The park was once part of the Romilly estate, with origins as far back as 1412. The council took over management in 1929. There's a miniature golf course and café at the coast end where a raised pebble beach keeps the sea out. The backdrop is the spectacular sixteen arch viaduct built by the Barry railway in 1897, which still carries the line west to Bridgend. The green here is home to extended families running barbeques, throwing Frisbees and walking dogs. The coast path at Porthkerry has been designated by the Vale Council as part of their Millennium Heritage Trail. This is a circular trek that takes in Cowbridge, Llantwit Major, Tinkinswood and the edges of Aberthaw. It leaves Porthkerry via the seaward end of Viaduct Wood to climb the point and emerge below the airport's runway end lights on Bulwark Fort.

The coast is littered with caravan parks, housing estates and industrial remains. Quarries that once gave readily of their limestone have lost their seaward walls to erosion and are now filled with static homes. The path rolls ever southwards, skirting the bulge that the village of Rhoose now makes in its search for property gold.

The land here, originally heath, has been pulled apart by hunters for first building stone and later blue lias limestone, a primary component of cement. Extracting lime, as I discover, is a feature of this coast. The Aberthaw and Rhoose Point Portland and Lime Company of 1912, which became the Aberthaw Cement Works in 1919, did most of the abstraction filling the landscape with holes. What they made was not just cement but asbestos cement. By the time the world discovered the health hazard that asbestos actually was, most of the blue lias was gone. Blue Circle bought what remained in 1983 and was perfectly placed to ride the nineties boom by reclaiming what it could of the site and building houses on it. Why should a world-beating cement company not branch out into replicating Brookside at the edge of the sea? Money was flowing and property development was the place to be.

With help from the WDA[26], Blue Circle spent a decade site-clearing and making things safe. They were not entirely successful. Fenced-off, water-filled pools and great stretches of former quarry remain. This has not stopped the developers delivering six hundred houses with plans for a further three hundred and fifty as soon as the market improves. Locals complain that planned retail units, a golf course and a nature reserve have not arrived. There are problems with run-off from the fields and with drainage. But the views of the sea compensate, just a bit.

Rhoose Point is the southernmost place in Wales. That is if you discount Flat Holm, the Welsh claims to Lundy, and the submerged lost lands off Pembroke that run south along the sea bed, church bells intact and regularly heard to toll at low tide, all the way to Italy. The Vale of Glamorgan celebratory sign is rich with rust and graffiti. Beyond it, between the extant sections of remaining quarry wall, you can, if you avoid the Vale's wire fencing, access the sea. There's no one around. A couple engaged in what appears to be a reader's wives photoshoot hastily scramble out of view, bra and camera flying, as I appear, notebook in hand, at the water's edge. I always wondered where they took them. They take them here.

The southernmost land tip is marked by a stone circle with central menhir brought here from Wales's most northern place. Land reclamation and New Landscape by Blue Circle Industries plc, 2000. They've tried. If you check the place from above you'll see more. Rocks here have been arranged in enormous spirals, fans, snakes, herringbones and as a finely-worked eight-pointed compass. You can barely tell what these things are at ground level, but get up there on the satellite and all becomes clear. It's unexpected and uncelebrated. View from the window of your next Rhoose Airport flight. It's worth a tilt.

Fontygary and Beyond

South of Fonmon Castle[27], the thirteenth-century fortified house now open for weddings to keep penury from the door, the land art continues. Brendan Burns is down on the beach. Graham Sutherland is in the lanes. The Fontygary vans run along the clifftops like Mondrian. The leisure park is so vast that it has districts. Fonmon Heights, Waverley Gardens, Devon Cliffs. It's all blues, reds, and yellows. The tarmacked paths are grey bars. The line of the hedge, which keeps frolicking holiday makers from plunging onto the limestone beach, is straight, green and dark[28].

There's an air of impressionism in the way the Vale's ordered fields chequerboard their undulating way to the sea. They cross a landscape that would have been entirely deciduous woodland before the Romans came. I can feel the history booming up out of the parked caravans, six-berthers, integral showers, finely manicured lawns, geraniums in tubs with, among them, wooden signs reading *Husband for Sale. TV Remote included! Watch out Dad's in a bad mood again! Enter at your own risk!* My heritage spread before me.

Carnaby, Senator, North Star, Aspen, Lyndhurst, Willerby, Santana. Maker's names for the vans I'm passing. Santana. Rhythm section the size of an orchestra out back, heavy metal lead guitar in front. I peer through the rain-flecked windows. Plush carpet, ceramic horse, teapot, copy of *The Sun* folded on the upholstered window seat. Silence.

Mark Boyle, manipulator of light shows and master of the UK cultural underground, made his name by chucking a dart into a map and then visiting the spot he'd hit. He would make an exact replica of the six-foot-by-six square of land he'd reached using fibreglass moulds. If his map led him to water then he'd take a cast of the surface or create a hologram. If it was air he'd film the sky directly upwards from the site. Streams of passing cloud, roaring sun or drenching rain. This was his 'Journey to the Surface of the Earth'[29]. He brought home parts of Liverpool Docks and great swathes of London. Far as I know he never ventured anywhere near Fontygary. Fonty, where the valleys hit the coast and the world has been sanitised.

I'm throwing my numbers by dice to get the OS co-ordinates for the seashore below. Access has been down the steepest of moulded concrete steps, half overgrown with foliage, onto Watch House Beach. Here grass-edged lagoons line the cliff edge behind a wave-driven ridge of amassed pebble that protects them from the sea.

ST 04519 65520 blue lias limestone
ST 03912 65830 blue lias limestone
ST 04956 65678 blue lias limestone
ST 05100 65510 blue lias limestone
ST 02945 65419 blue lias limestone
ST 04556 65781 blue lias limestone
ST 03818 66120 the Aberthaw Limeworks.

Aberthaw Limeworks, the remains. Opened 1888 to burn lime pebbles in its twin kilns, turning them to easily transportable lime ash. Ceased operation 1926. It is now a Grade II Listed Building and clad about with scaffolding as it undergoes conservation. The roof is in poor repair. Cracks in the walls are being filled. The tramway running east to Rhoose has gone.

The limestone on the beaches, known as Aberthaw Tarras, was once much prized. Victorian boats would land here to gather stock for the construction trade and for use as flux in the manufacture of copper and iron. Before the Aberthaw Pebble Limestone Company made the process simpler, boats by the score could be seen daily landed just to the west on the Leys Beach. At low tide their sailors would have dug out a hollow among the pebbles and marked this with a cradle of wooden stakes. The boats would sail into these when the waters were higher.

Aberthaw limestone, especially that from below the high tide mark, made hydraulic lime mortar which would set underwater. Quantities were used in the building of canal locks and in the construction of the first Eddystone Lighthouse in 1759.

The Thaw, which breaks the coast here, was once a great snake the shape and size of the Rhymney back in Cardiff. On its eastern side, set well back from the tidal thrash of the Severn, was the port of Aberthaw. In its day of some significance. It outshone both Col Huw (at Llantwit Major), and Porthkerry, especially when those two harbours were seen off by the storm surge of 1584 and the Great Flood of 1607. They built boats here, landed salt, dried fruit, broadcloth, kerseys, mercery ware, barley, evis seed, sacke, rozen, pitch, reap-hooks, tapping leather, cordage, apothecary requisites, Spanish wine and vinegar. Left with wool and butter. Went to Bristol, Somerset, north Devon, Spain, France. The Port Books list the boats by name. *Speedwell, Marie, Dove, Elizabeth, Long Thomas, Blessing, Patience, Endeavour, Harte, Jonas, William and Margaret, Fonmon, Speedwell.* Not a Welsh-sounding one among them.

In the seventeenth century smuggling was a main Bristol Channel occupation. The pirate Thomas Knight might have been pushed off Barry Island and sent back to his base on Lundy but this did not stop others. Local wreckers regularly lured ships onto the rocks right along this coast using false lights and set fake beacons on headlands. In the village of East Aberthaw the forti-fied Marsh House was in use as a smuggler's store. The Vale as Somalia. Local customs officers had a hard time.

At the end of the nineteenth century the Cowbridge and Aberthaw Railway (later the TVR), built to take away product from the Limeworks, began to carry day trippers to Aberthaw. The beaches were destinations. Before mid-Channel dredging became a regular activity, the sands at Aberthaw were extensive.

The great elephant on the shore, of course, is the power station. The structure dominates the rural seascape in a way that the twin stations at Uskmouth in the heart of industrial Newport never do. The sea defences are bulbous. There are wave return-tipped concrete revetements reminiscent of those protecting the Wentlooge levels. They have radiating groynes and fields of sea-stopping rock. It's an A level investment against impending overflow. If I were the sea I'd give up.

The Heritage Coast:
Aberthaw to Porthcawl

Aberthaw

Outside Aberthaw Power Station, since we've got there way too early, John Briggs is doing imitations of Lee Friedlander. He's shooting the Boys Village entrance sign through the car window. Wing mirror, door edge and wrecked Boys Village signboarding merging into a single chaotic take. Friedlander broke all the rules. His classic shots are bisected by trees and telegraph poles and crossed by the shadow of the photographer. He's simultaneously behind and in front of the camera. Taking the shot and in it. Scenes buzz with detail in an ambiguous mix of refection and divided reality. Friedlander was born in 1934 and I thought he'd died, but here he is with a new exhibition, *America by Car*, upcoming in London. Roadside views of all fifty States framed by the windscreen of his rental car. The wing mirrors, rear-view mirror, side window and the windscreen itself are all part of the finished take. Often as not they include reflected fragments of Friedlander himself and his camera shooting the picture. Seventy-six and still snapping. Top of his game. Gives you faith and restores your passion.

John, whose work is nothing like Friedlander's other than maybe a shared propensity for using black and white, claims the master as an influence. "He taught me not to be afraid of the mundane," he says. "Cities are full of the mundane. Signboards, roads, posts, poles, traffic, people, light and shade. Friedlander knew how to make it all work[1]."

Npower's Aberthaw B, which we've come to see, is a behemoth of an installation built in the 1970s, hard at the sea's edge. It fills the space once occupied by the Leys, the old Aberthaw harbour, the short-lived Barry Golf club[2] and a great slice of Aberthaw's river delta. The river itself has been canalised to run safely where Npower want it to. Aberthaw can generate 1500 megawatts by consuming 500 tons of coal an hour. And for something so enormously industrial – the coal mound itself contains more than a million tons and has its own railway for deliveries – the place is the next best thing to clean and quiet. There's a blue sky and you can hear the sea birds. Beyond the double perimeter fence, guarded by guards and cameras, the sea is flat. Minehead is visible in the blue-grey distance.

"Of course," says Amy, who is showing us round, "the plant isn't actually working today. Which might explain the tranquillity. But when it is, the noise isn't much greater. You see some plume from the stack and in my office there's a background buzz." Amy Sherborne is Aberthaw's Environmental Compliance Engineer. Increasing regulation, the need to reduce carbon emissions, and pressure to be greener from just about every lobby there is are things that npower's parent company, RWE, take seriously. This doesn't mean that they've abandoned the profit motive and have now joined in with those who breach the security fences and chain themselves to the coal conveyor belts. But it does mean they are seriously looking at ways in which a power station that works by burning coal can significantly reduce its impact on the environment.

Against this background Aberthaw B might have come to the end of its useful life if RWE had not opted to spend a few hundred million pounds of installing new seawater Flue Gas Desulfurization equipment which has reduced sulphur dioxide emissions by 95%. The centrepiece is a vast concrete-lined pond known as the jacuzzi, which bubbles just like one when in operation. Swallow and Peregrine Falcon fly across it. A double-fence protects the edge. If you fall in when it's effervescing you'll sink.

In the circular control room which looks like something out of a TV programme about nuclear disaster – all lights, buttons, screens, banks of telephones, and walls that have on them graphics depicting spinning electrons – Amy shows me a rack of emissions monitors. These are devices that measure generator temperature, the ph. and volume of the emissions from the stack, and the plant's operating noise. That can't be more than 10 decibels above the ambient level at the site's boundaries. "This place might look like something out of science fiction and that's because it doubled as such for the filming of an episode of the *Sarah Jane Adventures*," Amy tells me. "The crew put the atomic symbols on the walls and we've just kept them." John is photographing the incident chart and taking close-ups of the control desks. Unlike some other places I've been, npower are welcomingly open.

We're now on 275KV Switch House Road which, as Amy explains, is the level at which power is generated by the station. Further along is 132KV Switch House Road. "That's the level at which we import power. Strange isn't it, a power station needing to buy electricity from the National Grid? But we do. We need it to run the plant at times when there are outages or when market demand is low, like now, and the turbines aren't turning."

The plant centres on its massive coal-fired generators that use 75% Russian coal and 25% Welsh. This came originally from Tower Colliery at Hirwaun but is now sourced from Ffos y Fran opencast. Npower would like to see the Welsh contribution rise to make it 50/50. Local coal, however, has a higher sulphur content which makes it, despite the considerably shorter delivery distance, a much more expensive proposition. To help meet increasingly tough emissions regulations the plant also uses a small percentage of biomass – mainly woodchip and sawdust ground-up on site. The wood stacks resemble nineteenth century pit props waiting to go down the shaft.

History in this place has been completely flattened. Until comparatively recently Aberthaw A, the earlier 60s-built power station stood on the same site. That was demolished in 1997. The revealed space is now being used by npower for carbon capture experiments. They are installing a pilot plant which is expected to successfully extract all the carbon from the station's main emissions. Once operating, there'll be gallons of the fizzy stuff and nowhere to put it. The idea that it'll be successfully lost somewhere deep in the geology below is myth. Wrong rocks, apparently. It's the ones under the North Sea that we really want. The carbon will be emitted back into the atmosphere. Process proven if not exactly operational. Stage two – fix the geology. In the car park sits a HGV the size of which is something you normally only see on Ice Road Truckers. Another forty-metre carbon capture tower delivered and ready for installation. If all this is merely PR, as the environmentalists suggest, then it's certainly costing.

The plant ash mound, largely generated by the old A Station, has been capped and grassed. Rabbits live there. Under this, if you believe all you read, was once a castle, the unexcavated Bronze Age round barrow, Trwyn Llywelyn, a pirate's haunt, the entrance to a secret tunnel that ran all the way from here to Mumbles. Flattened and lost when the ash began to arrive. Ash from the present operation is filtered into high and low carbon residue. The high stuff goes back to the boilers for reburning. The rest to Lafarge Cement Works next door. There's a symbiotic relationship between these two Vale industrialists. The cement works quarries limestone and then fills the revealed spaces with Aberthaw low grade ash. Everyone wins.

We're in the vehicle now going through the car wash. Everything that moves down here among the mounds has to be sluiced down before returning to the main plant. John in his high vis, hard hat and plastic eye protectors photographs the high energy water jets through the front windscreen. Briggs as Friedlander, perhaps.

Creativity, of course, is never far away. Amy's boyfriend is Antony Lavisher[3], a self-published author of dark fantasies and a writer on the up. Unlike the boatman in *Shakespeare in Love* Amy does not produce a manuscript from her jacket and ask my opinion. She might well have done this. It happens all the time. Even a fireman, in my study a decade back helping put out a fire in the roof space, noticed the number of books I had. "You interested in this stuff," he asked, pointing his hose at my collection of author's guides and writer's directories. "It's what I do," I replied. "I'm a literary agent[4]." "Are you? Great, I've got this novel, see, and I wonder if you'd care to have a look." He put his hose down and began pulling papers out of his inside pocket. I stood there, quietly in my slippers, with smoke drifting past me, taking a speed read. It was about fire engines and flames and the excitement of his days. "Not bad," I said. "You should send it off."

The offshore caissons, looking like concrete Doric temples, are probably the thing that most people know the station for. The larger is a cold water inlet. The two smaller buildings put hot water back. There was once an inspection tunnel that ran out to sea but, like the secret passage to Mumbles, that's now been blocked off. We're standing on the top of Ace2, the most southerly building in Wales, Aberthaw's new education and interpretation centre[5]. Built on a foundation of pulverised fuel ash from the station, and with furnace bottom ash used for the car park, this place is greener than green. Rainwater capture feeds the toilets, insulation is with recycled papier-mâché and cooling is via ducts on the roof. On the deck up there, architects Loyn & Co have built great metal fins which can been seen for miles along the coastal path. They line up the cold water caisson with the station's tower. Only they don't, quite. You need to move your head to get the illusion to work.

In the generator hall, dimensions go up a bracket. The space is cathedral-like, with arrays of pipework reaching up towards heaven, turbines as the altar, and the blackened bodywork of the great boiler as god. God slumbering today but soon god once again burning. In the Tate Modern's former Bankside Station on the Thames they've ripped all this stuff out and installed great works by Louise Bourgeois, Anish Kapoor, Rachel Whiteread, and Ai Weiwei. The secular future.

But for now, here, it's still mainstream present. Coal to burn. Conversion to nuclear not yet happened[6]. No wind farms yet to ruin the tidal reaches.

Limpert

This place is Limpert rather than Limpet. Not the molluscs nor the mines. It was once a beach where day-trippers came. It had a café and an inn, both vanished, although a sixteenth century boathouse, once attached to the inn, remains. Today it has been extended and turned into the white-painted Limpert Bay Guest House. Busy Lizzie in pots, model yachts in the window. It's a picture of bliss were it not for the throbbing, coal-fired electricity generator so next door you could reach out of your bedroom and touch it. On the guest house website the leviathan does not appear in a single promotional photograph. If it were my guest house, I wouldn't include it either.

I've come down the track from Gileston. Thatch, ancientness, manor house. Population in 1841 was forty-three. It's not much more today. I diverted briefly via the Boys Village and am now parked in the small, pebble car park, watched by ponies, fishermen around me unloading their kit, seabirds whirling overhead.

The Boys Village was once part of Britain's obsession with bracing air, Christian values and healthy living. Built in the 1920s with grant aid from the Miners Welfare Fund, it was a place of improving recreation for the sons of pit men. It had a sports field, a gym, a swimming pool, activity halls, a refectory, dormitory blocks and a chapel of significant size. Everything was within easy walking distance of the health-giving sea. When the pits began to close the village opened its doors to other voluntary and Church organisations. New dormitories were still being added as late as 1982. For some time in the twentieth century, Christianity rocked. But as the world shifted on its axis and the values of outward bound, gender-separated, wholesome living fell from favour, the village went into decline. By 2008 the site had been abandoned and the vandals and graffiti artists had moved in.

Today the village is a dystopia of torn roofs, smashed windows and tag-painted walls. Full of ghosts and the ghosts of ghosts. The deserted, brick-pocked swimming pool surreally shimmers. The refectory's pre-War bamboo wallpaper rises from a tile-shattered floor. The accommodation blocks are a maze of smashed plaster and dissolving mattresses. The Church still points at heaven, but is a hell of wreck and plunder inside. The name Futuretown has been sprayed presciently across what was once the administration building's walls.

I'm taking pictures but I'm not the only one. Others lurk among the battered buildings, snapping the sights as though this was a tourist attraction. Checking on the web later, it's apparent that many have done the same as I and have been doing so for quite some time. The site's slow decline is charted on Flickr in considerable detail. You can watch the place, once tall, slowly crumble into the ground. History over, heritage gone.

Heritage gone – appropriate that, since I'm now on something called the Heritage Coast. This is the start of it. It's eighteen miles long, (or fourteen, depends who you ask), and it runs from here to Porthcawl. Heritage Coasts were set up by the Countryside Council in 1973 to mark out areas that excelled in their beauty. Local authorities were required to manage them, which meant adding stiles, waymarking and fences, and improving access. That word again. Wales has fourteen heritage coasts, including Pembrokeshire's Dinas Head and the whole of the Llŷn Peninsular in Gwynedd. The Glamorgan example crosses the land of two local authorities, Bridgend and the Vale of Glamorgan. To my amazement, this being the corner of the world that powered the Industrial Revolution, it is devoid of anything that could be considered urban. This is green country, cliff country, a place where the Severn has become the sea. Where the waves have white tops, where the distance melts into the west.

As a start it is not auspicious. Aberthaw hovers. But like the Limpert B&B you can often ignore what you are next to by turning your back on it. RAF St Athan, just to the north, barely flies a plane these days and the Lafarge Cement works in East Aberthaw are distant enough to not intrude. The path snakes off across the great delta that the River Thaw and its tributary the Kenson have down the millennia created. It's a flatland of massed pebble and drained pond. The pools here fill half-heartedly in winter, improved drainage leaking their content into the sea.

When the Boys Village was at its height, before the arrival of the power station, this coastal stretch would have been a joy of camp-fire, brisk invigorating bathing and uplifting song. Today it's a mess of deserted bladder-wrack and beached flotsam. For a mile and a half across it, wartime tank traps in the form of Ferro-concrete pebble cubes snake like a giant's abacus. Path maintenance is pathetic. Stiles are held together with rusting nails and blue yacht-rope. Waymarking is lost in the overgrowth. The way itself switches from pebble to bramble and then to field edge with the sort of illiteracy normally reserved for sheep tracks. As a coastal path it is a complete failure. For most of the way I'm striding either behind a land-defending wall of shingle or below a towering crop-protecting hedge. In the four miles between Limpert and Llantwit Major I see as much of the water as I saw of the Appalachians while doing my own walk in the woods[7] in North Carolina.

Where the land rises at the western end of the greater Thaw delta, is another wrecked outpost of Christianity, the Summerhouse Bay Conference Centre. This is owned by the South Wales Christian Outreach Trust. It was once known as Hafod Camp and was built originally as a convalescent home for miners suffering from silicosis. Its huts are now largely roofless, waiting for the storms to knock them down. On the headland, amid the trees and gyrations of the coastal path, is Summerhouse Camp[8], a Silurian promontory fort. This is maintained, apparently, by no one and has lost at least a quarter of its acreage to the sea. Its three ramparts are obliterated with trees and its centre is a labyrinth of encroaching undergrowth.

Within the fort, overgrown almost to the point of invisibility, are the remains of the Seys[9] family's octagonal summerhouse. Built in 1730 and reputedly in use as late as 1920, this piece of Georgian extravagance was used by revellers visiting the nearby and now ruined fortified manor house[10] a mile or so inland. Access was gained by knocking a roadway right through the fort's ramparts and by levelling its ditches. CADW, where were you then? High spot of this whole historical deal, for me anyway, given the total boredom of the walk to get here, is the much vaunted Seawatch Centre. This is a former coastguard lookout station with its upper room now done out like a ship's bridge and its roof bristling with maritime observational equipment. I approach it, late morning Saturday, high season end of hot July, to find its red bricks locked and boarded against vandals. A ship's anchor garishly painted black and yellow is cemented to ground. A chalkboard announces the centre's next opening time: Monday, 11.00 am. Worse than Dorset, which seems to close down immediately you approach. Worse than St Fagan's at its money-saving 80s nadir when it opened for about an hour and a half, mid-day on a Sunday. And certainly worse than all of France, which still closes for lunch, customers or not.

Llantwit is within reach and I continue to see more farm crops than sea as I hike towards it. This is the Vale where the fertile lands roll right up to the Jurassic cliff edge. The fields are big enough to land UFOs. The weather has drawn a vast crop of wheat and corn skywards. Fresh territory for the lads from Wiltshire to tackle with their crop-circle boards and midnight ropes. We could do with a revival of such ley line make-believe, a bit of fantasy to leaven the economic gloom that late capitalism has visited upon us.

The place arrives. Beach, cliff. Cliff, beach. Llantwit, beyond Stout Point, I see you. More the past hoving into contemporary view. Heritage sea, heritage coast, heritage town. How much more of it will there be?

Nash

I've crossed the gullies of Castle Ditches, the eroded hillfort remains that once guarded the eastern headland of the Col-Huw, and am now in the car park. This is the beach at Llantwit Major. Surfers, lifeguards, families. Great racks of pebble and tumbled stone. The Col-Huw, the river that's created this sea-reaching valley, must be the shortest in Wales. It's about a mile long and is made from the merged waters of the Ogney Brook and the Hoddnant that meet just south of the town.

Dave, rat catcher, laboratory technician, probation officer and failed itinerant teacher of English to the Russians of the Steppes should have been on this walk, not for where it went or what you could see but for the talk that might have been in the air. Right now we would have been discussing the collapse of society and how decades of socialism have led us to our present underclass-riddled impasse. Dave's fervent belief is that the rise and rise of our twenty-first century bureaucracy will see us down. The data spinners demand ever more data and that data spun ever faster. They enlarge their empires. They overdose on control. The system itself becomes the purpose. We've entered a world of pure administration where nothing gets done anymore. Outside Rome burns.

That's what we would have discussed sitting at the beach's west end, in the picnic-tabled café, drinking strong tea from real mugs, the Col-Huw gliding past and the blue sky above. To call it a beach is actually rather disingenuous, for this is mainly a cove of stones. This was once the port of Llantwit Major, population two thousand, bigger than Cardiff, a sanctuary for coastal shipping, lime exporters, importers of wine and hides. The storms of 1584 and then 1607 destroyed it. We might have talked about why it was, in those ancient days, that people couldn't have got their acts together and engaged in rebuild. Why abandon the port to the past? Looking around me I can't see a single sign of it. Same with Dave.

He couldn't make it. His knee is as bad as ever although he did talk about doing the sun salutation at home, privately. Book open on the table beside him, pushing his hands up towards the sky. Yoga was the future. Stretch towards god.

Llantwit is a knot of small streets which bend around a fifteenth century town hall, a thirteenth century dovecote, the remains of a monastery and a splendid thirteenth century church dedicated to Saint Illtud, the man after whom this place is named. How you travel from *Llan Saint Illtud* to the Anglicisation of *Llan Twit Major* I can't really say. Maybe medieval pronunciation was of the same order as that heard today in Brixton. Who knows? Tourist Information is billed as opening at 2.30. It is now 11.00. Can I wait three and a half hours? No.

Illtud founded a fifth century divinity school here. At the time that was the only kind of school possible, a madrasa of its day. As pupils, he managed to attract at least six future saints – David, Samson, Paul Aurelian, Gildas, Tudwal, and Baglan – along with the King of Gwynedd. Cor Tewdws[11], it was the oldest university in the world. The present church stands on the Tewdws site.

West of Llantwit, the path is high now. One hundred feet and more above the sea. Real Heritage Coast. The layers of lias and shales with their distinctive cracked, stratified, stacked appearance rise up from the wave-cut platforms below. The beach, which runs virtually unstopped for ten miles to the sands of Dunraven Bay, is all like this. Hard carboniferous limestone pavements, fractured and storm pocked, pooled and water-riddled, like canal bottoms on Mars or the Atacama Desert where once there was water but now there is none.

The problem, for conservationists, is the erosion. The sea slides up across the hard rock pavements to crash against the softer cliff bottom. These it undercuts, turning stone to shingle, bringing the whole face down. The coastline retreats, slowly, steadily. 'Holding the line', the Environment Agency term for fighting back the waters with sea defences, doesn't operate here. Caves form. Coast edge paths tumble into the sea and routes get re-established further inland. 'Rolled back' is the official description. Hill forts – and there are at least a half dozen on these along this coast – pour their ramparts into the Severn's sea waters. Thirty per cent of our prehistory is already lost. The remainder is heading that way.

Decades back a brave Vale of Glamorgan councillor suggested that the cliff faces should be concreted over to prevent further attrition. Lose the visual wonder of the frontage but gain a more permanent top. Officials chuckled at his naivety. But since then several further metres of irreplaceable national monument have slid into infinity. More will follow. The waves are boss.

Along here, among the cliff edge wild cabbage, wild carrot and samphire are innumerable World War Two pillboxes and the remains of gun emplacements. They should sit in their decaying brick and concrete glory, defaced and decrepit markers for what the world once went through. The example on the cliff edge up beyond Tresilian Bay has been laboriously repointed and faced with local rock in much the same way that former council houses are often covered with stick-on stone panels in an attempt to add distinction.

The path rocks and zings its way between field edge and precipitous drop. It falls across the front of what was once American newspaper magnate William Randolph Hearst's glory of restoration, St Donat's Castle. 'The Boathouses Swimming Pool Area Castle and Grounds are Private and Not Open to the Public.' You get in when you have a friend (see p.154 for a description).

For the average coast walker – and this is a day of pastel coloured anoraks and monochrome tee-shirts, walking poles and daysacks, trainers and sandals, kids carrying footballs, teenage girls with vacant pale faces, bearded ancients saying "you go past boy you're faster than me" – St Donat's is as far away from civilisation than they've been in a half-year. A place that somehow pulls its power straight out of the planet and has no need of cities or towns. To walk further is to enter the wobbling distance at the end of the universe, where the light is strong turning stronger and you need to carry water to ensure you remain alive.

But actually you don't. Nash[12] Point, hillfort, white light-houses and extended cliff-top car park loom up from the clifftop. Amazingly, the headland top café is open. Tea, cake, no beer. Dave could have saluted the sun here and almost touched it. High over the waters, watching the Nash sandbar, sinuous and golden, emerge from the ebbing sea.

"More sand there than I've seen in years," John, the Trinity House guide tells me. "They're not dredging much mid-channel now. That's the recession I suppose. Nothing much has been taken for at least four months and the sand, it's come back. Take a look at the beach." And it's there, too, sand covering the limestone pebbles at the mouth of Cwm Marcroes, the valley down which flows the Marcross Brook.

I've managed, with the sort of luck that is normally only ever in the possession of guide book authors, to reach Nash Point Lighthouse[13] on an open day. Fresh white paint, not a stone or grass blade out of place. £3.50 for a look inside the fog signal house. "Can we hear it?" "Not today." Then a self-guided climb up through the seven floors of the main lighthouse itself. "You can get married here. We've got another three coming in this week," John tells me. The third floor is devoted to the ceremonials. It has curtains, chairs and a maximum capacity of twenty-five, which includes the couple and the photographer. Half the guests sit, the others stand on the spiral stair. You get the fog horn sounded in celebration. Nine-hundred quid, including VAT. For the parsimonious this beats Cardiff Castle hands down.

The main lighthouse and its smaller companion were built in 1832 after the loss with no survivors of the paddle steamer *The Frolic* on the Nash sands the year before. The lighthouse is thirty-seven metres tall and was once painted with black and white stripes to distinguish it from its fellow. Mariners coming up channel would line the two up, and if they did that then the sands would not sink them. The main tower is automated today. No one lives here. The advent of GPS has meant that lighthouses are no longer what they were. There's a notice on the stairs that reads *The Association of Lighthouse Keepers Could Be For You.* £16 a year and access to all sorts of things that non-lighthouse keepers would be denied.

Outside, the former keeper's cottages are available for holiday let. They have names like *Ariel* and *Stella*. They are as perfectly white painted as the lighthouse towers. Their gardens appear to have been trimmed with scissors. I begin to feel that, rather than Wales, I've now reached Switzerland. On sea. I bend down and retie my shoes.

St Donat's

I'd come here in the sixties. So had John Briggs who is with me again today. We're entering from the main road. I'd visited once in that decade to listen to a MJQ sound-a-like playing cool vibraphone to a hall of polo-neck wearing youth. For the new generation, modern jazz was where it was, trad jazz was where it was not. The men were all in the early stages of long love affairs with Player's Navy Cut or Gold Flake, tapping their pointy shoes and thinking about women rather than jazz. In the next hall was a Dixie outfit knocking out stuff you could actually dance to but, being south Wales new-gen hipsters, all we wanted to do was stay sitting down. John can't remember any of this although he had to have been here at the time.

St Donat's, in those grainy black and white days, had only recently been bought-up by Antonin Besse II and given to the newly formed Atlantic College for the fulfilment of their educational ideals. It had opened in 1962 as the first of what was to be twelve United World sixth-form Colleges. This was an international pre-university finishing school of ivy league standard. John had been sent here from St Paul, Minnesota by a middle-class American family still convinced of the value of what they saw as an English education. "Coming here was a shock," John tells me. "They didn't have country lanes or castles in Minnesota. I was here to do my A Levels. I got them too. Trouble was, they turned out to be useless for getting into university back home."

John's current project is to return and shoot again versions of the photographs he took in 1964. He shows me a set of angular views through battlements, of the walls of the Hall, of the portcullis, of the Gibbet Tower. Karen, the commercial manager of the present enterprise, immediately rules out any return to the battlements. "We can't have you climbing up there." It's the usual story, regulation, fear, I suppose, of one of us falling off and breaking the limbs of the ambling students below. There are 350 of them, from eighty countries. They complete the International Baccalaureate studying language, math, science and the arts. They do it in one of the most amazing colleges I've ever seen. A medieval castle sitting right on the Heritage Coast, a Hogwarts-on-Sea with ghosts. There are towers, ancient barracks, a church with a fifteenth century Calvary and a Norman font, and Tudor gardens that step down to the pebbled sea in a measured, horticultural rush.

Karen is talking about weddings. You can get married here. Marry in a country church, a lighthouse, a pillbox or a castle. It's £3k a go at St Donat's but at least you can squash in more guests (137) than you can at the lighthouse on Nash Point. We pass the refurbished tithe barn that forms the theatre space for St Donat's famous art centre. Venue for the biennial story-telling extravaganza, *Beyond the Border* and countless other events. I read there in the 90s. I gave a gutsy performance full of verbal passion and Welsh diatribe to a well-heeled Vale of Glamorgan audience who'd come here almost exclusively from villages and towns which hadn't changed much since the war. Cardiff and Swansea, at about an hour away each, rarely sent anyone. Still don't. This is a sad thing for, like the Castle, the

Centre is a magical place. I did 'Breath'[14] which features me yelling into a tumble-dryer flexible extractor tube while simultaneously swirling it around me. Visually, the piece is unsettling as the unexpected spinning tube flies above the audience's heads. Sonically it adds Doppler to my voice, like a fire engine passing at speed. Not something you'd hear often in these deep Vale lanes.

We go down through the terraces, passing the Beast Garden where the Queen's animals, white greyhounds, lions, griffins, stand atop columns, watching you as you walk[15]. Below the Rose Garden and the Blue Garden are the restored Cavalry Barracks. These date back to the sixteenth century and were erected as security against invading Spaniards or marauding pirates, or maybe both, by Sir Edward Stradling, a man who at the time knew how to hold onto what he'd got. They fell to bits later but have today been comprehensively restored and are used as a base for Atlantic College's extra mural outreach work.

Beyond them are the swimming pools, one indoor, one out, the College's collection of fibre-glass boats and the lifeboat station. Castellated walls protect the enterprise from thievery but it often fails to work. Paul Dowling tells us this. He's the Seafront Manager. The boats have their engines removed and locked away while the hulls themselves are chained to large concrete blocks. Who'd come all this way to steal a boat? Shifty-eyed walkers, criminal fishermen, ne'er-do-wells from city estates strolled the whole twenty coastal path miles just to nick a fibre-glass smack. "We lose them," says Paul, shaking his head. "You come back in the morning and they're gone."

Centrepiece is the actual lifeboat, a three-crew Atlantic 75 named after the man who put up the money to buy it, *Colin James Daniel*. "It's all genuine," says Paul. "We train the students, they pass their RNLI exams, and we run the service. We get about a dozen shouts year. Real stuff." We look out at the windless, brown, eggshell-smooth and pretty shipless Estuary. Shouts today are unlikely. "From the great international mix here, who make the best sailors?" I ask. "Hard to say," says Paul. "We had a great Pakistani girl here last year, but it's probably the Spanish." Still invading then, after all these years.

John loops us back through the woods below the

Watchtower[16], to show me where the original St Donat's village once stood and beyond that where Hearst buried his dogs. William Randolph Hearst was the American newspaper magnate who was the inspiration for Orson Welles' *Citizen Kane*. He had so much money that in 1925 he was able to send a cable to his British agent, Alice Head, the editor of *Good Housekeeping*, which read "Buy St Donat's Castle". Ancient, available but, by Hearst at that time, unseen. In fact Hearst took a good three years to find the time to visit. Once he had, obsession took over. On the liner back to the States he made plans for restoration and wrote these up in a twenty-five page letter to his architect, Sir Charles Allom. Many involved installing new bathrooms – Hearst upped the number from three to thirty-five – and the piping-in of mains water and electricity. Ancient the Castle might be but Hearst lived in the modern world.

Controversially, however, Hearst also specified the buying up of all sorts of 'medieval' remains from elsewhere in Britain and France, and their incorporation into the St Donat's fabric. These included panelling from the Neptune Inn at Ipswich and from St John's College, Cambridge, a hooded fireplace from Beauvais in Normandy, a ceiling from the nave of St Botolph's Church in Lincolnshire, doorways from Eyre Court in Galway and a whole hall, Bradenstoke, brought here from the ruined priory in Wiltshire. There were questions asked in Parliament about the legality of losing part of England's heritage to Wales, but nothing was done.

Hearst's mistress, the silent film star Marion Davies, was a St Donat's feature every time Hearst visited. Rumour has it that she liked the place a lot less than he did. Their parties attracted the rich and famous – Winston Churchill, Charlie Chaplin, George Bernard Shaw, Clark Gable, Errol Flynn, Maurice Chevalier, the Mountbattens. There's a portrait of Lord Louis on the library wall. Bernard Shaw said the Castle was "what God would have built if he had the money". Hearst loaned St Donat's to Lloyd George in 1934 where, as Gorsedd Member Llwyd o Wynedd, LlG mounted a bardic pageant for the National Eisteddfod held at Neath that year. The Eisteddfod was in the Vale again in 2012. Did Carwen Jones repeat the exercise? He did not.

Hearst's good times ended when his financial fortune hit the buffers in 1938. He'd lasted thirteen years. The great Stradling family, who might not have started the Castle but were certainly responsible for most of its development, lasted four hundred and forty. The one-time promontory fort in a place known as Llanwerydd had a motte and bailey raised on it by the Norman de Hawey family in the early twelfth century. When his daughter inherited, she married Sir Peter Stradling. His son, Sir Edward Stradling, the first of nine Stradlings to carry the same name, took over in 1300. The line wavered through a history of capture by pirates, wars with France, pilgrimages to Rome, patronage of Welsh bards, imprisonment in the Tower, dalliances with Catholicism, and wholehearted support for the 1592 publication of *Cambrobrytannicae Linguae Institutione*. This was an early teach yourself Welsh course published in Latin, apparently in order to reach a wider audience. The Stradlings, who essentially built the Castle lost ownership in 1738 when the last of the line was killed in a duel in Montpellier.

Llanwerydd wasn't a name the Normans had much time for. Donatus, saint of seafarers sounded better. In Welsh today the place's name persists as Sain Dunwyd or Llanddunwyd. Written historical references refer to Sancti Donati, Sancto Donato and Sain Dondwyd. Catholic Online, source for all you need know about the world of saints, tells us that Donat was the patron saint of Llanddunwyd but that "nothing else is known". A lot of the past is like that.

The Vale Council has declared much of the premises as County Treasure. Up the road is Splot Farm. That's a treasure too. There's another Splot Farm just north of Aberthaw. Cardiff's Splott, another sort of treasure altogether, is not as unique as many think it is.

John is talking about his Art Centre exhibition of St Donat's – how it was in the 60s contrasted with how it is today. Atlantic College alumni have been invited. The famous and the powerful. Bank Chairmen, Arabian Princesses, investment bankers, TV journalists, heads of international corporations, authors, filmmakers. The show will be great. If he was still alive Bob Hope would attend too. He lived here, for a brief while. Hunting around the histories, it's hard to find anyone of significance who hasn't visited at some time or other. The Atlantic world washed onto the shores of Wales. Along with the rain.

The Hard Core Coast

Beyond Nash, I'm in the empty quarter. The Welsh equivalent of the Rub' al Khali that covers the southeastern wastes of Yemen and Oman. But green. Here, it's endless tractorless cornfields with barely a fence to break them. No sign of man. Not a building, telegraph pole, wind-turbine, tea stall, or surfer's lookout for many miles. And I'm alone. My fellow walkers have all given up.

Sue has gone on with Marilyn for some silver surfing in the roughs of Porthcawl. It's an annual pilgrimage that keeps the middle-aged young. Grit, slate-grey rushing seas, wet suits, bodyboards. Breaks the inexperienced can cope with. Not a single Beach Boys record playing the length of Rest Bay, apparently. But the dudes in their three-quarter shorts, their woven bracelets and their chapsticked lips, they're in place. It's what they do.

The cliffs here are classic coast, the kind they use in the brochure. The layers of fossil-rich Liassic limestone collapsing in blocks along their joints, fracturing, leaving great debris slopes. Their shuffled-card layers broken by hanging valleys where sea erosion has been swifter than that of the valley's watercourse, by seacaves and by cliff ledges that protrude over the sea's waters like the overhanging galleries of Tudor houses.

Out at sea, the bell on the buoy that marks the start of the perfidious Nash Sands tolls, rings out across empty waters, white dazzle in the western sun.

At Cwm Bach, a hanging valley, the official path routes a few fields in but the coast edge is open, so I follow that. When I later check the records for this deserted stretch I find the highest incidence of wrecks anywhere in Wales. Atlantic swell, sandbars, offshore reefs, hidden rocks. They've been going down here for centuries, ships. The *Royal Hunter* (1747), the *Indian Prince* (1752), the *Elizabeth* (1753), the *Prince* (1764)[17]. They wreck, you take what they've got. Down there today, on the hard carboniferous limestone shelf that serves for a beach, among the fossils and the clints, the pavements and the grikes, is nothing but empty, churning sea.

Ahead, beyond the faint waterfall at Cwm Mawr, is the promontory of Trwyn y Witch. Before it Traeth Mawr, big beach, Dunraven Bay. Dunraven, in Welsh *Dyndryfan* – fortress of the three rocks. This promontory once housed a giant circular encampment, a considerable proportion of which, as ever the case, has now been lost to the sea.

Here also are the still extant footings of what was once the seat of the earl of Dunraven, Edwin, Lord Adare. His great house, Dunraven Castle, reached prominence as a nineteenth century castellated mansion of considerable style. It had ivy clad battlements and sweeping drives. The remains of the Norman castle that preceded it, destroyed by Owain Glyndwr in the early fifteen century, are lost below the later remains. The Earl's Dunraven Castle, built in 1803 and much improved in 1858, lasted until demolition as uneconomic to repair in 1962. It served its time as great house, military hospital, convalescent home and, in the dismal days before its uncelebrated pulling down, the Workers Travel Association Hostel and Hotel.

Its walled gardens, ice tower and summer house, however, remain. They've been restored to something approaching their former glories and feature mystical and medicinal herbs, roses, a relic orchard, a croquet lawn, and Victorian, Tudor and plant hunters gardens. At the back of the summer house is a framed poem allegedly composed by two solicitors who stayed with the Earl of Dunraven in 1873. "Dearly I love Dunraven Bay, under its cliffs by night or by day", it reads with William McGonagall doggerelic precision. Are we ever elevated by public verse? Composed by the unable, promoted by the misguided for the edification of those who wouldn't be able to recognise real poetry even if their lives depended on it.

Down in Seamouth Bay more surfers are in action. Bronzed, wetsuited youngsters, standing on boards, barrelling into the curls. At the Heritage Coast centre, base for wardens, exhibitions and a small shop, I am their best customer so far this year. Among the racks of expected tourist leaflets, and hand-outs describing the coast and its features, are four Mary Gillham titles I don't own. Dr Mary Gillham, naturalist, geographer, inveterate walker, and author of the most comprehensive and detailed record of wildlife and landform along the south Wales coasts is someone I've been collecting for decades. These 1980s titles on the sand dunes, rivers, and coastal downs of the Heritage Coast are things I must have, weight no object. They are bagged and stuffed into my daysack where the waterproofs once sat. Those I wear, back-packing my new library the miles on into Ogmore. Some things you just can't get on the internet.

Ogmore, when I get there, is a change of compass heading. I've been walking northwest for miles now. The Ogwr River, and Ogmore-on-Sea beside it, bends east. The township here was originally known as Sutton. Off-shore the local landmark, Tusker Rock (with its name derived from that of the marauding Viking, Tuska) is a magnet for divers and blokes in kayaks. On Ogmore Beach, just behind the Sewage Pumping Station and the Surf Rescue garage, a community group from Bristol have set up tents and barbeques. They're playing cricket, football, chucking frisbees and shouting to each other in abandon. It's a sort of Whitsun treat with headscarves. I'm offered a cup of coffee which tastes like hot seawater. We watch the sun cloud over and then slowly the rain begin. Much more like the Glamorgan Heritage I'm used to. The visitors scatter while I stand there, waterproofed already, baggy blue and scruffily hooded, looking out across the Ogwr Estuary to the dunes of Merthyr Mawr and, beyond them, the lights of Porthcawl.

Merthyr Mawr

The B4524 up across the cattle grid from Ogmore by Sea car park is busier than a heading-for-nowhere B-road ought to be. Joyriders, roof-racked surfboards, pensioners wearing hats, couples singing in unison, kids with beat boxes, families with a back seat full of inflatable toys, picnickers, white van men on beach-view breaks, lone retirees dowsing the seaboard for something to do. The coast has people all of a sudden, people in droves.

This road bends inland here, running to the east of the Ogwr

River. Ahead of me are the ever-shifting sands of the Merthyr Mawr Estate. This SSSI of 932 golden acres fills the sea's edge from here to Newton, Black Rock and the static vans of Porthcawl. From where I'm standing, just above Portobello House and the swan-filled river, the estate looks accessible and, in the sense that you can see most of it in one go, totally knowable. On both counts, as it turns out, it's not.

Portobello Bridge, upstream about a hundred metres, looks an inviting and secure access, crossing straight into the Warren's sandy heart. Welsh Water Penybont Treatment Works, reads the sign, opened in 1970 by the Secretary of State for Wales, Peter Thomas. Remember him? Heseltine clone, Tarzan of the Gorsedd, right-wing foil for Cymdeithas during its 1970s most active of road-sign defacing periods. He was a Welsh-speaking Welshman and he lent an ear. And despite not much changing, it was hard for the Welsh world to claim that no one had listened. Opposite is a memorial plaque to a local who loved swans. The river is thick with them, lines of growing cygnets still following their parents. This is a bridge with public purpose. But on the sewage works western side it's obvious that I've been beguiled. Warren access is barred by yards of razor wire, metal spikes protruding over the river, high, mesh fences, mounted cameras, signs warning of deep water and explosive atmospheres. Below, another posse of range riders, hats and jodhpurs, churn their way south from Ogmore Farm's Horse Riding on the Beach operation a hundred metres further up. How can I reach where they are?

Upstream, clustered around the secured remains of Ogmore Castle[18], are the only concessions for miles to visitor leisure. Pub, teahouse, stables, and, rather unexpectedly, tipi rental. The distinctive cone-like frames in view through the drizzle look like a Sioux village after the raiders have passed. It's down season now, the campers are all back in the cities. You can rent an Ogmore tipi complete with Cheyenne smoke flap, rain catcher, barbecue pit and coir matted floor for £300. Sleeps eight. Please keep the noise to a minimum. Bring your own beds. Less fun than you'd expect in the rain. At the pub they have revived their heraldic origins by rebranding themselves as The Pelican in her Piety. A name you don't forget. You can see the pelican on the inn sign, plucking at her own breast, feeding her chicks with the stuff from her veins. Christian heraldics. The blood of Christ fed to the flock.

Beside the castle are the forty-two stepping stones of the Ewenny crossing. With the waters within an inch or so of their tops the whole deal looks dangerous, but as I'm preceded across by a man lugging a bike, two dogs and then a family of four with bags and shrieking kids, I can hardly not go myself. I could get to the Warren this way if I'd turned right and taken the track that crosses the Ogwr via New Inn Bridge. This has holes in the sides through which sixteenth century farmers once dipped their sheep. But in drizzle-filled error I head south through the horse riders churn and end up at the Ewenny and Ogwr confluence with no option but to turn back.

The Sahara-like dunes[19] of Merthyr Mawr, lost lands, a mirage rising through the rain.

I get to the Candleston Car Park by slogging it along the public roads. Merthyr Mawr village is green, thatch and great house, more like England than Wales. It's all humped bridges and twisting lanes. Candleston is a castle, or the remains of one, overrun by the Warren's ever-encroaching sands, crowded by buckthorn, alder, poplar and willow. It was once the fortified manor house of Tregantlow village but through the centuries overtaken by wind-borne grain. Its remains are overgrown and sunk now among the dunes.

The slopes, tongues and untold paths of the dune complex itself now lie in front. Coming here years ago had been easy. Kids in tow, loaded with folding chairs and picnic hampers. The struggle through the sunlit sands was a matter of do it for a bit and then you'll reach the sea. Today it doesn't look like that at all. The sky darkening. The ghosts of the long past coming up behind the scarps. The Beaker people with their axes, arrows, and sling-stones. The Romano-Welsh who once farmed the land above Candleston. Their great access road, the Via Julia, vanished now, sending in troops to protect them. The lost fort of Bomium and its warriors. The Vikings bent on plunder. The Normans, worried that the Welsh might triumph, slinging up fortifications in this forsaken, distant place. And constantly the sand, encroaching with its wind-wiped sting, covering what was, burying all.

The scarps themselves can rise to two hundred feet and in places the sands are twenty deep. The great storms of 1822 blew out enough of the drifted covering to reveal Tregantlow's windmill[20] to the west of the castle. Corn grinder for the now wrecked manor. There are rumours, too, of lost churches, wells, mines, and treasure hoards. Men with metal detectors have searched and searched. But the engulfing, ever-moving sands and their sea buckthorn fixers keep such things missing.

The paths switch and twist, fork, blend, and twist again. Direction's sense drifts like the sand itself. It's easy to see how this place doubled as Saudi for the making of David Lean's *Lawrence of Arabia*. I have no idea where the sea is. I climb a scarp to reveal further climbs, paths branching like the body's veins, rolling out ahead. Struggle on. Feet pushing at sliding sand, backs of the legs pulling, boots overtopped, grit in your eyes and ears, breath audible, and then, suddenly, it's there. Like land reached after the crossing of a great ocean. Wave crests. Breakers. The drizzle pressing its flat, grey brush across their collective surface. White horses, surf fleck, and the sound of waves softly thrushing. The coast, cold and empty for miles, but so welcoming.

Newton

There's a dartboard hanging in the porch and there's sand on it. There's sand on everything. There aren't any darts. There were, but in the somnambulance of the long hot days, I've idly thrown them into the dunes and they're lost. Behind the wooden door where the sand flows through onto the hut's one rug, the family is gathered. They are scattered across the put-up settee where I sleep and the rickety faux-bamboo armchair and are playing cards on the small low table and smoking. Players Navy Cut, Senior Service, Capstan Full Strength. 1955 and the red ensign is still dominant.

This is the family on holiday gathered together by the side of the sea, spending a week away from the dirty town. Here there's peace and air and you can walk among the dunes on the endless dry sand. It's sweet beneath your feet, blown in your ears and your hair, falling from your clothes, slowing you down.

My father is explaining what you do when you drink. Advice to his son. "Ask for bottles of Nut Brown Ale," he suggests. Sweeter than beer from the pump, smaller in quantity. You can sup it slowly and hardly anyone will notice. Drink lying down if you are going to, less distance to fall. Avoid rounds, leave the room when they're in the offing. Drink water when you've finished. Take aspirin before going to bed. Suck Extra Strong to cover your breath. Stay with beer, don't escalate. There's whiskey on the bedside table. Fire. Don't touch that.

My mother and my aunts are laughing. There's no radio but that doesn't stop them standing up, dancing, swaying each other round to the rhythms inside their heads. Jimmy Dorsey. Frankie Laine. Guy Lombardo. All of them have walked here across the Newton sands wearing high heels, shoes in shining 50s primary colours. My mother's heel has broken off and she's tried to stick it back with an Elastoplast but this hasn't worked. She no longer cares. My uncle is beating time with a pencil on the edge of the wooden-framed bed. I'm half-way through my dandelion and burdock – a thin glass with sand on its sides and grains at its bottom. The sixty-watt bulb that lights this scene flickers. "S'okay," says my father. "S'okay." Wind-borne sand rattles softly on the window. I peer again out through the dusk at the shifting, sliding dunes, but they're gone.

Today, housing from the encroaching estates that have expanded eastwards from the original village of Newton towards Wig Fach are giving the Newton Burrows a run for their money. The rentable holiday shacks, the ply and tar paper-roofed lean-tos, rickety caravans and bell tents that were here half a century back have vanished. The war-time rifle ranges, where in 1944 Eisenhower addressed the American 28th Infantry Division prior to the D-Day landings on Omaha, are still in place. The great American encouraging the troops from the back of an M3 half-track. Charlie Company, Able Company, Baker, Delta, Easy. Newton Beach a precursor to the Normandy horrors ahead. On the ranges, spent bullet cases still turn up. The pits where the targets were are just about visible. Mary Gillham reckons[21] that there have been rifle ranges in use on these burrows since 1882 and it is only comparatively recently that the shooters have given up and moved on.

With the ridges of Merthyr Mawr to the east and Kenfig Burrows to the northwest, the landscape here is considerably different from the stratified Glamorgan Heritage Coast I've recently been crossing. Soft replaces hard, change is constant, shimmer overtaking edge. The dunes began as Pennant Sandstone formed in the south Wales coalfields and, ten thousand years ago, were transported south by melting ice. Sand is created by the erosion of rocks by the sea. At the water's edge the sands mix with the shells of molluscs and crustaceans and then, as the tide ebbs and the surface dries, are blown back inland by the prevailing south westerly winds. Plants take hold. Sea rocket, prickly saltwort, sea beet, sea couch and lyme-grass first. The growth catches more sand and depth increases. Marram grass then follows. The ever-shifting dune systems flowing across, underlying the Triassic marls and limestones here and right across the south west of Wales, are the ultimate result.

Until 1825, Newton was a port, the only landing on this coast between Aberavon and Col-Huw at Llantwit Major. The creek that once ran down what is now Beach Road fractured the sands. Boats pulling up to take away wheat, butter and sheep were protected from the prevailing westerly winds by Newton Point beyond. This was "the Weare at Newton". Leland called it "a Station or Haven for Shippes[22]" and by the sixteenth century at least sixteen boats were regularly working here. As a port Newton eventually fell into disuse with the Industrial Revolution driven development of the docks at Porthcawl. Navigating the beach sands between Black Rocks and the Burrows, today it seems impossible that ships did anything other than sail by. At sea there are kayakers and wind surfers. On the flat sands, in their dozens, the dog walkers.

Away from the coast, just south of Newton's twelfth century church is the holy well of St John, the Sanford Well as it's called on maps, and on the slate plaque bolted to its side. Here the Latin text of Sir John Straddling's 1607 gobbledegook poem on the efficacy of the holy waters is displayed in all its glory. As poetry the Latin certainly swings a little easier than the English translation. Try *Te Nova Villa Fremens odioso Murmure Nympha Inclamat Sabrina; soloque inimica propinque*; against the clunky *With troublous noif and roaring loud, the Severn nymph doeth cry.* Even better, the Latin original uses semi-colons.

The well's waters offer a holy fix, although getting to them today would require locating the key holder, unlocking the barred and bolted door and then descending a covered flight of twenty steps leading down into a dark sub-strata of Keuper conglomerate. The well has the curious property of filling when sea tides ebb and draining when they flow. In the Middle Ages locals regarded this as a sort of magic and the well was much venerated. In the 1920s a local physician and snake oil sales-man, Dr Hartland, set up an open-air spa on the beach to exploit the curative properties of the holy waters. At tidal ebb, well overflow would spill onto the sands. Despite later scientific analysis showing that the waters actually contained no special minerals at all and were not that different from the stuff that came out of the tap, it was belief that counted. Those with bad skin, gout, rheumatism and aching joints walked away cured. Bolted onto the back of the present well-housing is a small and well-defended by razor wire topped mesh electricity sub-station. Down at the beach all that remains of Hartland's enterprise are a few unmarked rocks.

On my way to the Beach Road car park where the ice cream van (*We sell tea and crisps*) has a queue encircling it, I pass the sign marking the start of the Glamorgan Heritage Coast. The gate to Trecco Bay Caravan Park is a hundred yards off. A place where worlds meet, this. Out at sea Tusker Rock glowers.

Porthcawl

Across Trecco Bay the horses gallop the tide line kicking up plume. They're caught in silhouette by the unseasonable late sun like something out of high summer. This isn't a literary town although you'd think it might be with its somnambulant retiree suburbs and its hosts of sea-facing picture windows. But there's barely anything bar Bernice Rubens' gulls that climb up from the sands squawking "Cawl cawl cawl". She set her 1975 novel *I Sent A Letter To My Love* in the town, a soft Porthcawl full of sand, seabirds, death and memory. There's no commemorative plaque but maybe there should be.

I've met Robert Minhinnick, the poet and environmentalist, who has made Porthcawl his home for more than thirty-four years now and is virtually the town's sole creative beacon. His concerns with the wider world and the desperate state of the planet have driven him on for decades but the local is finally now supplanting the general. His novel, *Sea Holly*, named after the thistle grey seaside plant that infests the coast here, is a tale of love, loss, dissipation and despair. It's set in the Trecco Bay caravan park and the sandy warren of dune and half dune that flows out beyond it. His sequel, working title *The Limestone Man*, extends the narrative to the town where in the last week of the year the sea mist barely lifts while celebration rolls in an atmosphere of unsettling claustrophobia.

We're at Newton again, me standing on top of the pipe that spills what's left of Newton Brook onto the sands. It's autumn half term and the bay is dense with families. They have bags full of towels and sandwiches, are clad in anoraks and hats and scarfs, and their kids are digging castles like it was July. We go west entering the giant Trecco Bay Caravan Park, itself bigger than the entire township of Newton. Lines of static vans, prefab holiday accommodation, rentable, cheap, a part of past British holiday heritage still in action. The place is packed with working class vacationers from the south Wales valleys and the English Midlands. Extended families here for the sands and the beer and the doubtful weather.

The Park has its own main street of bars, food outlets, amusement arcades, and bowling alleys with names like Funtasia, Jungle Jims, and Splashland. Thin men smoking rollups drift. Kids go by on bikes. Inside beneath the ever-lit lights the machines thunk and click, spin and turn. On the Penny Cascade a man with an earring and veins broken across his nose slides in great handfuls of brown coin, three slots at once. He's not winning, but it's early yet.

The Trecco Park grew from a pre-War use of the dunes here for camping. There are old postcards which show the bay in the 30s dotted with bell tents like a Baden Powell Boy Scout camp.

When the trailer caravans started arriving in the late 40s the Council took the decision to remove the dunes inland from Sandy Bay. They flattened a natural landscape that would never return. Private developers bought up the land to the east for what's become the Caravan Park we are now crossing. Sand still blows up the roads, drizzles on the windows, lines its grit on everything you touch.

In what Robert calls the badlands, beyond Trecco where the Council's own Sandy Park Caravan Park once stood, all that is left are foundations, dune stubble and roads that go nowhere. The pubs, chip shops and stores selling giant sunglasses and bright inflatable beach crap have all been demolished to make way for a grand sea-front apartment development that never arrived. It's still on the way, rumour persists, with its attendant superstores and malls. But today it's not here. And there's still no sign.

Coney Beach, the funfair at Porthcawl's legendary centre, is a fenced-off ghost. Robert has charted the decline. He went round here in 2007 with the photographer Eamon Burke, between them capturing what was left of the fair's hamburger brite, lit bulb carousel, twister-shrieking one-time glory. There's a book, *Fairground Music*[23], launched in front of a couple of dozen holiday makers at the sea facing Coney Beach Hi Tide Inn. On the wall today, next to a sign announcing the imminent arrival of Wham Bam Duran followed by Fat Barry's Soul Band, there's a notice. This is from the fair's current owners, the Evans Family, and it assures visitors that the funfair will open again next year. Everyone looks forward to an *EVEN BRIGHTER FUTURE*. Inside the fence the past rusts.

A fair was established here as entertainment for American troops returning from World War One. Its name, Coney Beach, was added as a tribute to Coney Island back home. The land had been surfaced with ballast taken from the empty coal ships docking in Porthcawl's nineteenth century harbour. Attractions were housed in a converted aircraft hangar. There was a figure eight wooden slatted roller coaster and a bandstand, a skating rink and a pierrot stage. Excitement for all. Fame soon spread. Porthcawl's fun fair outshone that at Barry. The place filled with townies looking for fun, miners from the nearby valleys. They poured in by bus and by train. By its mid-century peak there were boxing matches, snooker tournaments, circuses, markets, cinema shows, fun houses, aerial acrobatics, and a hundred stalls and side shows and rides.

Coney Beach's subsequent decline was part changing fashion, part lack of investment, part bad luck. Safety standards were low and there were accidents on some of the rides. There was a death on the watershute. The fragile ferrous world of the funfair, as Robert calls it, began to turn to shreds.

Beyond lies the town itself. Porthcawl proper, slivered onto Porthcawl point between the two far more ancient townships of Newton, where we've been, and Nottage, up ahead. It could be that this place was the invention of the Industrial Revolution. Pwll Cawl Point was chosen in 1825 as the site for a new jetty, tidal basin and terminus for the Duffryn, Llynvi and Porthcawl Railway, exporter of the new coal and iron wealth that littered the nearby valleys. Porthcawl, as it became, would boom. John Brogden and his son, James came here from Sale, Manchester, in the mid-1990s and poured money into railway and dock development. Porthcawl, iron and coal metropolis, was born.

Boom it did but only for a limited time. When Barry and Port Talbot Docks opened in 1892 the already faltering export trade collapsed. Porthcawl, docklands with no purpose, an industrial township with no industry to service. Things fell apart.

The breakwater and outer dock are still in place, although the larger inner dock was filled in and turned into a car park decades back. We pass with the sun pulling higher in the sky and the gulls still whirling. Robert is pointing out Cosy Corner, the site of the bandstand, the place where the prefab cinema once stood, the site of the stalls and the entertainments along the front. Getting over its industrial-age kick in the teeth actually turned out to be a Porthcawl doddle. Porthcawl would become south Wales' Blackpool. Hotels and boarding houses were built, the town's extensive golden sands would be promoted as the gems of south Wales. Porthcawl, destination. Come here for the air and the joys of relaxation. The plan worked.

We round the rocks heading for Irongate Point. "This is the tarmac beach," says Robert. Ahead a slab of beachscape has been hard-topped black as if it were a sloping car park. Sea defences, seems to work. We're in the heart of Porthcawl now. Seafront guesthouses, cafes, all packed today in the late season sun. The hotels are here. The one-time Esplanade (now replaced with a set of post-Modern apartments, Esplanade Court, known locally because of its curved and aperture-filled frontage as The Bottle Bank) and the still extant Seabank Hotel. In the centre is the Art Deco clock-towered Grand Pavilion Theatre, venue for any number of Minhinnick-fronted poetry extravaganzas, Friends of the Earth Cymru promotions, and other community ventures. Its mainstream activity is as a location for shows featuring Chris Needs, the Manfreds, Elkie Brooks, Trextasy, wedding fayres and Miners Welfare brass bands. High spot is the annual Porthcawl Elvis festival held in September each year. The town fills with imitators of the king, all of them rocking their ways from pub to pub, the young teddy boy, the leather clad rocker, the white-suited sequined-monster, Elvis who goes on forever, rocking in the free world, still hound dogging, filling the stage with teddy bears and tears.

We cross Lock's Common, Rob giving me a gazetteer of Welsh names for the rock formations here. Hutchwns Point, Gwter Hopsog, and Gwter Gryn-y-locs, where roped rock climbers are in action as we pass. These are locations for plot bends in Robert's current novel, places that have set themselves inside his consciousness, home spots that act like lodes. Of all the writers from Wales in recent generations, Robert has been the one to take on the world's concerns and to travel to engage them first hand: Baghdad, North Africa, South America, the Far East. Nowhere has he not been. But now he's relocating his inspiration, moving back from the earth edges to the homelands where he's finally settled his feet. "I could write a whole book about just this one spot," he tells me. "Maybe I will."

We talk about books and writing. The forty-three issues of *Poetry Wales* he edited, the way that poets have skins as thin as onions, picking up slights where there are none. Forever unsure and uncertain. Was that last piece a fluke? Can I repeat it? Even after forty years the certainty of the muse remains a fiction, poetry hovering out there in the land of illusion. Only an editor's strong and unequivocal approval can make it real. "Best out of it?" "Yep."

At the Pavilion, he tells me, he dined with Joan and Dannie Abse the night Joan was killed. He'd had the two of them down to read. Small audience, but good enough for one of Wales' living greatest. Dannie, who lived just back down the coast in Ogmore had no distance to travel. At the end of the evening, meal done and darkness on them, he seemed uncertain of where the roads were that would take him back. Set off, ended up on the eastbound M4 and was driven into by someone out of control. Car written off, Dannie damaged, Joan dead. A tragedy that still reverberates. Dannie has been slow to return to the reading circuit but is back on form now. He lives permanently in Golders Green. Ogmore is too painful to contemplate.

From the long flat stretches of enormous Rest Bay, the sea has retreated miles. Along the coast itself, Porthcawl has shrunk to a line of upmarket housing which bumps up against the lifeboat station, the golf links and the turreted confection of The Rest, the one-time Miners' Convalescent Home, sited out in the sun and the winds where germs could never survive. When the tides are right the surfers gather here. Malc's, beside the car park sells boards[24], beads, wet suits and training. You can get tea and there's free Wi-Fi. No beach toys. No Beach Boys either.

Along from Ffynnon-wen Rocks are the sea caves, full of unexpected rock colour, seamed and cracked. Rob hunts for the one he's used for the cover of his *New Selected Poems*, published in 2012. But it can't be found. "I came here with Iwan Llwyd[25]," he tells me. "When Iwan was down researching his book on the coast of Wales[26]." Iwan, gem of a man, dead far too young, a Welsh language poet, an operator in the senior language, but happy to mix with those working the English tongue.

Gwter-y-Cwn leads us out onto Sker Rocks, a wave eroded, pool-pocked landscape like the lava flows of Timanfaya on Lanzarote. The ancient but restored Sker House, yellow painted for historical accuracy, home of the historian Niall Ferguson, stands in sea-facing isolation. The novelist R.D. Blackmore set his follow-up to *Lorna Doone, The Maid of Sker*, here. The Doone Valley on the edge of Exmoor lies directly opposite across the Channel (see p. 257).

We stand on the rocks looking northwest at the expanse of the Kenfig Burrows. It's as large as Merthyr Mawr, larger, with hills and valleys of sand running right up to the tidal edge. "The dunes here are different from those at Merthyr Mawr," says Robert. "Where Merthyr Mawr's shift swiftly, Kenfig's do not. They move and they do so inexorably but at a slower pace."

Out at sea, in the distance, is a single anemometer, a tower used to measure wind speeds and tidal pressures. A precursor to offshore wind farming. But like the Trecco apartments, the development has yet to materialise. "Probably won't," says Rob. "Uneconomic. There'll be no giant new generation pylons running here despoiling the edge of the Burrows, not yet anyway. The green movement doesn't know which way to go now. Almost everything is bad – wind, nuclear, coal. There are no easy ways out."

I can see Port Talbot in the distance, smoke and spark on the skyline. I'll get there soon, but it's Kenfig next.

The West: Kenfig to Swansea

Kenfig

The dunes at Kenfig would be different, Robert had said that, and they were. Grassier, with fewer paths. As big as Merthyr Mawr. Sunk in the slacks with the horizon gone and all points of reference with it, it was easy to see how Kenfig had become the land of the lost.

The shingle and sand coastal strip had been as spectacular as anything on the entire south Wales expanse – straight, unbroken flatness running for more than four kilometres from Sker Point, over the rocks of Gwely'r Misgl[1], to Margam and the steelworks further west. Stacks and tubular tanks and smoking towers breaking the horizon, reminding me that no matter how much of the wild world this place represents, the industrial one is just beyond.

These were once Viking lands as the names attest. Blakescerra meaning black reef from which the name Sker is derived. Tusker Rock out there below Ogmore by Sea.

Swansea's Sweyn's Eye down the coast. Scarweather Sands. The lost Danes Vale. Maybe even the name Kenfig itself. It would be easy to stride across them, rock up the unblemished beach, forging on to Port Talbot, to Aberavon, getting out of the prevailing westerlies that blow the sand from the sea's edge and roll it, unceasingly, towards the hills.

But there's too much here to miss, deep in the Burrows. Ernest Rhys[2], coming here in 1910, described the place as dispersed and silent. And there, in the centre of this world of rolling dunes lies buried Kenfig, a whole town lost to the encroaching sands. "Today it is a place apart, like no other that I know; an amazing place with an heroic record; the struggle of the community during hundreds of years with an irresistible army of sand whose tents and entrenchments you see all around it ... Today the drift still goes on: while six hundred years ago it was coming steadily inland, each storm bringing the sand higher." Built by the Normans – castle, church, a frontier town to face down the marauding Welsh – the place lasted a few centuries until it was abandoned to the sands. John Leland, passing through in the sixteenth century, described the town as "devowrid with the Sandes that the Severn Se ther castith up." How could this happen and what might be left? For myself I had to find out.

In the 1970s the Kenfig Dune complex was wrested from the Margam Estate by the Trustees of the Kenfig Borough and recognised as common land. To keep it that way the Kenfig National Nature Reserve was established. Bird preserve. A place for Bittern, Kingfisher and Mute Swan. You reach the interpretation centre by crossing the once fern-rich Kenfig Down, now largely the Pyle and Kenfig Golf club, on a back road out of Porthcawl. Below us lie the smooth and totally unexpected waters of Kenfig Pool. A wetland of seventy acres populated by migratory wildfowl. Canada Geese are in residence when we arrive. The pool was formed when the natural drainage system became blocked by the migrating sands. The now lost Blaklaak stream flowed from it towards the Kenfig River. Iolo Morgannwg claimed that a whole city is lost beneath the pond waters and that church bells could be heard chiming when conditions were right. There are other legends that tell of Kenfig Pool holding an insatiable central whirlpool which pulls victims right down to the earth's core, that there are seven springs feeding it, that it is full of fish of a kind that no one has ever seen before, that the waters have no bottom and go on and on forever. But all I can see are the waterlogged remains of a nineteenth century boathouse in use by cormorant as a resting place. Silence. No bells. Just the gentle wind.

The castle at Kenfig and, in fact the whole lost town, lie on the far side of the dunes, hard up against the abandoned rail yards that were once operated by British Steel. The M4, on its viaduct, crosses the dunelands in a distant, buzzing roar. It's hard to see how anything as complex as a town with fortifications could have existed here. The dunes roll and tumble. Grassed and rich with low-growing Salix. A medieval ordinance of the lost town was stern in its warning: "Noe manner of person or persons whatsoever shall reap any sedges neither draw nor pull any rootes nor cutt any furzes in any place whatsoever, nor do any other thing that may be to the ruin, destruction and overthrow of the said burrough." Nobody did and the green growth is currently rich. But the dunes continued to smear and spill and the town, sand in its rooms and climbing its walls, continued to fade.

Kenfig Castle, a rubbly stub of a keep, a few part-excavated windows with dressed stone at their edges, a doorway, and a wall that might have retained the inner ward are about all that is left. They are overgrown with buckthorn, willow and rowan. Of the town, west of the castle, there is no sign at all. Not a wall or suggestive hummock or mark on the sand's surface. All one hundred and forty-four dwellings abandoned along with the entire stone-built Church of St James. The residents given up their unequal struggle and allowing the winds to take all.

I'm looking for ghosts, for a sense of loss, or something hanging on from this medieval disaster, still there after all these centuries. Where human lives once spun their dreams there usually remain traces – marks in the ether, that glint subconsciously telling you that people once walked here. But among the dozing cattle and undulating dunes there's nothing. No CADW plaque, no historical society sign. Nothing to mark this place as anything other than a heap of abandoned rubble, hanging on simply because nobody has ever found it worthwhile to spend energy removing it.

The castle dates from the conquest, built of timber first and then later in stone. 1146 perhaps. There was a moat and traces have been found. A town to cluster around the castle's protection soon followed. But being Norman and out at the far edge of the conqueror's influence, Kenfig was constantly subject to attack. Its houses were largely wood and they were burned to the ground at regular intervals. This happened in 1167, 1183, 1228, 1232, 1243, 1262, 1295, 1316, 1321 and again and finally by Owain Glyndwr in 1405. On each occasion townspeople rallied and rebuilt. They fought against both the sands and their Welsh liberators. Neither attacker relenting once the battle had begun.

By 1439 high tides were pressing the coast and the dunes had advanced inland by at least four miles. The town was being drowned and it was reluctantly abandoned. The stones of the church were dismantled and a replacement built in nearby Pyle. Blocks from the Kenfig church can be seen at the foot of the walls of St James Church today. Townspeople moved first to a new village at Mawdlam and then dispersed to establish what became the communities of North and South Cornelly, further inland, safe from the sand.

Of Kenfig, the town, all that remained was the legal framework. The Borough of Kenfig. That itself came to an end in 1886 when Britain's historical collection of rotten and decayed boroughs was abandoned. Parliament would no longer be served by members representing towns that no longer existed or where populations had shrunk to single families.

The path on parallels the Kenfig River through extensive and waterlogged undergrowth, winding as rivers do like string uncoiling. This is bogland crossed by cattle mashed path, broken by earth outcrop and stuttering fence. Trees block the sightline and the peaks of the dunes press in from the sides. Sue is wearing a GPS runners watch which, although it doesn't actually tell us quite where we are right now, will show, later when downloaded, a neat map of exactly where we've been.

The bog path becomes untenable. Just as the woman at Castle Meadow Farm several miles back had said it would. We watch the sun and turn to face the dune complex and the distant sea. Just walk, easy. But it's not. Kenfig is no place for an easy stroll and certainly not one to traverse lightly without some solid notion of which way to go. We don't have that. We soon lose ourselves amid hollow and hummock, sightlines wrecked, sea vanished, the sun up there glaring its way westwards. We should follow this but we don't and after what seems like hours we are no further on, it seems, than when we began. We've skirted bog pool, waterlogged dune and climbed out of leg wrenching slacks beyond number. It's time to decide. There's the humming motorway in the distance, spotted from the top of the highest dune scarp I can locate. And in the long distance the tower of Maudlam Church. Line them up with the map, push on.

Kenfig Burrows, duneland of lost souls, the place where what you have vanishes and what you are ceases to exists. The landscape becomes you as you watch it. Sand gets in your teeth and your clothes and your hair. You can't make anything come together. Time to run but you know not where.

Eventually we emerge at the Prince of Wales. The oldest tavern in the district and once the 1605 town hall for the first resited town of Kenfig. Now a pub serving real ales and Sunday lunches, photographs of sea coast ship wrecks and the past that's vanished all over its walls. Sue's watch is still connected. When we get back and download the route and view the map, it shows a trail weaving in concentric circles, moving forward, doubling back, failing to reach the coast, wavering towards the castle out and back and then stopping for some time at the Prince of Wales. Well, stopping completely, because it's there we abandoned Kenfig and limp on some time later, past the Kenfig Pool caravan park (don't ask me who'd stay there, I have no idea – bird spotters, Prince of Wales pub fans, lost Kenfig souls) and back to where we've left the car at the Nature Reserve.

In front of me is Port Talbot, fire, fumes, blowing white pillars of smoke in the high blue skies, a place you'd have considerable difficulty losing. Although many would like to try.

Aberavon

After the airbrush of the Glamorgan Heritage Coast, what's ahead looks real. Clank and fire and gouts of smoke. I've been dredging my past to try to get hold of something that would illuminate the place I was approaching. On Wiki, as ever, it gave me the partial picture. Facts and suppositions stuffed together to fulfil their obsessive creator's idea of a balanced, informative whole.

The notable of Port Talbot include George Thomas, first Viscount Tonypandy who was born in Ty Draw Street. Andrew Vicari, the painter. Robert Blythe, Welsh actor, brought up in Tan y Groes Street. Currently (2009) plays Fagin Hepplewhite in the BBC comedy *High Hopes*. Paul Potts, an opera singer and the winner of *Britain's Got Talent* in 2007, lives in Port Talbot. Martin Ashton, British mountain bike trials former world champion and multiple British champion. Sir Anthony Hopkins, actor, was born and raised in Margam nearby. The Welsh actor Michael Sheen was born in Newport, but he did spend a lot of time at PT.

Sheen I came to see in 2011. That was when he created *The Passion*, a three-day theatre vérité extravaganza mixed with scripted interludes that took over the town and so entranced participants and audience alike that Port Talbot returned to the world map in a blaze of creative brilliance. Sheen, dressed like Jesus, arrived from the sea onto a packed Aberavon Beach where the town band, a male voice choir, and child gymnasts from the local school were entertaining the assembled in unseasonable sun. What you couldn't tell were which bits were real and which not. Was that the actual Mayor making public order announcements on the loudspeaker? Were the armed guards actors? Did that woman really have a bomb strapped to her belly?

The connections between this passion and the Christian original were slight, although the whole thing did retain a touch of biblical glory in the way it uplifted so many spirits. Owen Sheers, the scriptwriter whom I'd bumped into on the recently refurbished prom, was full of the usual authorial doubts. The crowd, however, felt differently. Sheen had been pretty inclusive in the way that he'd tried to involve them all. Schools, choirs, sports teams, police, lifeguards, dance troupes, the am drams, the boat enthusiasts. Although maybe not the fishermen. I'd met a few, lines cast, out at the end of the North Breakwater, the far side of several cans, faces hot red in the midday sun. Using the Gospel of St Mark as a loose template for the story Sheen had immersed himself completely in his character. He'd spent a night out of doors sleeping on the mountain and another in a police cell. The garden of Gethsemane was a corner of Council estate scrub. The crucifixion was on a roundabout.

But one Passion, a charge across Aberavon's golden sands and then a bus trip into Port Talbot's working-class centre for three days of impromptu theatre, pubs rich with thespians and a last supper of sandwiches at the Seaside Social and Labour Club, does not keep a town in the headlines forever. Local poet and historian Sally Roberts Jones wrote what is, I guess, the definitive *History of Port Talbot* back in 1991. There's nothing else like it for readability. Sally also wrote a guide to the town's pubs, a boozer's stagger from the Somerset Arms to the Globe, from the Corporation Green to the Shamrock of Erin and from the Forge and Hammer to the Hibernian Arms. It was an entertaining achievement that was strong on architecture and great on social history but never once mentioned beer.

I sold both these titles in the shop I ran, Oriel on Cardiff's Charles Street. I never bought a copy for myself at the time. Had to track one down last week on the antiquarian market: "ex-library, with usual stamps and markings, in fair all round condition and suitable as a reading copy". *Tynnwyd o stoc Llyfrgell, Coleg Normal, Bangor*[3]. No evidence that it had been loaned out, even once. Mine now.

I'm talking about bookshops to Lynne Rees who once ran one herself, Foxed & Bound, in West Malling, Kent. We've crossed Margam Moors, skirted the edge of Margam Burrows and have the smoking, fire-lit thunder of heavy industry before us. If the Heritage Coast in its twenty-mile, middle-class considered carefulness was the *Antiques Roadshow* then what's ahead is *Big Brother*. Four miles of delicate sand dune landscape, wildlife habitat, irreplaceable home to fen orchid, site almost certainly of special scientific interest, bulldozed post-War in the search for national recovery. Industry – Maker of Wales. Saviour of the town.

Port Talbot's shape, to Cardiff's lozenge, is an elongated iron ingot. It lies on a two-mile-wide strip of flat land pressed between the sands at the sea's edge and the hills of Mynydd y Castell, Mynydd Brombil, Mynydd Emroch and Mynydd Dinas. And the whole place is really Aberavon. The Talbot appendage came to prominence when, in 1837, Christopher Rice Mansel Talbot, landowner, industrialist and Liberal parliamentarian with an estate at Margam, put up the money for the diverting of the River Afan and the building of a new dock. So long as it bore his name. The port was a huge success. In 1921 a new borough incorporating the docks, a number of local villages[4] and, significantly, the historical heart of the area, Aberavon, came into being. Port Talbot, the town, the conurbation, was born.

My guide is a native. You can tell from her accent. Unreconstructed South Wales Welsh, unbent by years living variously in Jersey, Antibes and Kent. I am quite bowled over by the way, here on the coast, it makes the English language sound like something from the heart of the mountains. She's a novelist, poet and haiku writer of some distinction. I've recently signed her up as an author for the Real series. *Real Newport, Real Llanelli, Real Aberystwyth, Real Wrexham* and the others will be joined by *Real Port Talbot*. What you need for these alternative guides, psychogeographies and off-piste handbooks is an irreverent but informed attitude, a zest for place, and the ability to delve. You need to look where you are not supposed to, know the difference between information and entertainment and be able to manage both. Lynne possesses all of these qualities. *Real Cardiff*, you are taking over the world.

Lynne originally left Port Talbot to work for the Midland Bank in Jersey. She got into writing as a fulfilment activity, sold a story to *People's Friend* and never looked back. She did a Gillian Clarke-led creative writing MA at Glamorgan and then went on to teach at the University of Kent. Food is her big thing. She writes a weekly blog, *The Hungry Writer*[6], which mixes food and authorship in equal portion. "Are there any good restaurants in Port Talbot?" I ask. "You'd be surprised. I was. La Memo and Giovanni's in town are outstanding. And the Aberavon Beach Hotel does a mean Welsh rib-eye even if the dining room is more tundra with seating than intimate dining experience."

The circumnavigation, which is half for me on my coastal quest and half research for Lynne's forthcoming *Real Port Talbot*, involves getting onto the coast at the far southern end of the Borough. Port Talbot begins down there in the SSSI wastelands where the Afon Cynffig dribbles its way through the Kenfig Burrows to reach the sea at Margam Moors. On the map it looks clean white. On the ground it's gasp and dust. These southern reaches of a four-mile stretch of heavy industrial smog land are cluttered with ash tip, coke waste, conveyor belts, smoke stacks, coal mounds, crushers, tanks and pipes. You can't imagine dowsers walking here and, if there were leys once, then by now they will have fused right into the ground.

If you are a local then access, disputed by the steel company, is down Longlands Lane behind Margam Crematorium. This is the only house of the dead with its own signposted exit from a major motorway[7]. I was there last month to see Stan Barstow off. The Angry Young Man who made the English north famous but ended his days in Pontardawe's Welsh rain. In his books of love and lust and hand-hardening white man's work, the steelworks landscape would have been familiar territory.

Tata Steel bought the plant from Corus and have plans for expansion, the building of new power stations and other facilities to further enlarge their already much diversified industrial empire. They're not keen on intrusion, banning access on the grounds of health and safety, pollution, chemical and industrial hazard, ground contamination, air toxicity, and other contemporary fears where the intruder might sue and the plant owner have to pay. The signs say *Private Property – No Unauthorised Access – Keep Out*. In the uncaring past we were all free. In the concerned and caring present we do what we are told.

Although, in our case, we don't. I see no signs, although Lynne assures me later that they were there. The way ahead may well look unwelcoming but we walk on. The path hugs the coast running along the stacked stone of the sea defence. To the east is the Steelworks' Haul Road, a service road along which blackened trucks the size of moon launchers roll with abandon. To the immediate west is the sea. We are separated from it by a beach that most resorts would die for. Yellow, unblemished sand running flat for miles. Not a single person present. No one with a dog. No one digging for lugworm. No one with a rod. We're below the Morfa Coke ovens now. Rushes of smoke and fire emerging. Morfa Colliery[8], the pit that was once worked here, may open again. Seams abandoned as uneconomic have become economic again. Tata have identified them, stretching out under Mynydd Margam.

As we approach, the arms of the tidal harbour that grasp at the sea beyond the entrance to ABP's Port Talbot docks come into view. The roads of the steelworks bend inland to pass mixed stacks of ash and waste metal. Beyond are the blast furnaces. Signs designate the Blender Plant, the Sinter Plant and the Burdening Department. The furnace mists drift. The singe of hot metal is in the air. The sun is shining.

And then we are stuffed. A white pick-up with roof-mounted hazard lamps pulls over in a cloud of roadway dust. "You are on private land, do you know that? Can I ask what you are doing here?" I give him the full story, book, walk, research, which is clearly reasonable. But it's clear that the camera is the real problem. With my bulky Nikon D90 and its long lens hung around my neck I can hardly claim to be just taking snaps. And with security there's the ever-present threat that they'll demand your memory card and trash it right in front of you. Yet Roger Maher couldn't be nicer. I get his name from the calls he makes reporting our capture to base. He offers to drive us on rather than back and takes us through the dirt-ridden and pipe-crossed roadways that riddle the works' centre. We are dropped above the Port on the safe public highway of Dock Road just south of the main railway station. En route Roger acts as an impromptu guide. He talks of hot slab-steel moving through the plant on carriers and of the blast furnaces being refurbished. He points out the site for a future wood-burning power station. He shows us the sand wharf and the control centre for port movements. Finally there's the demolition in progress for the building of Port Talbot's transportation future, the new five kilometre road link between the M4 and the docks. That deal is financed by Europe. Sometimes it pays to be in an area of comparative deprivation.

On foot again going down the north side of the Afan river there are brown tourist road signs directing visitors to somewhere called Hollywood Park. I've seen these signs elsewhere in the town. The array of symbols – crossed knives and forks, theatrical mask, cup, beach, historic building – make this destination look quite something. I ask Lynne what they mean but all she does is smile. "I'll show you when we get there," she says.

Aberavon, north of the river, is in complete contrast to the smog belts we've just come through. What were once sand dunes that ran all the way to the River Neath have been levelled and transformed into a unique experiment in social housing. This is now a council estate of three thousand uniform brick and rendered dwellings. It was built after the War complete with lido and funfair and is fronted by a mile and a quarter strip of golden sands straight out of the brochure. At the height of Port Talbot's industrial fortunes, in the early 70s, when the docks were new and the steel works booming, the place was nicknamed treasure island. Just over the river at the south end, in an area once known as the Little Warren, was the Miami Beach Amusement Park. On the beach side was the now lost to fire[9] Jersey Beach Hotel. At the centre was the Afan Lido and an array of holiday-maker beach facilities, tea gardens, paddling ponds, a putting green, whelk stalls. At the north end, unexpectedly for a holiday destination serving a local population of industrial workers and a hinterland of mining valleys, have sprung up an old people's home and a mental hospital.

The present centrepiece is just beyond the 1980s painted concrete whale and somewhat before you come to the million pound grass-covered mound known as the Telly Tubbies Toilet (a set of new millennium facilities complete with motion operated hand dryers that don't work in the Gents and ones with a sign that reads Do Not Dry Your Feet Here in the Ladies). It's the much-vaunted Hollywood Park. It's the 3-D Apollo Cinema, a boarded-up burger bar, a never-opened bowling alley and the Afan Lido reborn but now flattened Aquadome. Some grass. No one on it. Lynne shrugs. That's

Aberavon, she says. Things open then they close. Or they get burned down.

The front does possess two splendid pieces of public art[10]. Both are by Andrew Rowe and reach for the sky as once did the steeples of churches. They stand as symbols of what could be if attitudes changed. But this is an area of multiple deprivation. High unemployment, substance abuse, graffiti, vandalism. Although walking through, the worst thing I see is a middle-aged man littering.

At the northern end where the prom runs out are what remain of the Baglan Burrows. Beyond them Witford Point and the estuary of the River Neath. Here the town's industrial brackets close – the once sprawling BP Chemical Plant might have gone but its ghost hangs on. The area has been renamed Baglan Energy Park. It has a bright new gas-fired power station as its centrepiece. Full ground work remediation is in progress. A rush of Super Cannes-styled, soft-shoed light industry replacements are already in place. But it's the size that stuns. 1500 acres of rusted railtrack and empty hardcore. Fenced, double-fenced, crossed by pipeline and rabbit warren. Waiting. Other than the family I momentarily glimpse in the distant bushes, blackberrying, there's no one about. Our route is a half official, half fence-ducking, rail-track leaping and bramble dodging haul, which emerges onto the brand new Central Avenue. This is where Baglan Bay, residential population zero, runs out. The end of the town.

We go back to Lynne's parents' Sandfields semi on Chrome Avenue for tea and talk to her father about how it once was when the steelworks rocked. He's been retired twenty-five years. Different back then. Certainly was.

Baglan and the Briton Ferry Bridge

I've got my bike in the boot of the car. I've spent most of my part of the twentieth century convinced that for travel of any distance motor should be the means. Yet here I am, unfolding the Brompton with two twists and a pull in a Lower Briton Ferry backstreet, clipping my trousers to my legs and sliding my pack on to my back.

Up above me are the twin bridges of the River Neath. These carry the M4 and the A48. Up there it's all concrete and dual carriageway. Now that the ferry at this place of the Britons is no longer, those bridges are the only way to cross.

On the long walk from Chepstow, fragmented by going home at night to sleep in a bed I know (which does on occasions make me feel a little like one of the anti-capitalist protesters outside St Pauls who abandon their tents at night for the comforts of home), I'd reached the Quays at Baglan. Here Brunel's 1861 Tower which housed the hydraulic accumulator that once powered the Briton Ferry lock gates has been restored and stands pristine in its splendid new pointing. The dock next to it is half filled-in and what's left is slurried with silt and debris. In its day the docks here, with their inner and outer basins separated by a floating lock, were substantial. When they opened, the first ships carried coal for use in the boilers of Brunel's steamship, *The Great Eastern*. The place buzzed. The docks lasted a hundred years before eventually closing in 1959. The last boat out was the sand ship *The Glen Foam*.

As part of late-twentieth century post-industrial redevelopment the local council have built new roads and offices, established a business park and put in a barrier-guarded car park. There are double yellow lines everywhere. This is why I'm down in my Briton Ferry side street, behind Winstone's Fitness Centre, next to the scrap yard. Already a young wag has come out and suggested that the bike I'm cycling on might be crap. "It's not crap, it's brilliant," I tell him. "It'll go anywhere, this will." "No. Not crap. Scrap. Is it scrap?" "Certainly not," I say. I head off.

My plan is to use what turns out to be a National Cycle Path – Route 4, London to Fishguard – Sustrans[11] – endorsed, mapped, labelled, surfaced, sign boarded – one of the principal cycle routes in the UK. Here it heads up the side of the A48 to cross the Neath River Gorge. The sea is to the south and Briton Ferry is to the north. The route then bends all the way down past the Crymlyn Burrows to head for distant Swansea. Sustrans' Celtic Trail West. I feel like an eco-warrior going up the slip road with artics and heavy carriers booming along beside me.

From the 1955-built A48 bridge itself the views are terrific. To the north are riverside scrap metal yards and Giants Grave, where they once broke ships. Beyond is the once industrial but now largely dormitory town of Briton Ferry. To the south the River Neath crosses the sands of Baglan to hit the Severn. There's a marina and a sand wharf, still working. A dredger, *The Argabay*, off-loads its cargo as I watch. Beside me the M4 crosses the same gorge, its concrete stations reaching the Swansea side at the precise spot where the remains of a castle built by Morgan ap Caradog ab Iestyn, the Welsh lord of Afan, Yr Hen Gastell[12], once languished. Gone now, most of it, carried off by digger, compressed as carriageway foundation, lost. The Iron Age hill fort that originally occupied the knoll below me is now used as a dump for wrecked vans. History and transport squash into this gap. A Roman Road originally came along here too, crossing the slow-moving Neath at low tide on stepping stones. For the future, and no doubt in actuality by the time you read this, the cycle path will double as the route through here chosen by Neath Port Talbot Council for their section of the All Wales Coastal Footpath. Cheaper than a new footbridge or a tunnel down there at water level and at least from here you can see the coast if not actually touch it. Now I'm cycling it and it isn't quite the crisp and uplifting experience I'd expected.

Noise levels are high from the nearby traffic, which although completely separated from the Route 4 carriageway, still manage to give an impression of unmitigated peril. The cycle track surface itself is riddled with patch repair and road dirt, loose gravel, fragments of tarmac, bits of lorry detritus. As a route it's certainly useable and a far better experience than actually trying to ride on the road itself with wheels passing inches from your ear at 70 mph. But if this is a cyclists' A-road then progress still needs to be made.

I turn onto the long slope down to Crymlyn Burrows. On the path I pass no one. The route is mine. To the north of A48 and on a sliver of well-lawned ground is Swansea Bay Golf Club, the 5th tee separated from the 6th by the road. They've built an underpass for the golf carts and it's down this that National Route 4 plunges.

Up front is Swansea Gate Business Park, much up for sale

and next to it the great Parc Amazon with its new access road, Amazon Way. The Welsh base for the world's best online retailer. You might even have got this book in a brown packet sent out from its doors.

In the early industrial age the Tennant Canal ran north of the present road, connecting the Tawe with the River Neath. Most of it is still in place, operated by the Neath and Tennant Canal Trust. It runs east of the River Neath through sleeping Jersey Marine and arrives opposite Giant's Grave in Briton Ferry. In front of me, to the south, the Port of Swansea begins. The A48 now has a name. Fabian Way. It follows the line of the Roman Road. It's named after Quintus Fabius Maximus Verrucosus Cunctator, said the *Western Mail,* the Roman general who came up with the Fabian Strategy of success by attrition, of getting there by harassment, of winning by delay[13]. Fabian Way, the slow method of arriving. But in my case it's not. Swansea is looming at wheel-whizzing speed.

Ahead is the single supporting mast of the new Sidings Bridge which takes traffic from Swansea's SA1 waterside redevelopment over Fabian's road of irksome impediment. From my angle of approach the tower looks like a Welsh-version of the Festival of Britain's Skylon. It's a capital adornment, that thing Swansea always wanted. I can see the city start, the glass pyramid of Plantasia, the roundabout-guarding anti-aircraft gun, Sainsbury's by the water, famous Prospect Place and the glorious Dylan Thomas Centre.

I could have walked all this. I could. But fun on a bike is so much better.

The Star Inn, Neath

It's the fag end of Christmas now, the grey sloping time that lies like a replete slug in the soft drizzle falling between the day itself and the barren wastes of the arriving new year. We're back in Briton Ferry, behind Winstone's Fitness Centre, closed today, the boys nowhere to be seen, the whole district silent and damp. The hail and intermittent showers are holding back but the evidence of their earlier presence is everywhere. We are behind the Wern Works, long riverside sheds, rusting to death and, like most of the south Wales's once industrial landscape, on offer for a much reduced price. The Wern Works are available at £1,300,000 for seven acres of brownfield light industrial. You could build flying saucers here or reprocess scrap metal or just knock it all down and construct flats. Clearly not a viable proposition. No one has yet taken it up. The Neath Canal flows here, bargeless but clear. It heads up country the three miles to Neath and then goes on up the Neath Valley to a terminal basin at Glynneath, thirteen miles and nineteen locks beyond.

Most of this waterway remains in place. Some sections are still navigable and only a few are infilled to allow for the crossing of modern roads. The canal has its origins in the 1690s with the industrialist Sir Humphrey Mackworth. He owned a copper works[14] at Melincryddan halfway between the Briton Ferry sea and the Castle at Neath. He canalised the Melincryddan pill to improve access from the river Neath to his works. As with much of the early industrial age, progress came in fits and starts. It wasn't until a full century later that the area's iron masters and mine owners finally got together to finance the construction of a navigable waterway. The new canal ran from valley top down to Briton Ferry's newly-created tidal dock fronting the sea. The barges were filled with pig iron, limestone, coal and silica. Some conveyed gunpowder from Curtis & Harvey's works at Pontneddfechan. Kingdoms rose and kingdoms fell. Fortunes were made. All lost now. The canal carried its last commercial barge in 1930. Mackworth's copper works are gone. Slag heaps by 1877. Overbuilt with houses now.

The shorter Tennant Canal, which runs back along the coast to Port Tennant at Swansea, opened a little later in 1818. The waterway entered the River Neath at Red Jacket Pill opposite the scrap metal wharfs at Giant's Grave. There should have been a linking lock to allow barges to access the Neath Canal by crossing the river but this was never built. The rival owners of the two canal systems were at each other's commercial throats. Microsoft vs. Apple. VHS vs. Betamax. Nothing is ever new. The Tennant Canal eventually joined the Neath via an aqueduct built upriver at Aberdulais in 1824. Combined operations allowed barges from up valley to choose between the wharfs and floating dock at Briton Ferry or the ever-expanding port at Swansea. And for a time there was enough muscle in the south Wales Industrial Revolution to keep everyone in business. Like its fellow, the Neath, the Tennant Canal carried its last commercial barge in the 1930s but for a time continued as a slow money earner by supplying water to the chemical works at Llandarcy and at Baglan Bay. The canal systems are now in the hands of a trust and are being redeveloped for what is known as leisure. You can fish and in some sections you can ride on pleasure barges. We live in a world of official joy and extended cleanliness. Estuarine Neath is no exception.

The local authority here now offers the towpath as a nature walk, a stroll beside trees and water. And it is that. For most of its route it is screened from the tidal River Neath and has the scrap metal quays and salvage operations at Giant's Grave tidied neatly away behind hedge and fence. There is water in quantity and wet clay everywhere. In the entire journey we are passed only once by another human being. That one a hoodie on a mountain bike, with a line of sprayed muck written right up his grey track suit back.

I'm justifying this short diversion inland on the basis that the River Neath is tidal all the way up to the town itself. It stays full of salt and waves above Brynhyfryd, the sports centre, Melincryddan, Neath General Station, and what still stands of the castle, bending on only to run out of power towards Tonna and Aberdulais. You can get significantly-sized ships up this far on the spring tides. This is still the Estuary, but only just. An echo of it, an outrider. What's more I have business up here. At the top end of the town the Star Inn still stands. A pub once owned by my family that I've never visited.

On the map there's a seamless blend between Briton Ferry and Neath. Briton Ferry's welcoming Earl of Jersey with its huge *Cymru am Byth*, the It's A Dog's Life grooming parlour and the tattoo shop give way to the terraces and small stores of lower Neath with no discernible gap. But on the canal path ground the two places are still miles apart. Open country, industry flattened, the Crymlyn bog come back. The towpath tracks a sliver of land next to the now surging river. In places the ground narrows to no more than feet wide. Industry is an echo, the occasional digger stilled for the holiday, its brightly coloured arms raised up like a contemporary sculpture.

As Neath arrives so, too, do the redevelopments. New housing replacing the wrecked old. There are historical interpretation boards in place, banks have been regrassed, locals are out pushchair pushing, dog walking and fishing. I'm as far from the actual sea as I have been on this entire trip.

On my mother's side, one of my great grandfathers, Henry Davis, son of an iron miner from the Forest of Dean, had moved to Wales and married his first wife, Jane Thomas. The Thomas family were publicans. They ran taverns in Swansea and in the nineteenth century owned the Star Inn and the cottage next door, then at a place called Tynycaeau on the northern outskirts of Neath. I've traced this family branch back in the pages of a Welsh bible through permutations of Thomas, Evans, and Morgan, to reach one Thomas Hopkin, Neath, 1753. This bible, his book. His handwriting there, the ink scrawl reaching up to me through two hundred and fifty years.

Jane, my great grandmother, was born at the Star in 1865. She married Henry, had four children and then died in 1897 of childbirth complications with her fifth. She was only 32. They lived not at the Star but in Pembroke Dock, where her husband had gone to work. She's buried in Swansea. At the Star in Neath, her family grieved. In the nineteenth century having children was always a risk but it's tragic that Jane should have managed four births, including my grandfather Edgar Henry John, and despite all her experience was a victim of the reaper with the next.

At the Star she's been seen. A spectral presence roaming the corridors, touching the living with her gentle hands, pressing them coldly, making herself felt. My great grandmother, the ghost. When my aunt visited in 1998 bearing a photograph of Jane, her likeness was recognised. She was the woman in the old fashioned dress who'd been seen floating through the walls. The picture went up behind the bar. An entry in Robert King's *Haunted Neath* brought the ghost hunters. Good for trade, for a while. But these are hard times for taverns, despite what you might think after seeing Swansea's Wind Street in action on a Saturday night. The Star, with no trade from canal bargees to rely on, isolated in the now renamed Penydre, with little passing custom, finally closed in 2009.

It's in a bad way when I get to it. Ground to roof cracks in its eighteenth century render, the car park empty, the garden overgrown with buddleia, the pub doors boarded and barred. The Star was a free house that once offered Worthington, Hancocks, Bass, and Carling. Its pillared and ornamented porch is covered with star images and the pub sign, a geometric stylised star, still hangs. It was regulation that finally did for it. There's a notice from the Council attached to the door closing the premises down. Rat infestation, food preparation carried out without adequate hot and cold water available, insanitary surfaces in use. Continuation prohibited.

A man over the road, cleaning his car between thunderstorms, tells me that the place had been sold and was about to be pulled down when the banking crash happened. "They were going to build houses there," he says, "they showed us plans, but that was five years ago and nothing has happened. It was a good pub, too. No trouble. I'm sorry to see it go."

Me too, I'm here years too late. Star no longer shining. Through the weather's bluster but with the sun breaking, low and bright, filling the towpath with long shadows, we walk back the three miles to the Estuary coast.

Canal Names, Some

Morgan Stuart Williams, Humphrey Mackworth, William Jones, William Kirkhouse, Richard Jenkins Squire Edward Elton, Lewis Thomas, Thomas Dadford Junior, Alexander Raby, Thomas Sheasby, Thomas Cartwright, Evan Hopkins, George Tennant, John Dillwyn Llewelyn, John Thomas, John Thomas, John Thomas, Jane Davis (nee Thomas) in there floating.

Crymlyn

The problem with a book about the coast is the sheer ubiquity of the sea. After a time it becomes just there like the air, in its unnoticed wonder and endless crashing. But recently as I've negotiated great bridges and the remains of Wales's industrial past, the salt waters have seemed to recede. So I'm approaching them again now by walking directly at them, south across Crymlyn Burrows. This is a declared SSSI[15] of dune, saltmarsh and intertidal habitat, protected by the weight of the law from caravaners, off-road marauders and men out shooting. As burrows go they are better than nothing but not a patch on the desert expanses of Merthyr Mawr or the Amazon-like basin that is Kenfig. There's no sight of the sea yet, either, just the rumour. The River Neath and Baglan Power Station are to the east. The sails of yachts glide by like feluccas. In the far distance through the haze are the dock cranes at Port Talbot.

But as I top yet another sandy ridge, suddenly and totally unexpectedly in its dazzling light, it's there, waves breaking, foam and froth, white water and the sound of the ocean. Sho, Shoosh, flut, ravad, tapavada pow, coof, loof, roof, shhhhh[16]. The shipping channel up the Neath is marked by a line of posts that step out steadily into the slow flowing Severn Estuary. Is this the Severn River or the Severn Sea? This is no longer a freshwater world, it has to be the latter.

The beach here is one of the undiscovered marvels of Wales. A great and largely unoccupied stretch of virgin sand, scattered with shells and driftwood. Great logs and broken hunks litter the dune line. In Victorian times when the octagonal tower and camera obscura were built at Jersey Marine in an attempt to develop the place as a resort, this would have been the leisure beach for trippers. The tower now forms part of the Towers Hotel, a spa pool and conference centre complex offering guests enough diversion never to have to leave the grounds. The beach is safe from visitors.

Walking west towards Swansea the beach loses none of its wonder. Stretches of coal lost from ships unloading at Port Talbot litter its surface. The incoming tide makes lagoons around its sandbanks then floods them with waves. Ahead, where it reaches the rock defences of the seawall protecting the docks, there are great white-topped breakers and showers of foam. In the late and low autumn sun it's a vigorous and exciting place.

Out at sea I watch *HMS Diamond*, the Navy's latest and most expensive destroyer, leave the port of Swansea where it has been on a goodwill visit. The burghers have been charmed. The ship's radar towers scrape the sky, its pointed prow cuts the waves. The white specks of birds spin in the air behind it.

Where the Burrows run out, BP's complex of storage tanks, clear and present on my OS map, is gone. This is now a huge cleared expanse of flat earth. It is protected by a pretty impenetrable double fence – the original 1950s Ferro concrete-posted barrier with a new high-duty mesh sewn on top. Inside there have been attempts to use marram grass to stabilise wind erosion. Stretches of the sandy soil have been marked with post and string, and hung about with bird deterring CDs – 80s disco finally put to new use.

This empty land waits. BP have offered it entirely free to Swansea University as a site for the education giant's second campus. There are plans to build a huge science and innovation precinct involving private partners such as Rolls Royce, so long as the Welsh Government comes up with matching funds and the local authorities give the project their blessing. BP has already offered £10m as partnership support. But this being Swansea the expected shower of delay, distrust and disinformation inevitably applies. Offered match finance is unaccountably withdrawn. Local planners object on the grounds that this development will interfere with the flagship development at SA1. Private partners rethink. Public partners have their budgets slashed. Heads are held in hands. Meanwhile the land sits, vacant and vast, the wind blowing across it. There are security cameras but no guards, no huts, no tracks. Empty. Nothing. Swansea Zen.

There's no way of crossing it either, bar breaking in. The only way out is back.

In the carr[17] woodland at the back of the Burrows, where BP's fences end and the SSSI returns, the traffic noise from the main road is never that far off. But you can ignore it. There are walkers out, amblers, horse riders. Two camouflage-wearing men exercising their birds of prey. One has a two-year-old goshawk and the second a yearling harris hawk. Unnamed yet. The goshawk, the bigger bird, splendidly bright-eyed and wearing a tail-feather protector, is called KP Nut. Well, she might be. That's the name her owner tells me is hers but he might be making it up. The goshawk thinks it's human now. It's what's known as imprinted on its owner. The Harris Hawk has a way to go. The men use whistles and electronic sounder to control the birds, which swoop and dive, soar and circle.

This flatland interzone between Neath and Swansea, where local authority control changes hands and traffic does little but pass in flight, is still largely fen. North of the road beyond the Neath and Tennant Canal, the Crymlyn wetlands run on as far as Skewen and east as far as Llandarcy. It's a piece of the past that largely missed the Industrial Revolution and remains preserved and unused today. A museum of how the Estuary coast once was and still is. Little visited, overgrown, blown by the wind.

Back on the road the coast has once again vanished and with it the sea. Among the traffic you can't smell it nor hear it. Around here this is an urban estuary.

Swansea

"Boom boom boom, Santana's in the room." It's the voice of someone called Big Boi coming at me through my earphones. Santana still in action on the player in my pocket. This is the comeback after the comeback album he made in 2005, Carlos endlessly riding up the Latin rhythms, as he's been doing for five decades now. The Duke Ellington of rhythm. The Count Basie of rock. The contemporary formula is to have on the album with you as many of the new generation fast risers as you can get, in the hope that some of the way music now bends will rub off. Bo Rice, Michelle Branch & the Wreckers along with that unforgettable rapper, Will.I.Am[18], all appear on *All That I Am*. Not a great critical success, I have to say. Where our man once held the intellectual high ground he's now down there in what might have been all-day disco if only the heart, kiss and mix it up pap stations would put him on their play lists. I'm sticking with him out of sentiment. Con Santana. El Fuego. Turn it off. Swansea's up ahead.

I meet Nigel Jenkins in the park-and-ride car park built on former railway sidings half way along Fabian Way. Nigel blames the myth of this road being named after a Roman general as being down to invention on the part of a Western Mail reporter. It's actually named after Daniel Fabian who came from Llanrhidian, Gower, in 1639 to farm at Glanybad Farm in St Thomas. The farmhouse became a marker used by arriving ships and the bay they were heading for as Fabian's Bay. The farmhouse was knocked down in 1850. It's all in the book, he tells me. He's referring to *Real Swansea Two*, the Jenkins master-piece that explains the city in a way that no one else ever has.

Actually, this doesn't quite happen. I meet Nigel not in the park-and-ride but outside the Dylan Thomas Centre in Somerset Place where he stows his bike for safety. Then we drive back to Fabian Way and walk. The DT Centre is the much-celebrated Swansea Council literary outgrowth estab-lished in what was once the town's town hall which lay derelict until European money was winkled out of the system in the early 1990s. It's been, if not the jewel in Swansea's firmament, at least a sort of literary Hilton following the town's hosting of the Year of Literature in 1995.

The Dylan Thomas Centre was almost built anew in spectac-ular creation in a car park opposite the Grand Theatre by the architect Will Alsop. But as a sort of forerunner for what was to happen later in Cardiff with Zaha Hadid, was declared to be 'Lego on sticks' and dumped. The old Guildhall redevelopment complete with restaurant and facilities for weddings was a much better bet. And so it has been for more than a decade. Everyone from John Ashbery to Owen Sheers has read here. The future, however, looks shaky. The bookshop has closed and building ownership will transfer to the recently rebranded University of Wales[19]. What will they do with it in our present impoverished times?

Controversy in building things haunts Swansea. The Docks, which the place needed simply to get on in the industrial world, were developed late simply because vested interests opposed progress, or to be specific, opposed the spending of investment cash. While Cardiff came on stream in 1839, Swansea's first North Dock with its half-tide basin didn't enter service until twenty years later in 1859. There is some advantage, however, to late development. Swansea's current array of docks, the Westside marina, formerly the South Dock, and the three Eastside expanses of water – The Prince of Wales Dock, King's Dock and Queen's Dock – are reassuringly large.

I've skirted ABP's endless chain link fencing and stern warning notices on my way in from the east. But size is no longer everything. Of ABP's five south Wales ports, Swansea is now the least used. The dock basins lie empty. If water could echo then down here facing Fabian's Bay, it certainly would.

The plan is to walk from Swansea's east to its west and to do this by keeping as near to the sea as possible. Nigel, full of anecdote, literary backdrop and local knowledge, is the perfect guide. He's a poet, primarily, and possesses a voice in the Richard Burton mould that quite often sends women shivering. I've known him for almost as long as I've been writing. He was born on Gower and has managed to remain a vaguely local resident almost all his life. He went to a public school in Cheltenham (which might have something to do with the development of the Burton gravitas his reading style betrays) and set out as a journalist only to end up first as a professional writer, then an editor (he famously compiled the English half of the Welsh Academy's *Encyclopaedia of Wales*, known to Nigel as Psycho because of the way for almost a decade it disrupted normal life) and now works with the novelist Stevie Davies as co-director of Creative Writing at Swansea University. Poetry is his mainstay, haiku a primary obsession, writing topographical psychogeographies a close second. With photographer David Pearl he compiled the landmark study *Gower* (Gomer Press), is author of two volumes of *Real Swansea* and is currently working on *Real Gower*. He's a supporter of underdogs and the alternative and, for a man on an institutional salary, has one of the healthiest suspicions of officialdom I've come across.

We cross the bridge over Fabian Way and descend towards the Prince of Wales Dock, soon to be marina but not yet, and the working port beyond. Nigel is talking about the Swansea-Cork ferry, the friendly ship that until recently left every day from the East Pier, boozers, travellers and families on board. In recent times profits had tumbled and service was withdrawn as a cost saver. Ferry owners, the West Cork Tourism Co-Operative Society Limited, couldn't save the ailing line. Another cultural link onto the scrap heap. Something is being lost here, the past going from our hands.

We are in SA1, the brash Swansea apartment, water sports and restaurant post-industry redevelopment, all sail roofs and ship detail in the architecture, unique to this city, but actually same as everywhere else in the UK. It's Swansea's eastern gateway, a sweeping expanse you can't ignore as you arrive. It's full of light and air and feels as if it's still on-going. Which it is, of course. The finish date of 2014 will be missed following the recession. The bars don't all function, the diners don't come here in their hoards just yet. It looks splendid but lacks heart. Mothballed incomplete. Like parts of Ireland. All we need now is that economic upturn, that tiny lift and we'll be off. But there's no indication of that happening yet.

As we walk we discuss ailments. It seems this is the thing you do after a life of writing, well a life of anything actually. Kids and houses when you are middle-aged. How death looks after that. Nigel's specialty is paroxysmal atrial fibrillation. This is a heart thing, high blood pressure and irregular rhythms, the most common such condition, apparently. When it struck Nigel first, a year or so back, he cycled to the hospital to be checked out and was told that his bike ride there could have killed him. All controlled by drugs now. Cut down on life's good stuff. Less drink. You know the score. I do. My own urology difficulties and, more recently, the early arrival of muscle wrecking polymyalgia have put me on a diet that is so healthy I should be getting younger. But I'm not.

Any atrial fibrillation poems yet? No.

Beyond the redevelopment we pass the resited Norwegian Church, which is smaller than the one in Cardiff, and the wartime bombed J Shed with its restaurants and New York-style loft apartments. The marble paving slabs we walk on were quarried in China. Cut price, made by workers paid slave wages. Mirrors the copper manillas that were once made pretty near here when Swansea was the great Copperopolis. Manillas were horseshoe-shaped bars used to barter for slaves in Africa. Swansea full of echoes of itself.

We cross the Tawe and hunt out the site of the original North Dock and its half-tide basin. The stones that made the dock's edge are still visible in the paving just east of Sainsbury's. They curve across the surface, unlabelled, unremarked. Just beyond lies a chunk of Ferro-concrete, all that remains of the Weavers Mill. This was the first structure ever to use a reinforced concrete frame. It was built by the French engineer François Hennebique in 1897.

Just behind Morgan's Hotel in Pier Street, an arm's stretch from the water, is Childe Roland's concrete poem 'YOUUUU-UUUUUU'. It is set in a brick wall at eye level and these days rarely viewed. But it says something about Swansea' ambition. Concrete poetry in use as part of an extensive public art offering. This was something the city did early. As a place that incorporated new art into its developing fabric, for a short time in the 1980s Swansea led most places in the Western world.

Swansea's extensive commitment to public art is the responsibility of architect and artist Robin Campbell. His role in the 1980s as the Council's Head of Environmental Design and the man responsible for coming up with the idea of reflooding the old South Dock, half filled with rubbish at the time, and then using it as a marina cannot be overstated. Having got that redevelopment in train he then went ahead to cover the entire seafront central area, the Marina as it's now known, with public art, much of it his own. We pass example after example. Fish shapes, stylised crabs, sand marks, heads on poles, wall engravings, Egyptian fantasies, reproductions of the eye of Horus and Cleopatra's needle and the container barge that brought it right across the Bay of Biscay, anchor chains, signal flags, bits of poems, philosophical quotations, then whole sculptures, standing in splendour facing the sea.

Out here, beyond the quay where the fishing fleet ties up, run Swansea's East and West Piers. These are the two arms that protect Swansea's dock's entrance and which stretch out for a considerable distance into the sea. Not only are the views back to the Tawe barrage, its outfalls and fish passes, appropriately dramatic, but the view on to the wider waters takes your breath away. There's no charge for access and no health and safety rigmarole and regulation. No one checks that you've got your pier familiarisation certificate. No one demands that you wear steel-capped pier walking shoes. At the far end are a couple of fishermen with rods plus the best views of the Estuary I've had so far which don't come from being on a boat.

We cross back onto Swansea Bay sands and walk just below all that remains of the burrows. These once ran back from the coast here for at least two kilometres. A small triangle, sand hummocks held in place by marram grass, hang on. On the shore side were once factories now replaced by bayside apartments. Sea vistas guaranteed. As we know so well, the sight of water always increases price.

We're heading out along the promenade where the bathing machines once stood and the stalls selling whelks and cups of tea. Swansea began as a sort of fishing port with beachside recreation potential, a Brighton of Wales to Porthcawl's Blackpool. That notion got put in a bucket when the Industrial Revolution took hold. The coal exported from the developing docks dirtied everything. Then the logistics of copper smelting (you need five times as much coal to copper ore) made it an economic nonsense to send the coal to South America. Better was to bring the copper ore here. Swansea coal exporter became Swansea copper refiner. Then tinplate and spelter[20] maker. A place full of fire and smoke and desperation. A town that made money like fury and for miles inland turned everything dark.

Out at the sea line, metal detectorists creep, headphones on, eyes down, hunting for coin, the past, stuff lost that may still have value. Their love-hate relationship with the archaeologists repaired somewhat now that detectorists have been responsible for finding Iron Age and Bronze Age trackways out there in the deep mud.

We're heading for the 'Tower of the Ecliptic', a Robin Campbell creation at the water's edge, built as an observatory for the Swansea Astronomic Society in 1991. Nigel describes it as a "hymn to light" with its staircase, alongside the tower that hosts its rotating telescope dome, surmounted by a woman as weather vane[21], its Mad Max heads on poles, and its gnomic verse[22] (created by Nigel) on plaques around its sides. The Astronomic Society couldn't keep up the rental payments and have vacated. Right now the tower stands empty[23]. Next to it is the Scots concretist Ian Hamilton Finlay's half-finished folly, 'Tower of the Nets' from 1987, a six-sided brick guard box with Aztec pyramid roof, which serves no purpose other than to support Finlay's philosophical plaques. These reproduce stylised quotations from Wittgenstein, Epictetus' discourse, Matthew 4, Theocritus's Idylls, and Plotinus's Enneads. "The cosmos is like a net." So it is.

The Campbell-originated art flood ebbs and flows. Along the seawall are engraved the names of some of Swansea's Cape Horn-rounding ships – *The Jonas of Swansey, Blithe de Swanseye, Mohican, Zeta*. Here plaques which once contained Campbell texts and symbols have been sandblasted empty by the prevailing winds. In twenty years the art has returned to dust.

On Marine Parade sculptures still stand, weathered and stained, fitting their locations perfectly. The 1988 'Copper Flame', the 1985 'Zeta Mnemonical', Rob Conybear's 1987 'Lighthouse Tower'. "It used to move and light up once," Nigel says. Corroded solid now. The Boat Shed doors with their rusted harpoon on the sea floor emblem did not go down too well with the Sea Cadets whose boat shed it is. The council had Nigel write a poem for the opening brochure. There was conflict over Jenkins' use of language and censorship followed. Nigel's relationship with authority up against the wire once again.

We head for Meridian Tower, at 29 storeys currently Wales' tallest building. Cardiff has at least three rivals, all taller, on the drawing board but the recession has held the Capital back. Instead Swansea, Wales' second city and with considerable aspiration, shines. We go up the rocket lift, the thirteenth floor, unlike those in American structures, solidly in place. On the top, Brains operate three floors of pub and restaurant under its Grape and Olive brand. Decent beer and half decent food, too. We take a window seat about as far up as you can get. The views run for miles. Below, on the flat mud and sand now that the tide is out as far as it goes, the arrow heads of the ancient fish weirs are visible. To the west Mumbles is touchable. Nothing sways, as skyscrapers often do. At 29 floors we are a pygmy in world terms, but we're getting there.

Back on the Mumbles Road next to the Bay View Hotel and Thai Dining stands the Slip Bridge. Or non-bridge, actually. This pedestrian crossing once brought visitors from the town and deposited them right on Swansea Bay's golden sands. It did so right up until 2004 when amid great controversy the council, in a fit of public concern, removed the metal work. Rumour is that the ironworks of the crossing were taken down to allow residents of the then brand new Morgan Court apartments a view of the Mumbles and the sea. Denied, of course. Local uproar resulted in a city-wide vote being taken on what to do with the structure. Restore it, was the decisive result. But by now the metal work had become too damaged to be simply put back so it has been set out as part of the Swansea to Mumbles cycle route, a few hundred metres up the road. There are plans, the council says, to replace the crossing with a new structure built onto the existing pillars. An illuminated glass bridge, perhaps, overhanging the sea. But, again, lack of cash has intervened and nothing has been done. The old pillars that once supported the bridge on its way across road, Mumbles railway and the LMS tracks, stand forlorn and scaffolded. Sand beats up against the bases. The dunes forever trying to come back.

The Mumbles Road

It's the end of the 1950s and my grandfather has brought me to Swansea. We've come in on a smoking train all the way from Cardiff General. A train with clang and spark that filled the fields with steam and the air with smoke. In the corridored compartment in deep GWR brown with faded, out of focus shots of Paignton and Torquay above the seats, I've sat and studied the passing countryside. The telegraph poles zooming, the green of the Vale, the fields of cows. And then I've been shaken, even at my uncaring young age, by the broken and desperate wreck of brick and stack and desolation that is mid-century Landore. The source of Swansea's wealth. Now gone into dust. Swansea, golden town of the west. I'd always imagined it to be this. But passing through Landore on the town's eastern outskirts it's obvious that it's not.

We're going to Mumbles, on the train. "It's a tram not a train," says my grandfather. And so it is. A bus on rails, standing at the terminus at Rutland Street. It's a trolley bus with tracks. Red and cream with a signboard saying 'Mumbles' on its front. On the hoarding behind it are the words Drinka Pinta Milka Day and an advertisement for the motor show at Earl's Court.

We board and my grandfather buys the tickets with a flourish. "You should collect these things," he advises me. "They'll be of value someday." We rattle off along the Oystermouth Road to Trafalgar Arch, the Slip and Brynmill, Ashleigh Road, Blackpill, West Cross, Norton Road, Oystermouth, Southend and on to our destination at the far end of the sea's westwards sweep, the Pier at Mumbles. There have been unparalleled views of the bay and the sea. Boats, water, sand. We alight. Smell the air. Then we get on again and rattle all the way back.

Today there's nothing left. Not a single extant reminder. The Rutland Road Depot has Swansea's Leisure Centre built on its site. The tracks have been obliterated with a precision that the World War Two bombing Germans would have applauded. The Mumbles Railway was the oldest in the world, established in 1804 as a horse-drawn tramway to carry limestone from the quarries of Mumbles into Swansea. In 1807 it expanded to carry passengers. In January 1960 the South Wales Transport Company, a bus fleet operator and the line's eventual owners, closed it. They did so in the search for the greater profits they could make by shuttling passengers back and forth by motor coaches. How we get from A to B and who can make a buck from us so doing. History not important. In its time Mumbles trains had been moved by horse, by steam, and by diesel. They ended using the fuel of the future, electricity.

Preservation of the remains was pathetic. Car Number Two went to a museum in Leeds where it was vandalised and subsequently destroyed by fire. The rest went for scrap, all of them.

Apart, that is, from the front end of Car Number Seven, which Swansea Museum acquired and several decades later have finally restored and put on display in the Tram Shed beside the National Waterfront Museum near the Marina.

Today I'm alone in the Oystermouth Road Car Park, the bike is once more in the boot. This is the Slip Bridge stop, just up from Rutland Street, beyond which the trams would start to pick up speed and rattle and rock. The route here is now known as Swansea Bike Path, doubling as Sustrans' Route 4 (which I've already encountered on my way into Swansea) running all the way to Fishguard. Half of it doubles, anyway, the other half is the promenade which takes walkers the four or so miles to Mumbles Head, its pier, lifeboat station and lighthouse.

Behind me is Percy Thomas's 1930s Swansea Guildhall in clean Portland stone with, as a nod to Swansea's alleged Viking origin, bits of Viking Boat as decoration sticking out from its clock tower. On the Oystermouth Road among the b&bs and small hotels is an apartment development that has taken this Viking ship thing just that little bit too far. Serried balconies in coated, coloured steel resembling the prows of longboats, protrude over the pavement. They do so with a down market lack of subtlety and lost opportunity that fits them in well among enterprises called The Beachcomber Guest House and the Abertawe Alehouse. This is the holiday seaside so we'll have boats. Visitors probably think they are something to do with pirates.

The path is patched with blown sand. On its seaward side there's marram grass and a build-up of dune that marks the burrow's return. The beach in all its slowly curving arc is a Swansea attribute that should be exploited far more than it is. Passing by car, as most do, this sight is denied. The tide is out again and the eye sails on for miles to a distant scratch on the horizon that might just be the tide line. The bay, a real bay unlike its rival at Cardiff, is a vast and almost entirely empty half-moon of flat sand marked by stretches of pebble and occasional rocks.

I pass the Patti Pavilion on the corner of Victoria Park. The Patti – a place celebrated in rock history. For years I kept as precious my copy of Man's *Christmas at the Patti*, a double ten-inch album put out as a limited edition. This featured a whole run of 1970s south Wales psychedelic heavy metal guitar bands including Dave Edmunds, the Flying Aces, Ducks Deluxe, Deke Leonard, the Jets and, of course, the album's centrepiece, Man themselves. It was a thundering headbanger of a record, recorded at the Patti in 1972 on a night when everything went brilliantly well until the police closed the concert down due to the noise.

The Patti Pavilion is named after the nineteenth century soprano Adelina Patti, who donated the structure to the city and would no doubt have been game enough to appear on stage with Man had she still been around. The pavilion was originally sited on her estate at Craig y Nos but moved to its present location in Victoria Park in 1918. The building was already in decline when Man performed there and, despite a *Challenge Anneka* minor makeover in 1994, continued to fall apart. There was an attempt to burn it down in 2006. But in 2007, powered by a National Lottery good causes grant, the building was comprehensively restored with a glass-covered wing housing The Patti Raj, an Indian restaurant, added at the street-facing front. Man, with their signature extended guitar jams, have aged less well, although they have their fans. I sold my double album on eBay to one of them. He was beside himself with pleasure. Further west is St Helen's Rugby and Cricket Ground, Taliesin Arts Centre, and the whole university complex at Singleton Park, but my eyes are south, on the bay. I've put on my hat, it's so cold.

I go by the War memorial, metalwork not yet stolen for scrap, the polished marble memorial to Ben John Bellamy, the young lad murdered near here in 2005, the trig point near where the Clyne River enters the Severn. Inland is Clyne Castle and the route up the valley once taken by the LMS railway. When we had railways. That's another one ripped up by Beeching and covered with regret ever since. The Black Pill Lido is empty and full of chill. High above are the districts of Uplands and Killay.

On a prominence at the entrance to Mumbles stands Oystermouth Castle, once the residence of the Lords of Gower. Mumbles – such a well-named place for the one-time haunt of Dylan Thomas and the town where poet Nigel Jenkins currently lives. Below the Castle there are pubs. Runs of them. The famous Mumbles mile[24]. More pubs in a line than I've seen anywhere recently. The two Dylan drank in, the Antelope, which has certainly seen better days, and the Marine, now renamed the Village Inn. Then the White Rose, The MCC Club, The Hancock, The George, The Pilot of Mumbles. Mumbles Rugby Club. Oystermouth Social Club. No reason not to be happy here.

The path passes the Mumbles boat moorings at Village Lane, the V Slip and Knab Rock. There's a sign designating one area for water skiing although this far out of season that's no more than a memory. Ahead is cluster of pirate-scrap amusement arcades, cafes and fishing tackle shops. Finally the pier itself. Built 1898. Today closed for refurbishment. It will be worth the wait, reads the sign. I sit on a bench below a notice that warns me not to sit here unless I am consuming produce purchased from the café. The café is closed. Check the map. Gaze out to sea. Turn round and cycle back.

Gower:
Oystermouth to Worm's Head

Oystermouth

I've cheated this time. I've come down the M4 by car, back to
where I'd last left off walking. There's a gap now in what's
passing for winter. There has hardly been a single frost this
January. Today is full of bright sun with one of those clear tall
skies you see in brochures for Scandinavia. On the road in I
could see Port Talbot ahead, a line of stacks across the vale's
rolling green. I counted them. There were at least twenty plumes
in grey and white – smog and steam escaping, allowable efflu-
ent, brand new cumulus hammering the sky. The past is still
with us, things don't change. It's been like this for as long as I
can remember. Coming down here in the 60s with a car full of
second aeon poets bound for Swansea, – Parfitt, Jarman,
Callard – haiku up their sleeves. Passing in the 70s with
Cobbing and Chopin taking language's microparticles to places

they'd never been. In the 80s with the performance poets, loudhailer and chainsaw packed in the boot. Again in the 90s drawn by the literary glow of renascent Swansea. Then in the new millennium making psychogeography of the places all these poets had been. Every time I pass, Port Talbot is smoking, retching up its plumes into the ever-supplicant sky.

I'll get walking again as soon as I hit Oystermouth, right where I turned my bike round at the end of that spin along the arc of Swansea Bay. Mumbles. Where does that name come from? I ask Nigel, who has re-joined me, offering once again to be my guide. "Y Mwmbwls. Mamillae, a word for breasts," he offers but then tells me that no one really knows. The whole place is actually Oystermouth – Ystum Llwynarth. The bear grove which bends, the corner thick with trees, trees like the back of a bear, the meandering headland, the headland full of trees, the oysters which mumble. Mummess, mommulls, mombles, mommells, y mwmlws. How places get names. Language flows around them, flickering, catching, falling away. Doing this until something gets written down and sticks. For a time.

There were Oysters here, once. Right up to the 1950s the place was famous for its catches. At the trade's height in the middle of the nineteenth century there were at least a hundred skiffs working the patch, each with its designated perch as the individual grounds were called. Oyster catchers used iron dredges which they hauled along the seabed scooping up everything in their tracks. Today there's nothing, not one shellfish left. Overfishing and pollution have seen the Mumbles oyster off. Roaders, they were known as, named after the Mumbles Roads where they were caught. They had shells as big as tea plates. Emerging from the receding tide are the skeletal lines that mark where ancient skiffs have been abandoned, one, two of them, three, four, five. Easy to spot when you know the shape you're looking for. Nigel does.

Oystermouth. No oysters now, no mouth either. There's no river at Mumbles. It's a bit like Gower as a whole where, because of the porous nature of the underlying rocks, there are no watercourses of real significance. There's just a bit of seeping from the Mumbles cliff face above the sewage pipes that still run out from the headland to the deeper sea. Walking up the

Mumbles Road with the houses to my right tight against the much-quarried cliff and the reclaimed sea's edge where the railway once ran, I get the feeling that this is Fishguard writ larger. It's a Milkwood place where Polly Garter, Rosie Probert, Utah Watkins, Mrs Organ Morgan and all the rest still stalk the streets. Where the beer and the voices flow and the world is still rich with unaccountably poetic dreams.

Oystermouth Castle, from where we've just come, is closed and shrouded in scaffolding. A repointing job of significant scale is underway. The Norman castle, a William de Londres early twelfth century creation to keep the Welsh out of their own lands, is now up there in John Davies's *Wales: 100 Places To See Before You Die*. Swansea Council is working hard at restoration. The grounds have been trimmed and repathed. There's an incredibly naff set of new entrance steps replacing the old wrought iron gates at the end of Castle Avenue. These were described by Robin Turner, the *Western Mail's* Swansea correspondent, as being much like the entranceway to a football player's mansion. There is also the suggestion that, once fixed, the repaired castle walls might again be repainted in the same white they originally were eight hundred years ago.

"They should put the roof on again," says Nigel. We're round the back, sliding among the fallen leaves. We are inspecting the towering scaffolding, totally workmanless, which looks out from the medieval fortress to the twentieth century allotments beyond. "We could use it rather than just view it." Reroofing, however, is a CADW non-starter. Fix the walls, add entrance metalwork, replace the doors, yes. But keep the weather out, that would be tampering with the past. So no.

Next to the Castle is what remains of the Colts Wood Limestone Quarry. Soon to be filled with what the Council describe on their affixed notice as "foamed concrete" in order to stabilise the surrounding ground. Above the kilns a new housing estate presses itself into the fragile soil. Mumbles, which grew to fame as a source of limestone, is a source no more.

Down on the seashore we go looking for the second-oldest road in Swansea. Archaeologists have discovered the remains of a Bronze Age trackway here leading out into the rock-strewn wastes of the Bay. Nigel knows just where it is. We plunge out, boots sinking, eyes intently staring down. "What are we looking for?" I ask. Wooden slats, a metre or more wide, laid like a path. There's the fossilised remains of a tree stump, several thousand years old, evidence that this was once a fen landscape with plant growth and freshwater. There are rocks. There are sea delivered ripples in the fluid mix of sand and mud. There is mud. And more mud. But no track. "It's here somewhere," says Nigel, kicking a boot at a watery hummock. "It's at right angles to that lilac house." He points back at the properties which edge the shoreline. "But it might have been dug up or maybe the sea has buried it again." Like the champion psychogeographers we are, we do not give up yet and spend a further half an hour scouring the pools and the outcrops. Hunting the ripples, gazing at the mud. But there's nothing. "I'll have to ring the archaeologists," says Nigel. You will[1].

"If this lost track is the second oldest then where's the first?" I ask. "That one's 4000 years old," Nigel tells me. "This one is only 3000. The oldest is at Brynmill, that way." He points. "Might still be there, might not." This is clearly how ancient trackways behave. On the GPS when I look later, our route shows us marching off piste out into the blue of the Bay. Pointless but liberating. It's what psychogeographers do.

On shore again more recent relics, in this case those from the lost Mumbles Railway, are far easier to spot. A distinctive sleeper (two parallel wooden slats with concrete lumps at each end) lies, junked, at the foot of the seawall. Not worth preserving today. But they'll find it again and declare it as amazing in a few hundred years. The Square Café (closed) at the end of the car park is not what I originally took it to be (a concrete block cheapo build) but what remains of the original Oystermouth train station. The poles which run near it once held the trams' overhead electric supply. Nigel points out rotting fragments of more wooden sleepers embedded in a wall. Gone but still here. Just.

We divert briefly from the Estuary walk to cross the road and enter the cleared graveyard of Oystermouth's All Saints' Parish Church. Here, still extant, and flanked by two Polaris missile-like marble pillars is the grave and slab of Thomas Bowdler. 1754-1825. "Above all things, truth beareth away the victory."[2]

Bowdler, who came from Bath, was a physician and philanthro-
pist, and famous as the man who invented bowdlerising –
expurgating original texts to remove from them any hints of
violence, lewdness or impropriety. Bowdler did this to
Shakespeare to make it more suitable, as he saw it, for the ears
of women and children. "Out, Damned spot" became "Out,
Crimson spot". In *Hamlet* Ophelia accidentally drowned rather
than committed suicide. The prostitute vanished altogether
from *Henry IV, Part 2*. Bowdler also rewrote parts of the Old
Testament and then went on to remove much of the death and
violence from Gibbon's *Decline and Fall*. After a long life of
making the world clean he retired to Swansea where he died.
His extensive personal library of unexpurgated originals was
donated to the University of Wales at Lampeter.

"There's stuff worth seeing in the church too," Nigel tells me.
We try the door. Locked. The glory of God appropriately
Bowdlerised.

We reach the yacht cubs. There are two, the people's 60s-
styled Mumbles Yacht Club and, next door, the red-brick Bristol
Channel Yacht Club. Kingsley Amis was once a Bristol Channel
member. He'd stand outside next to the twin cannon, smoking.
Gone now, both Kingsley and the guns. I wrote to him once
asking him to contribute a poem or two to my literary magazine.
The great man sent a postcard by way of reply. "Mr Amis
regrets that he is unable to do as you request" was printed on
one side. A bit like the postcard from R.S. Thomas found among
the late John Tripp's papers. And the same to you, that one read.

Outside, stacked in the sea-fronting car parks are boats, pulled
from the water for winter. Mumbles' cultural dichotomy is
eminently visible. The first boat we pass is called *Ysbryd Y Môr*[3],
the second is *Itchy Pussy*. Kingsley would have hated them both.

Beyond the pier, still closed, still awaiting refurbishment but
with large notices now attached telling all that it'll be worth the
wait[4], are the islands. The two humps of land that form
Mumbles Head. On the far one stands the 1794 lighthouse built
to guide ships around the hazardous Mixon Shoal half a mile
out to sea. It still works, although like most Trinity House light-
houses it does so on automatic. There were houses in number
out here once, Nigel tells me. At least forty people were in

residence manning the wartime guns. As the tide is now out we've crossed the sound, walking along what remains of the concrete walkway and the railtrack along which supplies were once sent. The lighthouse, still painted white but sandblasted like much of this region, was once lit by coal. Since 1995 it has relied on solar power. There's a barely legible plaque to its architect, William Jernegan, on the landward facing wall.

Around the headland lies Bracelet Bay. Still Mumbles but with a totally different feel. Here the view is southwards and full of light. There are stretches of grass, a glow of green mingling with the blue-grey thrash of the sea. A sense of Gower rather than post-industrial Swansea pervades. A windsurfer crosses the distant Mixon sand bar, marked at its extremity by a buoy. "That's the buoy in Edward Thomas's poem[5]," says Nigel. 'Sweeter I never heard, mother, no, not in all Wales'. It's set here, I'm sure."

I photograph Nigel standing outside the apple, the 1930s Ferro-concrete structure shaped and painted like a large Bramley. It's actually a café originally opened by the Whiteways Cyder Company of Devon as part of the countrywide promotion for their new non-alcoholic apple drink. The Mumbles apple, still working but naturally closed when we reach it, is one of the few extant examples. When they are open do they sell cider? Who knows.

Ahead is the land I don't know despite having lived within an hour or so of its grasp for most of my life. I think it was that time in some hot, hot summer of my youth that put me off. So many city escapees came here looking for respite that the local authority shut off access. *Gower Closed Sorry* was a sign they erected across the road. Did I really remember that? Or have I made it up?

Nigel goes back to Mumbles, I head on.

Where Gower Begins

Up here on the headland, just beyond the rusty railings that protect the slope back down into Mumbles Gower begins. That's not me talking but the local authority. They've erected a tasteful blue and green welcome sign and affixed it to a chunk of headland rock. Gower – Area of Outstanding natural Beauty. English first, Welsh underneath. Gŵyr? Ardal o Harddwch Naturiol Eithriadol. Welsh hasn't been strong in these parts for hundreds of years.

For those from further east, Gower has a pull and mystery equal to that of Pembrokeshire. It's a distant yet accessible land of yellow beach and palpable peace. But for those who live nearer, and for many this place is a mere dormitory for Swansea, it's a municipal park without park-keepers. Paul Ferris[6] reckons Dylan Thomas thought of it like this. He came here many times but allegedly never took his socks off. Yet there is a photo of the young him, fag in mouth and his arm round Pamela Hansford Johnson, standing in a rock pool at Caswell Bay. You can't quite tell if he has his shoes still on or not. The photo was taken in 1934 by Hansford Johnson's mother. Dylan has his trousers rolled up right to his very thin thighs. Pamela looks as if she's going to bite off the end of his cigarette. They knew how to enjoy themselves in those days.

The Gower coast path is a fine thing. It begins just beyond Fortes Ice Cream Parlour on the corner of Plunch Lane. Along here it's a mix of concrete, tarmac and reinforced step with a handrail protecting the seaward side. Fall off and the local authority are worried you'd sue. The countryside pasteurised. And as it's a fine Sunday in usually dark January the hordes are out walking. In fact there seem to be more people making their ways from Mumbles to Caswell than there often are on Wind Street in Swansea. The only difference is that today's crowds are all wearing anoraks, wool hats and boots, and not one of them seems drunk.

As a peninsula Gower runs for some fourteen miles due west from here to end out at sea, at my destination, the Tudor far reach of Cardiff's maritime authority, Worm's Head. It's a dry land of gentle undulation. The Welsh, those very few who remain, are confined to the northern half in what's known as the Welsherie, Gower Wallicana. The dominant English with their racial mix of Saxon, Flemish and Norman blood occupy the south, Gower Anglicana. It's Pembrokeshire all over again. Pembrokeshire without quite the same number of prehistorical

cromlechs, stones and tombs. Although Gower is not bereft –
there are at least eight menhirs here including the famous
Arthur Stones at Cefn Bryn.

The sea coast feels like a sea coast and not a watercourse
bank. That's brine out there, its waves thrashing. Any ideas of
the Severn as river have now long gone. I'm on the Welsh equivalent of the well-maintained and similarly railinged paths that
run from Lynmouth out to the Valley of Rocks. If I flew like a
seagull over the water southeast from here that's where I'd
beach.

What many do not realise is that there's an inland Gower of
similar size to the sea-surrounded peninsula I am currently on.
Upland Gower, part of the original Lordship back in Norman
times when this place was a sort of self-regulated March,
stretched back right up to Betws. Bounded by the Llwchwr, the
Aman, the Twrch and the Tawe Upland Gower is a place apart.
In *Real Gower*, Nigel Jenkins will ensure that Gower's disparate
components are fully reunited. He's astute. Make the place as
big as you can, I told him, at an editorial meeting. That way we'll
sell more books.

The walk from Bracelet to Limeslade Bay is short. A splendidly positioned but soon to be closed Coastguard Station
protrudes from the limestone cliff-edge rocks like something
out of James Bond. 'Francis Kilvert came here on holiday in
1872' proclaims the tourist information signboard at the path's
start. Kilvert clearly is a better known name than, say, the poet
Vernon Watkins who spent his life here, or the contemporary
concretist and word spinner J.P. Ward who has kept a house at
Gower's western end for decades.

Over the next headland Rotherslade merges with Langland
and looks almost like the French Riviera in its controlled
overdevelopment. There are abundant cafés. I am passed by a
couple drinking coffee from branded plastic-lidded paper cups
as if this were an inner city on a workday morn. Langland Bay
was once dominated by six hotels of which only one, the Little
Langland, now remains. But what really catches the eye here are
the 1920s beach huts. In a uniform faded green, all closed and
utterly unembellished they await redevelopment. The Council
are offering them on ten-year leases for £10,000 a time. All-

year access, no overnight stop-overs possible, no parking and a question mark over water, electricity and gas. Could be that if you want to sit here all day watching TV then you'll need to bring one that runs on batteries. Will there be council tax on top? Be sure of that.

Behind this throwback to an earlier age stands the structure that actually does dominate the tiny resort. The Merthyr iron master Crawshay's Scottish Baronial-style court with its conical towers and multi-gabled roofs began life in the nineteenth century as the summer residence known as Llan-y-Llan. When the iron trade fell from grace the building became a hotel and then a convalescent home for miners, finally reaching the twenty-first century as a refurbished top-end, gated apartment community known as Langland Bay Manor. You can't just wander up to this place, you need to be invited to get near. From here Langland spreads west with the neatest of golf links at its sea edge and jet-age residences that step back into the cliffs much as they might if this were Lanzarote.

Caswell Bay, over the next headland, doesn't quite have the same style but it tries. The front here is just as manicured as that at Langland but with the addition of both a chip shop and a takeaway. The ice cream shop in expansionist mode advertises itself as operating in Caswell, Milan and London. Outside the surf hut (closed) is pinned a physical fitness readiness question-naire. This offers seven questions which need to get a yes before you can rent a board. Have you had chest pains this month? Fair enough. Have you fallen over as a result of dizziness? Not sure about that.

Out at sea, and from where I'm standing apparently in the heart of the sun, a lone surfer pushes himself back out into the crashing waves. The beach is in deep silhouette and the sands glisten. Not river, this. Not at all.

Caswell has a few big seafront mansions, one of them with a helicopter on the forecourt but is dominated by a 60s-styled block of apartments that reminds me a little of the Balls Road shops back in Cardiff's Llanrumney. A giant glass and metal box with added balconies. It's a style that hasn't really aged that well. But then this place isn't about architecture, it's about sea and sand. Back home I check the webcam, located on the Surf

Side Café. No surfers visible but the waves are still rolling. They roar and crash. What else would they do.

Pwll Du and on into the West

At the western end of Caswell, beyond the lifesaver's hut with its flag and noticeboards, and the carefully placed stone blocks that protect the Redcliffe holiday apartment block, its perfect lawns and its straight-edged paths, is a set of steps half hidden by trees. They lead up through the woods onto the high clifftop where the ridged remains of Redley Cliff Iron Age fort have just about hung on through the centuries. Brandy Cove reads the sign. It's where the untrammelled begins.

If I had an idea of Gower then it was driven by the peninsula's proximity to the suburban sprawl of Swansea. Viewed from Google Earth's perspective you can see it, the grey-brown built-up edging out the green behind Mumbles and Rotherslade and Langland. That smear pushing on, too, towards Caswell. But there it ceases and the wild world returns. The real world. Where the rains fall and rocks erode and green things grow and grow.

Brandy Cove might once have supported smuggling but all that tomfoolery of shoot outs with customs officers and hauling illicit drink up across the pebbles has long gone. So, too, the nineteenth century lead mining that took place just up the valley. Not a trace remains. The Cove is carparkless and hard to get to. Deserted as I cross. Like much of February Gower.

John Updike, who I met once at a conference in what was then Yugoslavia but Serbia now, splashes his suburban novels with news reportage. The headlines of the day come in on car radios, are glimpsed in newspapers left on tables in coffee shops, arrive by bulletin on TVs hung on stands above bars. At the conference he was always seen with his head in a paper, flown in for him by the American Embassy. The Russians read *Pravda* and knew nothing of the real world. Updike would take them on in plenary by arguing the case for information. As writers you need it. He told me in the bar that as a young man starting out I should be like a sponge. Suck up everything, there is nothing that is not useful. Would he like to come to Wales to talk to us about this, I asked. He said he wasn't sure. By which he really meant no. So like a sponge I've been, since then.

The high limestone cliffs of south Gower wind towards Pwll Du. The concrete steps of the Langland/Caswell suburban Gower have been lost and the path is more as it should be, rich again in boot-clogging mud and instep-cracking rock.

Like much of Gower Pwll Du, black pool, is famous for things that are no longer there. Smuggling, quarrying, the shipping of limestone, having a working population of two hundred heavy-drinking men. But when I arrive there's nothing. A high pebble storm beach blocks the Bishopston Stream causing it to lagoon before disappearing seawards. There are two houses hidden by trees. Seawards, the bay, protected by outlying rocks known as the Needles, once offered safe harbour to dozens of small ships – barques, muffies, row boats – but today it's empty.

What they did here in the nineteenth century was a concentrated and very successful version of the trade that much of Gower engaged in. Limestone extraction. And in Pwll Du's case, limestone export and in quantity too. As much of Gower consists of a limestone plateau surmounted by red sandstone summits, finding the rock was no problem. At Pwll Du it was quarried from the cliffs themselves and lowered to the beach where it was broken into transportable blocks. Its destination was Devon – Lynton, Lynmouth, Appledore, Bideford – where the soils were acid. Limestone, burned to powder and spread into the topsoil in a mixture known as marl, improved drainage and brought forth "fine and sweet grass" as George Owen of Kemes wrote in 1603. Agricultural yields significantly increased. In Devon they couldn't get enough. There were few roads. Limestone came over the Estuary by boat. And as burned lime was known to damage the wooden hulls of transporting boats it was carried whole.

Ships would beach at Pwll Du and their seacocks would be opened. On the incoming tide they would fill with seawater. Quarried lime could then be loaded safely. The water in the holds would prevent the rocks from gashing holes in the ship's wooden sides. At low tide the seacocks would be opened again and the holds would drain. The cocks would then be closed, the ships refloated, and off they'd sail, bound for the ports on the Channel's further side.

You could use lime for many things. Lime kilns dot the coast. There's evidence of at least five at Pwll Du. Lime to sweeten fields, to disinfect earth closets, to mix with paint as a defeater of damp, as a medicine against gout and scurvy, as a treatment for ulcers in cattle. Lime the wonder drug. Vanished now, almost totally, in this our chemical future.

The five taverns that serviced the lime trade workers have also vanished. So, too, the boats and the stacks of blasted stone that once lay across the storm beach. Out on the Needles are iron rings once used as moorings. All that remains of two hundred years of trade.

Pwll Du Head is the highest point on the south Gower coast. There's nothing higher until you get to Rhossili. Crossing it passes Graves End, named for the sailors from *The Caesar* which came aground here in 1760 carrying at least sixty-eight handcuffed press ganged men in her hold. Further on are the rocks which wrecked *The Lammershagan, The Lutece, The Mercia, The Parry's Lodge, The Tours, The Dunvegan* and *The SS Fellside*. And before men wrote these things down countless others. George Edmunds tracks them in his shipwreck guide, *The Gower Coast*[7]. In the book they sit in black and white grainy photographs, merchant leviathans from another age. Out at sea there's nothing. The Estuary displays its expected shipless calm. Grey Welsh water matched only by the grey Welsh skies.

Below me are caves. Bone caves. Bacon Hole. Mitchin Hole. A few of Gower's many inaccessible, limb-breaking, sea-protected and not for the faint hearted repositories of the bones of Palaeolithic animals. Straight-tusked elephant, bison, soft-nosed rhinoceros, cave bear, reindeer, wolf and hyena – now viewable at Swansea Museum. In addition they've found traces of Romano-British use in the form of cooking pot fragments, spindle whorls, combs, spoons and bronze broaches. In winter, right now, the caves are full of bats. There are rumours that one along here has cave paintings, a thing denied by protectionist archaeologists. Do I climb down to check? This time, no.

In front of me are the Pennard Burrows. Sand dunes. Last

encountered in civilised manageability at Swansea but here, it seems, spread out again in all their foot-slogging, sliding, view-zapping and unmapable glory. Worth it[8]? I guess.

Hugged Again by the Burrows

With my partner Sue I cross Pennard Common, south of Southgate. If I'd been alone and had the player with me then I would have put on Phil Tanner. 'Fair Phoebe and The Dark Eyed Sailor'. 'The Oyster Girl'. 'Barbara Ellen'. The finger-in-ear scat diddley diddley of Four Hand Reel. Tanner was Gower's pre-eminent recaller of bygone folkways, a singer of unaccompanied traditional songs. He had a cracked and authentic, high and anglicised voice, which he used to tell us how it once was in Gower centuries back. Tanner was born at Llangennith in 1862, descended from a family of Flemish weavers. He lived and sang firmly of Gower Anglicana. English Gower. He recorded several songs for the BBC and these were subsequently issued by Topic Records. His fame came late. He died in 1950. His is a voice of the long past now. It would have fitted these south-facing cliffs, Pobbles Beach below me, Swansea leisure seekers exercising their dogs. As different from Gower Wallica as Cardiff's Splott is from Windsor.

The rush to beat the incoming tide which might have short-ened our coast walk by allowing us passage across the front of the bay ahead's famous three cliffs promontory fails. Too much water, arriving too fast, as tides have done for the entire length of this walk. Pobbles becomes Three Cliff. The headland here, which holds the three limestone landmarks, is officially known as Great Tor. It has to be climbed.

Three Cliff Bay is famous. Blue Flag status. Britain's best beach, reports the BBC. "It gives me the feeling of being hugged", says hyperbolic Katherine Jenkins. We rush the cross-ing knowing the dunes ahead will do their best to zap whatever energy I have left. And they do. Slithering paths, marram grass in clumps, vistas arriving and leaving at the whim of the land, half-buried wooden slats, posts with no signs on them. I rise once and catch sight of golf being played in the green distance and then it's a slip back towards the unwinding and lagooned Pennard Brook as it slowly turns itself into Pennard Pill before emptying into the sea.

Inland, a little up the Pennard Valley are the remains of Pennard Castle. These stand half buried by sand, half falling into the Pill below. As a castle it offers much less on close inspection than it does in romantically glimpsed vista. What's left are crumbling skeletal walls. It's a twelfth century Norman powerbase abandoned to the encroaching sand by the fourteenth. Not everything the conquering warlords built managed to last.

They did better at Penrice Castle, a few miles to the west. The Normans spent much building time on Gower. Penrice is the peninsula's largest and the structure with the most to see. As it's on private land access is restricted. At the great house today, a neo-classical villa built in the 1770s on ground below the Castle, you can get married. I got that information out of the estate's website[9]. Getting married on Gower turns out to be a feature. But more of that anon.

Atop Great Tor, eventually, the sky darkens and threatens rain. It's been cold enough on this whole Gower journey so far to wear a knitted cap and gloves. But the rain holds back. Great Tor holds the half-buried remains of a medieval church, ring work from a onetime Norman castle and Pen y Grug, what's left of a Neolithic burial chamber. The only structure that shows much sign of managing the future is a restored double-fronted lime kiln, itself now well into the process of becoming besanded. Dunes do that, right along this coast.

The view due west of Great Tor is magnificent. A great two mile sweep of sand, arcing from Little Tor to Oxwich Point. Here Nicholaston Burrows merge into those of Oxwich. A significant stretch of Gower sanding its way inland, the dunes advancing towards the Oxwich marshes and on to the ridged backbone of Cefn Bryn.

Apart from a brief detour inland to cross Nicholaston Pill by the footbridge, we get two miles of flat beach walking with no need for any further energy-draining engagement with the mighty dunes. The land here is National Nature Reserve and rich in pyramid orchid, bloody cranesbill, rare lichen and fluttering skylark. But my legs won't hack it. We follow the wave edge instead.

Sea fishermen, wrapped in waterproofs and waders, sit by their rod-holding tripods. Each has his own fishing patch. They are spaced out, fifty metres apart, all the way from Nicholaston to Oxwich. Conversations are shouted, catches slow.

At the water's edge three men work the sand with rakes, scooping their catches of abundant cockles into buckets. "There didn't used to be such a quantity here," one of them tells me. "We all thought pollution had seen the cockle off. But now they're back. Here anyway. The trick is to steep them overnight in clean water with salt added to remove the sand. Then steam until the shells all open." Free food and a million times better than the version that comes in jars.

Sue, ever the hunter gatherer, can't contain herself. From the Oxwich Bay Hotel, where we've rented a tiny but very well equipped room called Great Tor[10], she rushes to the waterline equipped with a plastic bag and the snow scraper from the car. She returns half an hour later with a borrowed child's bucket filled to the brim with beshelled cockles and a salt cellar lifted from the dining room below. The cockles go into the bathroom sink from where they seep their sand into the hotel's drains. She sprinkles them with Saxa from the lifted cellar. Tomorrow she'll be back at the waterline for more.

In the bar the dune sand is diligently removed by staff using vacuums. Here hugging is regularly practised by those attending one of the hotel's many wedding fayres or, more likely, to actually get married. I ask them at reception how many they do. One hundred and fifty a year. Hell. That's three a week. The hotel has a wedding-friendly manicured lawn and set of well-clipped bushes. There are ribbons tied to door knobs and white silk covers over the backs of chairs. There's a soft-lit marquee nestled among the trees. Hugging bliss. Roll on.

Headlands

Inland at The King Arthur in Reynoldston the Gower obsession with weddings has peaked. Offers to provide me with places I can get married in have been following me around ever since I picked up a leaflet advertising the lighthouse as a venue back at Nash Point last summer. Pubs, community centres, halls, great houses, council offices, exhibition facilities and hotels brushed passed on the route west have all been fulsome in their advertising of forthcoming wedding fayres. This is never fairs I notice, but always fayres. Fayres sound traditional and reassuringly olde.

What is it about the south Wales coast and Gower in particular that makes it attractive to wham bam ceremonies involving long white dresses, blokes in shirts with weird collars and guests looking uncomfortable in big hats, new suits and shiny shoes? The hospitality, the scenery, the drizzle? At Oxwich they were going for it with sea views. Here, at the solid, expansive and ancient-looking King Arthur it is clearly the rugged upland rocks. There's a sign-boarded parking space *Reserved For The Registrar* and a wedding reception in action round the back. "You wouldn't think there were one hundred and twenty guests here all enjoying themselves, would you?" says the barmaid. I would not.

We're in the body of the pub where they serve sizzling steaks and real ale. Kingsley Amis would have felt entirely at home. In fact this deep Gower pub could well be the model for the Bible and Crown, celebrated in the one-time Angry Young Man's 1986 Booker Prize winner, *The Old Devils*. In this masterpiece Amis reinvents Gower as the island of Courcey linked to the mainland, rather like Barry, by a causeway. It is a place, in Amis's depiction, that might have a deep-seated ambivalence about being part of Wales but is Wales just the same. "There was no obvious giveaway, like road signs in two languages or closed-down factories, but something was there, an extra greenness in the grass, a softness in the light, something that was very like England and yet not England at all, more a matter of feeling than seeing but not just a feeling, something run-down and sad but simpler and freer than England all the same." In the King Arthur the past merges softly with the present. There's a sign near the gents that advertises a forthcoming Wedding Fayre as if it were something the locals regularly enjoyed, like a quiz or a karaoke night. Maybe that's what they do round here, on long winter nights, they attend weddings. On the open fire logs burn.

On the table next to us a middle-aged red-faced man in an open necked shirt cuts into his sirloin. Beside him are eleven open bottles of wine. He's working his way slowly along the row. Fork of food, gulp of wine. He's either an alcoholic or the father of the bride here to check out the venue. After a while he's joined by a black-suited female carrying a clipboard. She smiles enthusiastically. A King Arthur wedding planner. The couple sitting on our opposite side, up to now enjoying a night of mutual eye-gazing and ice-bucketed champagne, have also been joined by a clipboard-wielding suited official. There are smiles everywhere. Excited talk of dress fittings, horse drawn carriages and cake delivery drift across the bar. Amis would have had apoplexy. Outside the Gower night twinkles full of stars.

The King Arthur is named after the somewhat damaged but still impressive Neolithic burial chamber of Maen Ceti which sits in the centre of the nearby Cefn Bryn ridge. This, in English, is Arthur's Stone. It's so large that, according to the Welsh Triads, it is one of the three mighty achievements of the Isle of Britain. How it was erected and how the top of it subsequently became smashed are lost to history. And as you might expect with such an ancient structure it's surrounded by myth and legend. It's a time portal, a door into the otherworld, a centre of druid worship, part of giant astronomical calendar, a marker for arriving saucers, or even a stone hurled there from the shoe of Arthur when he crossed the Burry Estuary. Giant King Arthur, man of legend, hovering still.

Back on the Oxwich coast, Arthur recedes. This is a peninsula now of headlands and jagged cliff, of waves that roll and land that fragments. St Illtyd's Church hugs the rocks that face back across two miles of sand towards Great Tor. St Illtyd who founded the great centre of learning that was once Llantwit Major, was here as well. Already the land seawards has crumbled taking with it the rectory and the rector's garden. On the storm beach great boulders stand stranded. The tiny whitewashed church in its picturesque splendour might appear a creation of Gower's new wedding industry but it predates that by almost fifteen centuries.

The font inside is a hunk of barely carved rock allegedly put there by St Illtyd himself. The walls betray their Norman origin.

In the churchyard are gravestones marking death by misadventure, by drowning, by war. One is in Irish, marking the final resting place of Patrick Russell, lost when the barque the *Tridonia* went down in 1916. Next to it is the grave of the unknown sailor, lost at sea in the same year but now known only to god.

Oxwich Point is extensively wooded with the ramparts of the expected Iron Age fort sitting out on its southern most extremity. Beyond, the path turns back along National Trust land, green and clear, running all the way to the sands at Slade with the lifeboat station and village of Horton and the sands of Port Eynon beyond. A clear run now to Rhossili with Worm's Head, the end of this long psychogeographic ramble of mine, almost within reach.

But no. At Slade there's been a landslip with the coastal path now dumped onto the beach thirty metres below. Negotiations with the landowner who has a field of sheep at this place have not yet been completed. There's a temporary diversion in place which takes travellers miles inland. We decide to cut my losses and inspect Oxwich Castle[11] instead. This is a des res dream home of the Tudor period, according to CADW's promotional material, and it is atop the ridge twenty minutes ahead.

As it turns out this side visit is worth the effort. Sir Rice Mansel, who built the present structure in the sixteenth century on the site of an earlier stronghold, has his coat of arms over the entrance. Inside is the soaring three-storey wall of the East Range looking like an Elizabethan version of a Glasgow tenement, the still roofed South range and an extensive assortment of towers, halls, fake battlements, basements and galleries. For a wrecked castle, even one that's more a fortified manor house than a Norman war machine, there's an impressive quantity still in place.

Outside are the whitewashed remains on the largest dovecote I've yet seen, and Gower has a few. The front has crumbled revealing a mesh of inner nesting places looking like a medieval version of something the artist Richard Long might have created. Pigeons, as all year round meat, were a staple of the well-to-do. Not a bird in sight today, however. In the empty car park where I might have expected to see a notice offering the castle as a wedding venue there's nothing bar a small chalked notice informing visitors that the site is closed for winter. You view from a distance. Or you climb the fence and take a tour for free. I'm not saying which I did.

Salt and Rock

Port Eynon bears all the marks of an over-trafficked holiday destination. Car parks have stern warnings against overstayers. There are huts in which attendants and their money-bags can cluster at every gate. The roads have never-ending double yellow lines. Everywhere you look there are notices warning cars not to stop. In the centre there are chip shops and cafés, stalls that might, in season, sell surfboards, beachwear and ice cream, and places that look like they might retail sunbeds and inflatable crocodiles. But this being February everything is closed. Unmanned. Including, unfortunately, the Smuggler's Haunt, an enterprise that looked promisingly like a pub[12] right down by the bus stop and mini roundabout at the seafront.

Port Eynon is named after the eleventh century Prince Eynon, whose castle was here somewhere but has long been lost. The village rose to prominence as a fishing haven – in the tiny churchyard there's a statue of a man in sou'wester and waterproofs commemorating those lost at sea. It was also, like many places in south Gower, a port which exported limestone. It sits at the western end of another glorious mile-wide arcing curve of sand. Horton is opposite. Below the car parks, caravans, camping grounds and the well maintained sea-touch-ing youth hostel are the roofless walls of a structure that once stood among cottages inland from Sedgers Bank. The cottages are long gone. Sea erosion has seen them off. The tide now pushes at the structure's edge. This is the famous Salt House (rems of). History in the sun.

A primary school are visiting when we pass. The male teacher is interrogating his assembled flock. They are neat in their uniforms and have pens, pads and lunch packs strung about them. "Can anyone think of anything round here that might have a lot of salt in it?" he asks. There's a silence and then a tentative hand goes up. "Fish, sir?" "Almost. Try again." "The sea." "Yes, the sea. Full of salt. They let it in here." He points down to the remains of a large enclosed reservoir. "And then they heated it until the water all boiled away and all that was left was its salt. Valuable, salt, back then in the mid-sixteenth century when they had no fridges and needed the stuff to preserve their food. Salted fish. Anyone tried that?" No.

The Salt House began life as the base for pirate and privateer John Lucas's smuggling enterprise. Port Eynon was as good a base as any to be used for the import of duty-free tobacco and taxless drink. Customs Officers controlled from distant Cardiff devoted a huge amount of effort to bring Lucas down, but failed. There were rumours of secret caches and tunnels which ran underground from the Salt House to the town. All unfounded, as it turns out. In 1986, Glamorgan Gwent archeological Society investigated and found no evidence. They looked in the wrong places, was a local response.

Lucas shifted from smuggling to salt extraction when the excise men eventually got the upper hand. His operation, and that of his descendants, ran until the mid-seventeenth century when the building's use changed to that of accommodation for quarrymen working the lime on the cliffs behind. The structure fell into disrepair in 1900 when limestone extraction ceased as an economic enterprise. The ever-encroaching sea then brought most of the buildings down. Restoration and signboarding has been carried out by the local council working with CADW. A local landmark saved.

The path across Port Eynon Point runs up through the scree-like shale of quarry waste to emerge on a wind-swept, gorse-covered southern extremity. This is the nearest to the Devon coast Gower gets and the wind is blowing. On the western side of the headland, beyond the quarries, on National Trust coastland is the famous Culver Hole. No dis or rems on the map for this one.

The high cliff edge here gives not a clue as to what lies beneath. Only the marks on the map betray evidence of some viewable structure. I discover what looks like a sheep run down the face and onto the sea-dashed rocks below. The sea roars here, completely non-riverine and full of white-topped waves.

About time the Severn showed some salty teeth.

Culver Hole is a man-made structure of mortared limestone blocks. They are walled across the narrow gulley of a pretty inaccessible inlet in Port Eynon Point's cliff face. It can only be safely accessed at low tide by coming at it across the rocks from the sea. But I'm not doing that. I'm on the sheep track, or rather, on the razor sharp rocks that break like fractured glass at the track's end. I'm wearing leather gloves to prevent the further slicing of my hands. I'm no real rock scrambler but the Culver experience is one I am determined to have.

The structure's frontage is impressive. There are openings for round and for square windows, and a doorway at beach pebble level. Inside are the remains of a staircase and internal rooms. Nobody is really sure who built it or why it's here. Smuggler's haunt? But pretty far from any accessible quay or landing point. Castle? Sea defence against raiders? There's talk of another secret passage that runs from here to Eynon's Castle but no one has yet found either. Could the Castle have been built on the headland above with Culver Hole as a sort of medieval sea-washed basement? Unlikely given the total lack of any evidence to support this theory on the clifftop above.

Most speculators have settled on the notion that this is a dovecote similar to the one at Oxwich Castle. Pigeons would be kept here for their meat. But I can't imagine that fat slow grey bird being up to flying in and out in the face of the prevailing westerlies. Maybe it's another time portal left here by the Martians and disguised as a castle? Or a hermit's cell with many floors, a sort of early religious pod hotel? I take a few photos and then, clinging hard to the vertiginous rocks, edge my way back.

Out to sea are the Helwick Sands where the Helwick Lightship was once stationed to warn off shipping. That lightship is now preserved as a floating Christian Centre and moored in Cardiff's Roath Dock. The banks it once marked are being extensively dredged, and with the usual consequence of sand also disappearing from local beaches. There is no formal admission on the part of the scientific community or the dredging operators that there is a connection between these two events. Time will tell, is the official line. And in a sandless, barren future Gower, so it will.

The name Helwick comes from the Norse. More Viking evidence. Helwick: the hidden, the covered up. The place where Eynon's castles stood when the land ran out this far. Graveyard for mammoths. Site of a great drowned forest. Out among the waves the bell of the East Helwick Buoy clangs and clangs.

Paviland

West of Overton, the Gower coast gives up any pretension it might have had to being day walk territory for city leisure seekers. Instead it takes on the status of full-blown National Geographic sea cliff littoral replete with fractured anticlines, sea caves and churning waves. Gower the great. Gower full of power. Gower at the edge of the world. The track, now marked with its new Wales Coast Path[13] badges, flows on, empty of users, save us, bright in the morning sun.

There's a wrecked lime kiln at the edge of the Longhole Cave Nature Reserve where the red fescue grass thickens up around our boots. Feral Rock Dove and Herring Gull nest on the cliff ledges. The famous cave itself is ten metres long, ancient and unspectacular. Excavation has revealed Palaeolithic flint tools and traces of Pleistocene fauna. There are rumours that a cave near here has Stone Age wall paintings, stick men fighting mammoths, hyenas leaping, spears showering through the air. Could it be Long Hole? Who knows. I've no torch with me to find out.

To the west the limestone plateau is crossed by ridge and gully in profusion. Blackhole Gut, Ram Grove, Horse Cliff, The Knave. This is Pomland, Monksland, Panylond, Paviland. Fields once part of the monastic grange of Paviland and owned by Neath Abbey. There is evidence of both prehistoric flint scrapers and medieval boundary markers. In the sun it's all green and empty. In the prevailing driven rain it would be as bleak as an upland moor.

The grange itself has now vanished with nothing left bar a few earth banks next to the seventeenth-century farm buildings of the present day Paviland Manor. Medieval fields have been amalgamated to suit contemporary agricultural needs, but for the most part this is still an unchanged and ancient landscape. Paviland we're almost on you. The Welsh past as far back as it goes.

These sites are much celebrated by ley line followers. This is a place for aficionados of the antediluvian, the ancient King Arthur Warband, and the operators of the Megalithic Portal, guide to the universe of henges, funerary roads, standing stones and places of unaccountable power. The ground should shake but I guess it won't.

Paviland's celebrated cave I last glimpsed in a film on the history of Wales[14] written by Jon Gower and starring the newsreader Huw Edwards, who was shown striding up from the sea to confront this four metre cleft high on the rocks at Foxhole Slade. Edwards spoke of the remains found here, The Red Lady of Paviland, as being the oldest Welshman, of how the red ochre ceremonially spread on the body still stains the bones red today, thirty thousand years on.

This is actually Goat's Hole but calling it Paviland after the nearest habitation somehow adds authority. Its eighteen metre depth is accessible for two and half hours either side of low tide. You need to clamber the length of the Foxhole Gully to access the cave from the sea. Coming down from above will bring death unless you know how to rock climb. The bones found here in 1823 by the early geologist and clergyman Dr William Buckland were incorrectly identified by him as female, Biblically dated from the time of the flood, and declared as belonging to a prostitute or a witch, a woman of low morals. The British Camp above – the Paviland Iron Age promontory fort – would, two thousand years back, have been occupied by Romano British soldiers. They needed sport. The Red Lady provided.

Buckland was actually looking for animal bones. The fact that those he discovered were human came as a considerable surprise. The teeth of leopards, and mammoth jaw bones found buried were evidence of bodies swept here by Noah's flood. Biblical-age humans did not die like that.

Buckland's account of the finding, *Reliquae Diluvianae*[15], has an illustration of his excavations at Goat's Hole. Workmen inside clamber the cave's height using ladders. Access is from above using ropes. Buckland stands by and directs.

Contemporary bone analysis has shown that the Red Lady's body was left here around thirty thousand years ago at a time when the River Severn was no more than a stream snaking along the bottom of a valley and the sea's ocean was sixty miles distant. As bones go the Red Lady's remains are not much. One leg, no skull. Devoured over time by hyenas or bears. They went to the Natural History Museum in Oxford where they were declared too valuable for open display and kept below in a box. Replicas adorned the display case. Today they've been repatriated and are in the hands of the National Museum of Wales. Our own Elgin Marbles. Source of our people. Much older than England's.

We struggle to see where they were found. Tide is high. The rocky cleft full of onshore wind. Access impossible. I try for that sense of something that ancient places should have, a feeling of otherness in my feet, palpable age in my rock-grasping hands. Behind my eyes there should be something. But there's not. Red Lady moved on.

On towards Worm's Head the frequency of Iron Age fort increases. This place where the Gower finishes was easy to protect. Caves proliferate. Deborah's Hole. Twll-y-Flwyddyn. Red Chamber. Places where animal bones have gathered.

The inlets widen. Beyond Thurba Head are the sands of Mewslade and Fall Bays. Kayaks beached, figures in wet suits clambering the rocks. Then I can see it. Offshore now, an island again. The green tops and bent backs of the Worm. The end of Gower. Reach it. Touch the Coast Guard Lookout hut. Too late now to cross. Come back another day.

Wurm

The village of Rhossili faces down its tourists in better style than Port Eynon. There are fewer signs saying don't, and a vague layering of hippiedom brought on by the presence of surfers, Tibetan flags, and cafés selling black-eyed bean and mango burgers. The dunes flow north where the early Rhossili village with its ancient church once stood. That was before, much like

Kenfig, it was besanded and had to be moved out of nature's reach and rebuilt on the rocky headland.

The replacement church, St Mary's, is still old enough to have a square tower and a Norman doorway complete with scratch sundial. Inside is a memorial to Petty Officer Edgar Evans who died with captain Scott in the Antarctic. The wall on the south side is letting in damp and the paintwork is flaking badly. "We're having it redecorated today," the woman tidying the hymnbooks tells me. There's a ruckus beyond her as a great bearded blind man, white stick in action and carrying a gallon container of white distemper, heaves into view. This is certainly a new approach to painting. But actually it's the rector helping prepare the ground. The Rev Cannon Joe Griffin looks after a run of churches in the Parish of South West Gower. Like everywhere congregations have dwindled. They're lucky to get six locals here. How much longer can they continue? Dumping the paint the rector turns to help bring in a heavyweight decorators table. St Mary's will be bright again soon. For a time.

South is the Worm. The whole walk has been pointing at this. Here it is sodden with rain and shrouded by fog. Wurm. The serpent's head, the dragon. The snake of land bending out from the end of Gower like the small remaining finger of a severely damaged hand. It's an iconic place, a world's end, a far westerly reach where the land finally succumbs to the endless sea rising and the blasting winds.

I'd set my mental sights on it more than a year ago and now here it is. A phantom in the Welsh mists, a drizzle-drenched place full of air and grass. Just like most of Wales actually is. Worm's Head is what remains of far Gower now that the tides have risen and the estuarial forests have all been drowned. It's a series of three westerly islands, connected to the land by a bridge which emerges at low tide, a place that faces the prevailing weather and is eroding fast.

Access is supposed to be easy. On his website *Weatherman Walking*, Derek Brockway describes it as a long and winding trail through an area of outstanding natural beauty. Nothing about mist or the sound the storm makes. On the clifftop the Coastwatch Guards sit in their heated hut watching what they can through binoculars. They tell me later that their biggest problem is visitors from countries with no coastline or from places like the Mediterranean where tidal rise and fall is slight. Here on the Estuary the process is extensive and dramatic. Access to the Worm is by crossing a causeway that only emerges from the waters for two and half hours each side of low tide. If you've no experience of a real tide then the Severn's ferocity can surprise you. People get stranded and they have to be taken off. How? Lifeboat from Horton or, in extreme cases, by helicopter. Do you pay? Not yet.

My first attempt got me soaked, my glasses misted to blindness, and seawater in my boots. I reached only the end of Inner Head. The causeway was like a place bombed, pool and razor ridge and a wreckage of rock, pebble and heaped mussel shell with no discernible path. Most of the time this is the seabed, I had to remind myself. What did I expect? I gave up when I could no longer see where I was going. The wise thing, the Coastwatch Guard told me. Do it again when the weather is better.

And, by luck and co-incidence, it is only three days later when the National Trust, whose land this actually is, organise a guided access. Walk to the end, lunch on the top. £4 a go. Give your money to Ranger Al who checks all twenty-two of us off. Walk leader Chief Warden Sian Musgrave who, it seems, was Weatherman Derek's guide back in 2008, gives us the safety procedure talk and checks our boots. A fat woman wearing tracksuit bottoms strengthened with gardener's strap-on knee pads is decked out in sandals. You'll struggle in those, she's told.

The whole stretch of Rhossili Beach from Kitchen Corner to Llangennith Burrows runs off to the north. Halfway out, below Gower's highest point, Rhossili Down with its cairns and burial mounds, stands the white painted Old Rectory. Built in isolation halfway between two parishes, this is now the National Trust's most desired holiday rental. The most popular in their entire portfolio. Above it a hang glider soars.

We walk the mile from the ice cream-selling visitor centre to the Rhossili headland. To our left is the Vile, the remains of medieval strip farms, now rented to tenants. To the right is Old Castle, a well-defined Iron Age hillfort, hummocked and grassed, hanging on in its twenty-first century future.

On the cliffs overhanging the sea below are the remains of further limestone extraction, the cuts and terraces of small quarry work. At the sea's edge are the ledges known as the flot quas, the floating quays, from which the quarried stone was loaded to boat. Port work. The furthest west Cardiff ever went.

In a group and with a guide, the sea passage is easy. En route we pass ill-clad visitors making their way in deck shoes and heels, carrying handbags and plastic carriers filled with crisps and coke. The Inner Head looks like a green sharks fin. It's been farmed for centuries. Corn. Potatoes. And sheep grazed too. It's that now. The sheep will stay until March when they'll be herded back across the rocky causeway.

As we scramble up the path above the Inner Head's storm beach a yellow helicopter clatters in. Already someone has fallen and broken a bone. The Worm is a dramatic place.

The crossing onwards over Low Neck to Middle Head is far from simple. The rocks are wild and crevasse-filled. It's a fifteen minute two hands and two feet scramble. What is a scramble? Alfred Wainwright, the great Lakeland rambler, had it that a scramble was when walking the knee ended up actually making contact with the shoulder. On Low Neck that certainly happens. Below, the sea has receded exposing a great flat reef of seaweed-covered rock. The rollers to the west are white and huge.

Halfway across Middle Head itself is a great stone arch, carved by the eroding sea. Devil's Bridge. Five foot wide and an easy stroll. Dylan Thomas was stranded here once. Came out with a bottle of pop and a pack of sandwiches, forgot himself and had to wait for the tides to cycle themselves in and back out. "I stayed on that Worm from dusk to midnight, sitting on that top grass, frightened to go further in because of the rats and because of things I am ashamed to be frightened of. Then the tips of the reef began to poke out of the water and, perilously, I climbed along them to the shore." Like all good writers he got something out of it. His short story 'Who Do You Wish Was With Us'[16] is set on the Worm.

To the west of Middle Head is the end. My target destination. The far westerly extremity of all this coast walking, this folded bicycling, this Port of Cardiff artifice which I set myself more than a year ago. This is the Worm's Outer Head, where it all finishes. From here you can see Ireland or the Azores or the world curving out there on the horizon. It's a thrilling clamber. More causeway and the blow hole, and then the scramble up to the high grass-covered head itself. Access to this spot beyond March is banned for the sake of nesting birds. But it's still Feb and I'm up there, my famous vertigo bottled, chicken pastie in hand, smiling like a fool.

At the far end of the Worm is a great sea cave, bones have been found there and salvaged to Swansea Museum. As the sea-driven air rushes in, the island's blow hole sounds. We all gather around it to listen and feel the air rushing up from below. Walkers standing over it do Marilyn Monroe impersonations, the flaps of their anoraks sailing up in the air. John Leland (1503-1552) reports that the sea cave once had a great wooden door at its end, one with nails in it[17]. A passage beyond led to inland. But like most Gower secret passages nothing has ever been found.

What now? Watch west for seals, ships, storms. See none of those things. Tell the crowd I've come with why I'm here. We are a shrunken group, a third of our number have given up part way, stayed on Inner Head to avoid the stress, eaten their sandwiches on Middle Head to avoid the heights, decided the rocks were too much for ancient legs. I could do a dance, wave my hands. Sing the victory song hey hey hey hey. But don't.

Inland there's mist now over Rhossili Down, a line of grey-white cutting land from air. But there's no mist here. I take another bite of pastie. Just the stuff.

England: The Tidal Limits to Lynmouth

The Tidal Limits

On the road to Maisemore north of Gloucester, I pass at least one flag of St George, the famous red cross on a white background, flying sideways from a scaffolding poll. Out here I am more than thirty miles from the Gloucester/Monmouth border where the Wye enters the Severn at Chepstow. From there it's a further twenty-five miles back to the real Welsh border at St Mellons where the old power-base Glamorgan begins. I'm searching for the tidal limit, the place where the salt of the Severn Sea finally finishes. There's a place up here on the serpent river where the twice-daily ebb and flow finally gives up. It's reputedly at Maisemore. Part of Wales once, when Wales, like Poland before it, was empire large, before the conquerors got working with their armies and their chieftains and their lords, slicing off the bits they had decided to own.

But there's no sign of Wales now, even if you discount the carefully graded anthracite sold at Young's coal wharf and the White Hart, which offers beer, curry and chips just like they do in Port Talbot. If ever a land knew how to retreat into virtual invisibility then Wales is it. We've lost the courage to be what we are. We let the English dominate our border towns with their gift shops selling Welsh fudge made in Cirencester and postcards printed in Manchester. The greater trader seeps, the nation of shopkeepers manages ours with style and skill. The Welsh accent thins as it heads east. By the time it has reached the border it has lost most of its nasal distinctiveness. Its vowels begin to bend as if they came from the heart of England's west. I've met people, many of them, declaring their firm Welsh nationality in voices that sound as if they'd be more at home in Tewkesbury than in Pwllmeyric, Portskewett or Llanfihangel Rogiet, which is where they were born. That's what happens at places where lines have been drawn in the landscape, differences melt and merge, atoms leach over by osmosis.

Heading upstream towards Gloucester the River Severn engages in that thing that rivers love to do. It starts to make serpentine, bending and winding loops. It is as if, south of Chepstow, lies an estuarine territory where salt and sea make the waters behave. While here, up river, with no great guiding hand in place, the river can do what it likes. And it does. It bends and it hoops. It meanders like Duchamp's Standard Stoppages over its floodplain of water meadow and sediment. It builds its banks, makes them strong, grasses them over and then, as if by whim, begins to wear them down again. The road, the A48, sights water at Lydney, at Newham and again at Minsterworth as the river bends towards and then away from it. Still tidal. Still subject to twice-daily gushes of inward bound saltwater.

Boats sail here, sea ships, traders. A few still do. They come up channel from the south Wales ports, from Bristol, from Ireland, from France, from beyond. The larger the draft, the heavier the ship, the greater the difficulty. Only at spring tides could many of the early trading vessels penetrate as far as I am now just beyond Minsterworth, where Jon Manchip White, writer and direct descendant of the Cardiff martyr Rawlins White, once lived at the Court, just south of Gloucester itself.

Near here, where the remains of Llanthony Priory still stand on the edge of a trading estate full of half-demolished concrete, dumped hard core and scrap metal resellers, the River Severn divides. Rivers don't normally do this. But the Severn has. It splits into two, bends and turns, and then re-joins as one river again. On the map it looks like an eyelet of water, the river breaking to flow around an island of land. As if there was something special about this place. Locals will tell you that there this. This is Alney, and other than those in middle of road, the only island in Gloucester.

Here the Severn gets new names. The Severn Western and Severn Eastern Channels. There's a weir on the east just outside Gloucester's old docks. Here the eastern tide stops. On the west it runs a little further, as far as the weir at Maisemore. That's it, then, the tidal limit. That's where I'm heading. North of Gloucester the Severn has no further claim to be sea. Up there it's just river.

The docks at Gloucester are almost a surreal enterprise. Here is an inland refuge for tall-masted ships that down the centuries have delivered grain, timber and wine to a place most imagine to be utterly coastless. The town's river quay has received seagoing traders since at least Elizabethan times. The docks were a development of the canal age and constructed two hundred years ago when the Severn's resistance to sea-going vessels was partially alleviated by the digging of what eventually became the Gloucester and Sharpness Canal. They lie off the Severn's Eastern Channel. Old photographs show them gloriously full of tall-rigged sailing ships, reminiscent of similar shots of mast-stuffed docks at Bristol and at Cardiff. Today they've been restored for leisure use. The old brick warehouses have been uniformly refurbished. The dock basins are filled with pleasure craft, rentable narrow boats and barges, old steam dredgers, barques and lighters restored as museum pieces. Not that past enterprise has entirely vanished. Ship repair continues in the dry docks. There's a flourishing bespoke narrow boat building operation and Tommi Nielsen's traditional rigging repair has many customers.

Today the docks are full of ice. That it's still mid-winter I need not remind myself, dressed as I am in thick gloves and heavy coat, woollen hat pulled over my shaved head. The museum is great if you have kids and love canals. It has more barge boat history than I really need and is oversupplied with 'how many boats can you find in this picture' instruction panels and games you play with floating bits of coloured wood. I don't try my hand at seeing how heavy a sack of corn would be to lift. Nor what I'd look like if I donned bargeman's clothes. In the café, full of the retired dozing over their tea and baked potatoes, Radio One blares and crackles. Outside the gulls sit mid-basin, walked there on water. A woman returns to her narrow boat by bike, Tesco carriers on the handlebars. There's smoke snaking from the boat's on-board chimney. On deck are potted plants and painted kettles. Waterway domesticity still lives.

The path to the river's southern divide at Lower Parting is barred by the gates to a scrap metal trader's yard. I try instead for the northern split at Upper Parting. Access is over a gate up beyond the White Hart and across the Ledbury Hunt's muddy field above the weir. Here the great river can be seen opening its arms. A road sign on the opposite bank warns boatmen that the western channel is no longer navigable and that Gloucester Lock is three miles on, bear left. Call up to let them know you are coming. There's a phone number or you can get them on VHF Channel 74.

Why am I here? I suppose I needed to see where this river's estuarial existence ended and where the tides ceased their bearing on how the river flowed. If I've been asking right along this coast, as I have, how do you view this water? Is it a river or is it a sea? There's only one answer possible standing here.

All the way up I've passed the hams, the tidefields, the water meadows – Arlingham, Newnham, Minsterworth Ham, Mean Ham. The land I now stand on at Upper Parting is Maisemore Ham. Maes Mawr Ham. In English that's Big Field Tidefield. Just like the River Avon is Afon Avon. Translated back into English that's River River. So much water they named it twice.

Wipe the mud from my boots, pull up my jacket collar, head on back.

The English Border

The whole time I've been walking, getting myself slowly from Chepstow to the Port of Cardiff's Tudor extremity at the end of Gower, I have had a constant companion. Visible most days, sometimes crisply, sometimes clouded and fuzzed by fog. On grey days the coast on the far side of the water seems too distant to bother with. But when the sun hits it can be almost touchable. Buildings can be seen with the naked eye. Power stations, farmhouses, towns and towers. Boats in the harbours. Out there where Gloucestershire rolls through Somerset and on into Devon lies south Wales' twin. A place that is not London metropolitan, not a power base, is sporadically industrialised, has a population that speaks with accents that make you laugh. It's a land that is constantly bracketed with Wales, as one economic, political or resource-using place. Wales and the West. Source, in part, of the buzz-saw accents of Cardiffians. The west of Britain. The UK beyond the east. It should happily hang together. Somerset doesn't mind. Nor the Devonians. But ask them in the industrial valleys and in the Swansea hinterland and you'll find that people rather value their political and social independence. Wales, the nation. The west country, a region of somewhere else.

I'm standing near the border, where it runs below the water. I'm in South Gloucestershire now, in the place that used to be Avon, looking out over the Severn at Wales beyond. It's only barely Wales, it has to be said, that part that I can see. Buildings clustering around Portskewett, holding onto the coast at Sudbrook, wavering into England the wrong side of the Wye. I thought I might detect a sense here of a boundary that had to be crossed. A psychic mark. A touch of something in the air. Where England ends and Wales begins. But I don't.

If anything the border is not actually to the north before me, but is the line of coast running away west towards the Atlantic sea following the direction of the Severn's flow. I'm on the land between the two bridges. The English levels where the drainage reens have become rhines although, largely, the language remains the same. The Old Splott Rhine lies a few hundred metres back. More Splotlands, these, but lacking the Cardiff district's working-class touch. This is not Wales, the place I've just come from, nothing like. The fields behind me are bigger, the sweep of the levels smoother, the grass-topped earth bund acting as sea defence stronger, somehow more definite.

This is England, and this part of it was never really anything else. Even at the time of Wales's mythic giganticness, when the country ran out over land now lost to sea towards Man and to Ireland and deep into the Atlantic swells. When there were land bridges that crossed to Ynys Echni[1] and the great Sabrina itself was a mere dribble meandering in its centre channel bed. Back then swathes of what are now the Marches and the English Midlands were part of Wales. There were Cymric claims to lands in Scotland and to the hill line that ran the length of Ynys Prydein. Even then this place was still England, or the land that eventually became that place.

The river is in flood, a slowly moving mass of brown water much wider than the levels I'm standing on. It's no threat in its current state but a rise of a few metres would bring it to me, swamping the ground. I can sense its strength out there. Waiting.

The country I am now opposite is the one imagined by everyone who doesn't live there to be permanently swathed in moving mists. It's a land of fantasy, where Arthur Machen created the phantasmagorical Avallaunius, where women become birds and men turn into rocks, the trees are at war, giants stalk the land, warriors mutate into grains of corn and the valleys all drown under the tumble of water. A place that many revere as the true heartland of Britain while others imagine to still be full of bearded throwbacks desperately trying the get their outmoded ley lines to function and their dope pipes to light.

There's nothing quite like it where I stand right now. Although I need to remember, when making these great sweeping statements, that not that many English miles west of here stands Glastonbury Tor, the grave of Arthur, and all that that means.

This is actually birder territory between the two Severn Crossings, the old bridge and the new. South Gloucestershire is establishing a new wetland reserve at Pilning for the Dunlin, Redshank, Sandpipers, Turnstones and Oystercatchers. There's a half-constructed observation and interpretation centre on stilts and extensive landworks scraping away acres of field that will be shortly flooded. The bund-top coast path, part of the Severn Way Path[2], will run behind the wall so that the shadows of walkers will not unsettle the nesters.

I'd arrived at Aust, historically the site of the first services on the M4 heading east from Wales. When the original Severn Bridge opened in 1966 the services moved from their original purpose as a comfort stop for drivers to become a fully-fledged destination. Scores of trippers in their faux sheepskin car coats and wearing string-backed gloves came for tea and a look at the Severnside view. Scores more sat with thermos flasks and paste sandwiches in the car park. The drive here from Cardiff and from Newport was thrilling. My father, a regular, brought me once. We stood gazing at the gulls. I couldn't really see the attraction.

Aust Services are gone now. Like the ferry the bridge itself replaced. Instead there are the much smaller Severn View Services. All day breakfast but no view. There's a sign in the car park threatening car parkers with a charge if they stay for more than two hours. Another avenue of joy destroyed.

A couple of kilometres away across Northwich Wrath the second crossing launches itself on a verdant translucent frame that hangs in space, a wired road straddling a run of concrete caissons that take measured steps across the flat brown river. Clustered around its base are the villages of Pilning, Redwick (an ancient English echo of its Welsh brother just across the water) and New Passage from where ferries once sailed to Portskewett and the wildness of Wales. The coast switches from levee to concrete bulwark. There are hard-surfaced paths and seats and couples dressed for the Barbour countryside taking the air.

The New Passage ferry from which this tiny hamlet drew its name was once the terminus for the Bristol and South Wales Union Railway. This was a Victorian venture that brought passengers bound for the wastes of Wales to a pier and ferry crossing to Portskewett on the other side. There was accommodation, offices and a whole thriving community dedicated to fulfilling the needs of travellers. The great New Passage Hotel is long gone but the guest house that is now Severn Lodge Farm hangs on, being refurbished and up for sale as I pass.

The Estuary edge is well revetted here with a road and a concrete walkway. This is the Binn Wall. The river flooded in 1815 and again in 1920, 1976 and then enormously in 1990. On each occasion the wall was strengthened. It looks almost nuclear proof today.

The pier which once extended five hundred metres into the river is now a truncated stub. Steam ferries, paddle tugs and paddle steamers with names like *Saint Pierre, Gem, Relief, Chepstow* and *Christopher Thomas* plied the tidal waters. They survived the 1881 Portskewett Pier fire and stopped only when the Severn Rail Tunnel opened in 1886. There's a memorial plaque to the railway along with one celebrating the fact that in the eighteenth century those Methodist dynamos, John and Charles Wesley, crossed the water here on their way to convert the backsliders of Wales and Ireland.

Backsliders. Ah, Wales is full of those. I had this idea once that I might compile a lexicon of insults used by the English about the Welsh and assemble this into a swirling sound-scape of meshing verbiage and spiked invective. Invective can work brilliantly on stage. Well-chosen a crashing catalogue of irreverent descriptors can be made to sound like Roman Rhetoric or John Cage on speed. I'd done this before, breaking open the poet and miserablist R.S. Thomas's work set in the gogledd hills and turning it into a diatribe against incomers.

Gwint gap grog gap
gap gap gap
Immigrant slate mirth grot gap
Bald grass, non-essential waste gap,
Rock docker, slow slate gap, empty rocker ...[3]

The poem, when I delivered it, chanting and swaying, certainly rocked. With my voice I could make it do that. And did so once in the presence of eminence grise, the great Welsh poet and theorist, Emyr Humphreys. I would present him with my credentials, simultaneously both nationalist and modernist and he would have to be impressed. In the event he sat there, impassive, throughout the whole performance. Not a flicker crossed his face. When I finished he didn't clap.

I had some of the insults lined-up in my head. Sheepsters. Pugnacious little trolls. Cheese bellies. Foreigners. Dyslexic work shysters. Barbarians. Verbose short-arses. Shifty sniffers. Oversexed dribblers. It was a list that could run a long way and one that would have had audiences adding to it and that's, maybe, where the problem lay. Irony is not a poetry audience's strong suit. Someone would end up imagining that I was on the side of the insulters and cheer me on. I put the idea back in the box.

Near where the bridge makes landfall, beyond the delightfully, if inappropriately named Sugarhole Sands, the Severn Tunnel surfaces and the track is visible, briefly, before plunging on into further rail tunnels leading the eleven and a half miles to Bristol. Where the Welsh-side portal remains a secret the English side has its own road direction sign, RVP Severn Tunnel. As a completist I check it out but the view is obscured by embankment and dense undergrowth.

Heading for Avonmouth the coast turns south. This is still South Gloucestershire, just. In front of me now is a piece of surrealist Severn Estuary history, Severn Beach. An impossible venture from a hopeful past that seemed pretty unbelievable even then. Severn Beach, with a foreshore well below sea level, was a fully-fledged 1930s holiday resort, created because the railways came here and largely as the result of local entrepreneur Robert Stride's big idea. A Blackpool of the West, he branded it. There were advertising posters on the walls at Paddington. Everywhere in sight of water wants to emulate Blackpool, it seems. Stride brought in sand and turned the mud and rock foreshore of Severn Beach's river-facing frontage into a shingle beach. He built a boating lake, added cafés, a hotel, shops, and deckchair rental. He opened changing rooms, a funfair with slides and dodgems, a paddling pool, a cinema. He put on donkey rides, encouraged the establishment of tea shops and whelk stalls. He ran bathing beauty competitions, seaside revues and water carnivals. His centrepiece, next to the Rustic Tea Gardens, was the great Blue Lagoon, an art deco-treated salt water lido that in the old films I've seen was as full of swimming-costumed revellers as Marbella. Visitors flocked, arriving by train from Bristol, Birmingham and from Gloucester. For miner's fortnight when the south Wales pits all closed families would arrive in droves, their cases sent up in advance. People came by bike, four hundred were once recorded in a single day. A beach on the edge of the salt sea. What more could you want.

Things began to fail only when motoring took the place of rail as the way to travel. Leisure seekers sought variety and became willing to travel further. They went to Bournemouth and Brighton and then they went to Benidorm. The days of Severn Beach were numbered. The lagoon closed in the 1970s and was then, along with many of the other failing attractions, demolished. Today, remains are scant but there is a heritage trail. Looking down from the concrete and railinged river edge walkway at the rock-littered flats and sewage pipes that extend out into the Estuary, it's hard to see how anyone would ever want to sit down there, handkerchief secured to their head, drinking tea from a thermos.

At Shirley's Café, open Sundays and serving meals as well as tea and cakes, they are advertising line dancing. Wednesday evenings, bring your own drinks. Severn Beach not quite dead yet then. On a wall outside someone has affixed an engraved plaque. *Lost One Wife & Dog. Reward for Return of Dog.* The spirit of Blackpool still evident. Avon, still a place with which to grapple.

Singing

'Down river.' David Ackles sang that, back in 1968 when he was a real alternative to Leonard Cohen. "...times change I know, but it sure goes slow, down river when you're locked away..." He had a voice like the Severn flowing. Deep and dark. Never came here. Died in 1999. Left four albums none of them recorded later than 1973.

But out there what is there? 'Aloha Severn Beach' from Adge Cutler, 'Severn Beach' by The Blue Aeroplanes, a song somewhere about riding on the Severn Beach train.

'A Suite for the Severn' written by Elgar in 1930. Brass Band music for the twenty-fifth anniversary championships held that year at Crystal Palace. Elgar had a house at Malvern and could see the river. Same river but so different in its snaking up there. Elgar banging out the notes for the bands to blow.

Six pieces for orchestra, 'The Severn Bridge Suite', created by six composers, three Welsh and three English, in 1966 when the first bridge opened. Malcolm Arnold, Alun Hoddinott, Nicolas Maw, Daniel Jones, Grace Williams and Michael Tippett. All based on Song of Praise Hymn No. 505, *Braint* in Welsh. Fanfares and satisfying sonorities. Short. Tippett wound it all together. Malcolm Arnold's only lasts 1 minute 39.

Gerald Finzi's 'A Severn Rhapsody'. Ivor Gurney put to music: 'Severn Meadows'. The Albion Morris Men's 'Upton On Severn Stick Dance'. Jim Jones's Severn. Pandora's Box's 'Severn Suzuki', Causing a Tiger's 'Severn Tunnel'. The Declining Winter's 'Where The Severn River's Tread'. Adam Haley's trance three versions on the same EP his the best, 'Severn Bridge', the original mix.

More of this Severn music out there than you'd think.

As far as the Estuary is concerned everyone from Yusef Lateef to the Banana Slug String Band. Into the Estuary. On the Estuary. Up the Estuary. Along the Estuary. Astride the Estuary. Avast the Estuary. Actually the Estuary. Stepping the Estuary. Besides the Estuary. On Top of the Estuary. Bop The Estuary. Rock the Estuary. Rip the Estuary. Sambamba Samba Samba Estuary. Oh Oh Estuary Oh Estuary Man. Rich Rich Estuary. Hit Me Estuary. Estuary Estuary. What Happened At The Estuary. Wild in the Estuary. Her Estuary Twang.

Estuary singing. Bound to catch on.

Avonmouth and Portishead

Portishead – that's a band, isn't it? Ethereal 90s disco, a scratchy space future for music that never really arrived. This was where it all was. For a time. When you look it up you discover that Portishead is a Bristol outrider, a suburb by the sea with a muddy beach, a place where the merchants of the great city came to retire. I'm standing at Battery Point on the sloping grass next to the seamen's memorial. "The closest place on the coast of the United Kingdom which large ships pass." Dedicated to those sailors from the West Country who have gone to sea by ship never to return. Given the fame of this waterway those are many. From Sebastian Cabot who opened up the lands of Ameryk and Master Andrew who sailed with Magellan, to the merchantmen by their hundreds who went down on the Atlantic convoys.

This is where the ship spotters come with their cameras and their handbooks. Port movement lists. Ship descriptions. Gazetteers of ship flags and ship line colours. But in the dull almost drizzle of this December day on the loping grass there's no one. A lone fisherman cwtched into the rocks below the beacon on Portishead Point. Denny Island out there in front of us, like the grass-haired head of a giant slowly emerging from the river.

Bristol itself is a few miles back inland. A place as far away as Ireland. It always was for most of the time I knew it. Before the bridge in the 60s you got there by water or you took the train. A steaming thrash through the two and quarter mile river tunnel to Brunel's Temple Meads. Rattle and rock the whole way. Bristol. Lord of the waterway, England's slave port, the largest docks anywhere outside London, strider of the Avon estuary, owner of the channel that took its name.

If anything dominates these waters then it's Bristol. For centuries a governing force in the affairs of western Britain. The port that colonised English America, won the war with Spain, fished the Newfoundland Banks into extinction, brought tobacco to Europe and wine to Britain, and imported more cars than any Western nation of our size really needs. Bristol, a city built around a snaking docks seven miles up the river that inspired the Bard, the place from which Brunel launched the *Great Western* and the *SS Great Britain*, the world's largest steamships.

The city docks, the floating harbour, well inland from Clifton on the Avon Gorge, closed to merchant shipping in 1991. The warehouses and storage tanks and sand depots relocated west to the newly expanded docks at Avonmouth on the north side of the Avon and at Royal Portbury on the south. Portishead's harbour closed to commercial traffic in 1992 and became a marina, trade drifted north the few miles to Portbury. From Battery Point the whole sea frontage is visible. The cranes and gantries, the wind turbines, the lock gates, muddy water surrounding them. Bristol has dug its new docks deep enough to take large container ships and trade has followed. In the 70s the deep-water docks at Portbury opened for the import of motor vehicles. There are plans[4] to build an even deeper container port at Avonmouth to take the new generation of Ultra Large Container Vessels (ULCVs)[5]. There's a future. They hope.

Avonmouth in the low drizzle feels like Liverpool. Gantries, railtracks, a sense of things being once much greater than they are now. A large and linear Severnside Industrial estate follows the A403 along the shoreline passing the Severnside Power Station and running all the way to Severn Beach. From the bridge crossing the tracks at the deserted St Andrews Station, Avonmouth's coal and bulk wharfs are all visible. The port is in full industrial swing yet it appears so still and so post-modernly silent. There's little here anymore to excite the breath and race the pulse. In their overalls the men at work get nothing dirty. Their hands no longer become ingrained with the oil marks of ropes or the grime of shovel handles. They're in a huddle around the tea stall, eating bacon rolls, downing hot coffee.

Across the Avon sit the docks of Portbury. The newest and largest on the Severn. Its forty-one metre wide sea lock can take ships with a dead-weight tonnage of 130,000. Its nearest rival is Newport, which can barely manage 40,000. Things are pulsing. Avonmouth's plans for its own redevelopment as a Deep Sea Container terminal are in place.

The Welsh ports in their run along the Estuary's northern coast may have dominated the iron and the steel trade, when there was one, and the coal when it flowed, but none of them ever had Bristol's history to fall back on, never got anywhere near its size or its UK dominance. Only Cardiff's Tiger Bay ever became a rival in the familiarity game played out in the distant ports of Empire.

When the bridge opened in September 1966 the dream was

of the two great ports it linked becoming so much closer. Road time was now less than an hour, if you hurried. There'd be Bristol voices among the stores of the Welsh capital and the Cardiff accent slicing away in the pubs of Bristol. Never happened. Not much. An hour in a car for us is clearly too much. Over the decades there's been about as much interchange between Cardiff Wales and Bristol England as there's been between Cardiff Capital and Swansea second city. Mostly we stay where we are.

Bristol. It recedes from view. You can't see it all from the Welsh coast, Or from the waterway. In the centre of its city docklands there's a district known as Welsh Back. In the Welsh capital there was once a hotel known as the Bristol. Behind the bar, among the rum bottles, was a model of a poodle made entirely from empty Woodbine packets. Spirit of the age.

In the Avonmouth Tavern, where I've retreated, the ceiling still shows its nicotine stains. They don't serve tea, this is a pub. How the world should be.

Weston

The loss of Birnbeck Pier in 1994 was a blow. It would have been even more of a blow if this had happened in 1963 in my years as a callow youth when I'd crossed the waters from Cardiff with my arms round Janis. Great name, redolent of the age to come. She was hip, smart, young and, as it turned out, Jewish. For a time her parents thought I was too. Something about the way I looked. To get on in Janis's world I had to keep up the pretence. I didn't have a clue.

We'd taken the Campbell's White Funnel paddle steamer the straight nine miles from Cardiff's Pier Head to land on the quay jutting out from Weston-Super-Mare's Birnbeck Island. A day trip away from prying eyes. The Weston we found was decayed but glorious. A melee of chip shops, kiss me quick hat stalls, funfair rides and donkeys strung out along miles of flat, perfect sand. There was nothing like this in Wales. The town jumped with visitors, people disporting themselves as only that generation could: shirt sleeves, handkerchiefs on their heads, trousers rolled up, ice creams. Speakers dotted everywhere pumped out music. Heartbreak Hotel, Be Bop A Lula, Da Doo Ron Ron. Please Please Me. She Loves You. Twist and Shout. Our world followed us round.

The day was magnificent. Sun that beat down and a sky that radiated joy. We got ourselves into the pleasure gardens and lay on the grass. Do that at home and we'd have been spotted. Janis – I could see my future here. But it didn't last. Almost as soon as we got back, the paddle ship making a deep whooping noise from its steam whistle and men trying to look like mods spilling their beer on the deck, her father demanded a meeting. He'd been making enquiries at the synagogue up on the Lady Mary Estate and the news was not good. Finch? Never heard of him. My greatest fear was that he'd ask for some sort of proof, insist I recite from the Torah or drop my trousers, and then I'd be lost. I didn't see Janis again after that.

Coming back to the town almost half a century on I expected to find its Victoriana even more decayed and the front looking like Porthcawl does – an admix of the cheaply fixed nestling against the forever unfixable, paint-peeled B&Bs with signs permanently announcing vacancies in their windows. What I found, in the midst of the recessional twenty-teens, was no half-repaired place hopefully waiting for the builders to someday return. Instead there was a gleaming town with all its stone frontages cleaned, a completely redesigned and replaced sea front with brightly-lit booming piers jutting out into the sea. Well, actually, on this occasion jutting out into the never-ending mud flats. The great Severn tide was once again out. Weston, a town on the up.

Weston on the Moor. Ar lan y Môr. From the Welsh for beside the sea. West tun. From the Anglo-Saxon for settlement in the west. Weston-Juxta-Worle. Weston near Worle. Weston-Juxta-Mare. Near the Sea. Weston-Super-Mare, a slice of Latin imposed by the Bishop of Bath in 1348. It's an ancient place.

As a town Weston is largely the product of the Victorian obsession with health and the saline sea, and the arrival of Brunel's railway, which brought in leisure seekers by the coach-load. In the early part of the nineteenth century the land here was still largely sand dune. Sand Bay, Weston Bay and the more southerly Berrow Flats below the Brean Down peninsula all face the prevailing westerlies. And just like their Welsh counterparts at Kenfig and Merthyr Mawr sand accumulates along their tidelines and then, wind-driven, moves steadily inland.

The flat and seemingly endless beach coupled with the location's proximity to the centres of population at Bath and at Bristol (not to speak of south Wales) made Victorian development an economic proposition. Using the distinctive Bath-like local stone, hotels were opened and grand houses with sea views built. In 1867 the pier linking the town with Birnbeck Island was opened. In 1903 a second, and much longer, 1300-foot Grand Pier running straight out to sea from the promenade was created by engineer P. Munroe. The new venture had a 2000-seat theatre-cum-music hall at its tip, although the whole thing burned down in 1930. After repair it was burned down again in 2008. The present pier is the third manifestation. In 1995 the, by comparison, stubby Seaquarium Pier opened, the first new sea pier to be built in Britain since the early 1900s. Weston, land of Piers. Even the sea damaged[6] and rotting Birnbeck Pier, the one I arrived on in 1963, has recently been sold to a new developer. Great things are expected.

Out at sea is the familiar sight of Flat Holm where Wales begins. Much closer and looking oddly humped is Steep Holm, the slopes we never see, the dark side of the moon. Weston has style and ambition not apparent anywhere on the Estuary's northern coast. This place is no mere Barry or Porthcawl writ large but a flourish of urbanity of a totally different dimension. It has space and is full of light. It faces the sea with bravura. There's no problem with identity, purpose, future, governance or delivery. This town knows what it is.

I walk along Marine Parade with its cafés, candy floss, and beach goods stalls, the sand beside me rolling out to sea so far you'd think the river had sunk never to return. Royal Sands merge with Uphill, turn into Weston Bay, become Knightstone. There's a plaque attached to the railings, one of the Wonders of Weston[7], *Build your house on the sand*, it reads. *Surrender conventional wisdom. Tunnel like a sandworm. Form an exoskeleton like a crab. The town a beach. The beach a town.* The Zen poets have been in action again.

The pristinely clean art deco Winter Gardens Pavilion outshines the Porthcawl equivalent by at least 3000 watts. Tim Etchells' neon art piece runs along its top. *The Things You Can't Forget* it reads. They like words here. At Knightstone Island where the causewayed Marine Lake is empty and full of Severn mud, the hotels bend in a stone arc as if this were purposeful Georgian Bath. It's a climate change day in mid-November where the sun is high in the sky and the temperature well up towards 20. There are leisure seekers everywhere. Weston as Marbella. Families with kids on bikes, elderly perambulators. Hardly a single person carrying a can of something or with their head behoodied, tattoos displayed on their exposed arms.

The sand dunes that once dominated this sea frontage were flattened in 1883 and a seawall built to hold back the encroaching tidal estuary. Great storms in 1903, 1981, 1990 and again in 1996 took their toll. Most of the town is below sea level. If the sea defence ultimately failed then almost everything would be lost to water. In 2006 the decision was taken to rebuild. And not just the wall but the whole sea frontage – everything from the Marine Lake causeway to the promenade paving would be upgraded. New walls, new drains, new frontages, new pavers, new benches and a grand beach entrance arc created in Saddam Hussein Bagdad-style but without the giant swords. The contractors worked with sculptor John Maine to ensure consistency of creative design. The results are amazing.

The granite promenade curves and steps in keeping with the smooth turns of its street furniture. The stone benches have wave-like shapes. The gates and drainage covers are fretted to resemble the shifting waters. What the town has now is clean space. No one has yet wrecked it with directional signage, regulatory notice or traffic calming measure. No one is panhandling. There are no buskers. A woman overtakes me on an electrically-powered carriage. There's a man walking three dogs.

I listen out for the music that was once here. Billy J, Beatles, Glad All Over, Big Girls Don't Cry, Hello Little Girl, Walk Like A Man. Yep. Done that now. Didn't then.

You can still get here by steamer or what passes for a steamer these days. The subsidised *Waverley* operates in season offloading visitors by connecting tender to Knightstone Harbour. No stepping directly onto pier heaven. On the Grand Pier itself with its Victorian tea shop (tea and scones £18, not for the faint hearted) and massive amusement arcade complete with ghost train and make-your-stomach-turn-inside-out-spin-through-the-air distractions they are playing Abba. Weston's take on music that lasts. Out to sea the late sun glints. The Estuary moves its mud about. The shelduck, dunlin and redshank dine. Above them the sky.

Watchet to Minehead

The view out from Wales, my part of Wales, is often of these very hills. Standing on the top of Penarth Head and looking not south but Atlantic west can take in a great swathe of Somerset's England. The Quantocks, a sort of imitation Vale of Glamorgan outrider to Exmoor, hit the coast to the east of where I'm headed. They are designated as an AONB[8], an Area of Outstanding Natural Beauty, not yet a National Park, but aspirational nevertheless. To their east is the nuclear power generation complex that is Hinkley Point. The gas-cooled reactor of Hinkley Point B is currently in action and the proposed new French-built European Pressurised Reactor (EPR) for Hinkley Point C has just passed the consent stage. In the wings are proposals for a future Hinkley Point D. There's opposition, there's always opposition, but it goes nowhere. In Nuclear-free Wales, sixteen miles over the water, no one is the slightest bit concerned. Concern is something we keep local. England is a foreign country. In Wales there are other threats with which to be concerned. Lack of burgers in school meals. The withdrawal of incapacity allowance. The state of the national team.

EDF, Electricité de France, will send their new nuclear energy along overhead cables borne by giant pylons of a kind never seen before in this part of the world. Huge striding monsters will cross the Quantock fringes. "Pylons, those pillars / Bare like nude girls that have no secret." Spender was right[208]. They'll be visible from everywhere as they trash the landscape with their concrete feet and gargantuan arms.

Watchet, a road sign off the side of the A39, has no pretensions to resortdom. There's no beach to speak of, although the mud and sand mix of Helwell Bay to the east might vaguely qualify. Watchet is an ancient harbour that goes back to the days of Ethelred. The town name comes from Wacet, a blue dye found in the cliffs. It once exported iron ore from the Brendon Hills to Ebbw Vale and commodities up and down the coast. But no more. The inner harbour is now a marina stuffed with pleasure craft. The First Watchet Sea Scout Group have their own gunboat here. *Gay Archer* it's called. It bristles with armament although I doubt the guns actually fire.

On the quay I spot the mayor, just along from the statue of the seated mariner that could well have been made by the same man who created the lounging sailor on the front at Cardiff Bay or Captain Cat in the Marina at Swansea. The mayor wears a business suit with his chain of office on top. He's preceded by a white-haired town crier in full regalia. They're moving west to where I can hear the unmistakable sound of a train whistle and the indrawn huff of moving steam. Watchet is a station on the restored West Somerset Railway. A heritage line of gleaming paint and polished metalwork, middle-aged volunteers wearing full railway uniforms, driver's caps, station master's hats, platemen's overalls.

Today the newly restored footbridge over the station tracks is getting its official opening. The uniformed Watchet Town Band cluster in a half-moon playing 'Congratulations' and 'The Dancing Snowman'. The Rev Clive Gilbert offers a prayer of dedication via loud hailer. On the station's platform there is wine. The restored 7828 Norton Manor in GWR green sends steam in sentimental clouds across the platform. M.H. Jones is launching his masterly and monumental volume on the *Brendon Hills Iron Mines and West Somerset Mineral Railway*. £25 a go. Black Dwarf Press. Both the Mayor and the Leader of the Council make speeches. There is cheering and the local press photographer gets everyone to pose. A ribbon is cut and the well-mannered and very English locals stream across the bridge. In the Methodist Church beyond they are running their Christmas Fayre. Five stalls, three selling bric-a-brac, one offering cakes and one retailing hand-made Christmas table holly and silver painted pine cone centrepieces for £2.50 a pop. The unvandalised public toilets are all open. I haven't seen a hood or a tattoo for ages. There's no one anywhere with a can in hand.

Out at sea, or where the sea will be when it eventually rushes back, the rock strata resemble the Glamorgan Heritage Coast but lying down.

West of Watchet, along this coast that's so much a mirror of its Welsh counterpart and yet so much unlike it, runs the seemingly endless shingle expanse of Blue Anchor Bay. Endless in that this stretch of clustered north-facing beach runs all the way past Kermoor Piling, the Dunster Nature Reserve and the West Somerset Golf Course to end at Minehead's Madbrain Sands. It is unrestrained by pier, outcrop, headland or groyne. There's hardly a caravan to slow you, the railway rushing alongside a constant companion. Steam and smoke in the skies.

Minehead is everything I had not expected it to be. Big, cheap, and in the November cold, unexpectedly bustling. It had a pier once, in its glorious Victorian past. That was when it was a resort for the genteel, the well-heeled from Bristol, the paddle-steamer passengers arriving from over the water, the visitors in their suits and dresses strolling the fine promenade, taking tea on the lawns, watching the channel waters slip by in their greyness. And the gulls in their swirling.

But in 1962 Billy Butlin chose the place as a site for one of his early camps. Today it is one of three that remain. Developed on flatland to the east of the old town, it has been refurbished regularly enough to ensure a constant flow of grateful visitors. The latest improvement shifts Butlins upmarket with a set of new sea-facing twenty-first century luxury holiday apartments known as Blueskies. On the streets the winter Butlins clientele stroll with cans and fags in hand. London accents, Midland voices, blokes with bags of chips, women with giant handbags, drink going down like fury as a bulwark against the prevailing winter wind.

The camp succeeds by offering a mix of inexpensive, all-inclusive family entertainment with adult weekends away that involve school reunions, rock revival shows and World Wrestling. Surprisingly it also hosts the annual Spring Harvest, the largest Christian festival in the UK. But that's at sunny

Easter. Visitors love it or hate it. They're either captivated by ready access to constant drink and the ease with which the alcoholic days flow by or they're so upset by the state of the accommodation, carpets, beds, bedding food and holes in the wall that they vow never to return. Yet they do. Butlins fills a need. Without it Minehead would slumber.

Minehead is also the terminus for the Railway that I'd encountered earlier. There's a whole sliver of the town devoted to shunting yards holding brake vans and passenger carriages and lines of steam and diesel engines, both fully restored and on the way. It's an enthusiasts' glory. The station shop does a good trade in Ian Allen ABC rail guides. These are volumes that list the UK's entire rail network of unit numbers. They detail the stations and the sheds. They show how to get access, and when and where your camera will be perceived as a threat. The ABC of how to see what you need to and how to avoid trouble. The complete trainspotters handbook. I buy a pamphlet on Brunel, the man who brought the broad gauge railway from London to Wales, and consider the prices of the model trains that sit protected by a perspex display case. Engines start at £150. Track packs the same. This is no longer a pocket money hobby.

But it's winter and despite the Butlins hoards on the streets the West Somerset trains are not running. They'll do a few Santa specials nearer Christmas and then stick to weekend working until April. In the dark months we stay indoors, watch the fire and the TV flicker. But not me. Onwards into the west. Pacing down the corn and sheep fields of Wales is the green and undulating bulk of Exmoor.

Exmoor

Back home they've leaked another paper. A planning consultant has told someone over dinner that he'd heard that the National Parks may soon be abolished. This on the grounds that their governing bodies are increasingly behaving in a way that is wholly against the economic ambitions of the Welsh Government. And we can't have that. The National Parks say no. They stop you building. They restrict your access. They deter change. They keep the lands as they were. They protect them from the incipient ravages of developing society, from men building burger bars and waste processing plants, housing estates and football pitches, dual carriage ways and airports, overhead pylon lines leading to wind farms the size of Caerphilly, oil refineries and open cast mines. In Wales there are three National Parks – The Brecon Beacons, the Pembroke Coast and Snowdonia – and they cover almost a quarter of the country's land mass. The Welsh Government are in hot denial but you can see that something here has come through the seams. All the National Parks are interested in is landscape runs the trenchant criticism. Well, yes. Good, good. Me too.

Over here, on Exmoor's 267 square miles of sea-bordering moorland, there are no indicators of imminent abolition. The coast road bends and turns. Across the water the twin chimneys of Aberthaw power station stand like beacons. Downriver sails a Grimaldi Line vehicle carrier out of Portbury. Bound for Europe. Almost five thousand cars plus six cabins for cruise passengers. The only ship I've seen all day.

At Porlock Weir the high pebbled beach is swarming with school children carrying tape measures and clip boards. This is a school geography trip from Watford. They're here to explore the fact that small stones roll further than large ones. From Porlock they drift with the tide towards Hurlstone Point. The Weir itself is a small but ancient harbour, recently repaired and full of pleasure craft. They once sent pit props to Wales from here and oysters to Bristol. There's a sign telling me that I've just missed the ninth annual conker competition at The Ship. *Three conkers (supplied) £1. Come and take on last year's champ Sarah 'Slasher' Withers.* Might have enjoyed that. Out at sea beyond the rotting groynes there's a submerged forest. Beyond that the grey-brown shine of my constant companion, the gloopy, glimmering, glabrous mud I've come to love and hate.

On the pebble beach World War Two pillboxes subside into the pebble drifts. A row of seventeenth century Gibraltar cottages with tall chimney stacks spill onto the beach. Above, high in the trees, is Worthy Manor, home of Byron's daughter Ada, mathematician and interpreter of Babbage's analytical engine, the world's first computer. There's a toll road which winds up through the grounds guarded by a toll cottage and a brick arch. A sign shrugs off responsibility for the owner's negligence, non-feasance, misfeasance, or, indeed, any kind of responsibility whatsoever for the state of the trackway and anything standing near it. But no one's collecting toll charges and it looks as if they haven't for quite a time. In their autumn colours the woodlands glow.

High on Exmoor itself, running north from that spot where the West Somerset Coast meets North Devon, is the line of longitude that cuts the Severn Sea to breach the Welsh shore at Sker Point and lunge on through the living room of Sker House. Turn south here and you are looking up the Vale of Bagworthy. On to Brendon Common. Up the Doone Valley. The man who connects these two spots is R.D. Blackmore, as I discovered when I visited Porthcawl (see p. 167). Richard Doddridge. The author of the world smash, *Lorna Doone* (1869) who followed it with the now forgotten *Maid Of Sker* (1872). Both Victorian triple-deckers of significant size. Available now for next to nothing in out of copyright reprint or free as an eBook download.

Blackmore, the last great Victorian novelist, won fame and fortune worldwide. For a time his Devon became as well-known as Hardy's Wessex. Yet his style has not weathered well and other than for Doone itself his score of novels are largely forgotten. His Welsh connection is via his mother who came from Nottage, the place where R.D. was brought up, although he spent his adult life living in England. He regarded *The Maid of Sker* as the better book but the public did not agree. It is *Lorna Doone* with its wild weathers and tales of betrayal, murder and revenge for which he will be remembered.

The valley path runs from Oare Church where Blackmore's grandfather was curate, over the seventeenth century humpback packhorse bridge, through the village of Malmsmead and up towards the moor. There's a slate memorial stone out there erected in 1969 by the Lorna Doone Centenary Committee. The rival private river path doesn't lead to it. *Please put money in box. 50p adults. 20p children.* The box is rusted shut. The path runs through mud followed by more mud, Bagworthy Water rushing gaily beside.

My Father, John Ridd the elder, says the younger Ridd in *Lorna Doone*, was a great admirer of learning, "and well able to write his name". And you can sense that, here where Cloud Hill rises above this tributary of the mighty East Lyn river. They'll be there, Blackmore's people, in their scattered cottages, pouring over their ancient books. In the single shop at Malsmead I buy a map, a history of the area, and a fat copy of *Doone*. Known by reputation and by television. Never actually read. Like so much of literature.

The road on zips and bends as it traverses Countisbury Common and Foreland point. Roads always go on. Except this one doesn't. Ahead is a great incline, road signs warn motorists to slow, to test their brakes, advise cyclists to dismount, and horses to give up. One in four is promised on a road down to nowhere else. But we come from Wales where such things are commonplace. We might have any number of things to consider but not fear of hills. The road slopes on down.

Lynmouth

This is the place that Shelley came to, and like Laugharne and its obsession with Dylan just over the water, the poet's name is living on. Overlooking the road bridge across the combined waters of the East and West Lyn stands Shelley's Hotel. At the back of the fourteenth century Rising Sun, overlooking the harbour, is Shelley's Cottage. Both places claim to be precisely where Shelley came in June 1812 with Harriet Westbrook, his new young bride. Here between conjugal duties and fermenting political change he worked on the outline for 'Queen Mab'. Mab, his masterpiece of revolutionary agitation and the virtuousness of humanity, is in nine parts. It is dedicated to Harriet, love of his life:

> "Whose is the love that, gleaming through the world,
> Wards off the poisonous arrow of its scorn?"

Shelley's Cottage, humped below the sheer rocks that fly six hundred feet to Lynton above, might appear at first to be the more likely location. Picturesque, ancient, with its reproduction available through the town on mugs and placemats. "It's widely believed that Percy Bysshe Shelley spent his honeymoon here with his sixteen-year-old bride Harriet in 1812," runs the website. And so he could have.

But as ever fog pervades history. Up the road at Shelley's Hotel claims seem firmer. The hotel is an extension of Hooper's Lodging[10], a property once known as Woodbine Cottage and renamed as Shelley's Cottage in 1854. It was turned into a guest house in the 1930s and known then as Shelley's Cottage Hotel. It was damaged in the 1952 flood, rebuilt, and was rechristened as Shelley's Hotel when sold to the present owners in 1998.

There are nineteenth century records which show a cottage on the hill behind the Rising Sun as being owned at that time by a Percy Bysshe enthusiast and renamed as Shelley's Cottage in his honour. The Rising Sun's Shelly's Cottage might still have legs. Except that in 1907, according to a North Devon Journal report, the nineteenth century building was destroyed by fire.

From his base on Lynmouth, the ever seditious Shelley took to distributing radical and revolutionary texts, including his famous *Declaration of Rights*[11]. He would wait for the winds to blow towards Wales or back at Bristol and then send the texts off in sealed bottles, casting them adrift from the Lynmouth foreshore. He made small boats from boxes: "carefully covered over with bladder, and well-rosined and waxed to keep out the water, and, in order to attract attention at sea there was a little upright stick fastened to it each end, and a little sail fastened to them, as well as some lead at the bottom to keep it upright". He tied copies to fire balloons and let them sail into the air. Shelley called these things "vessels of heavenly medicine[12]". He sent his servant Dan Healy into nearby Barnstaple to post up the pamphlets. It being a God-fearing town Healy was immediately arrested and fined £200. He couldn't pay and was instead imprisoned for six months. Shelley, who might have helped by paying the fine on Healy's behalf didn't. But he did visit. How are the seditious bottles going master? Pretty well. I check the foreshore for ancient glass. Nothing.

The great poet escaped to Swansea at the end of August. The Lynmouth fishermen wouldn't help him but those at Ilfracombe further along the coast did. To cover the cost Shelley had borrowed sufficient from the cleaner at Hooper's Lodgings. From Swansea he then headed north to the distant wonders of the Vale of Llangollen. Back at Barnstaple, faithful Healy served out his term.

At the Rising Sun I try to rent their Shelley's Cottage but it's closed. Out of season. We take a first floor pub room instead. Harbour views of bobbing boats, good beer and excellent food downstairs.

Lynmouth sits at the end of the Lyn Gorge at the foot of the towering Hollerday Hills. Meltwater from the most recent ice age once poured over Exmoor, dislodging rock and cutting great rents into the fabric of the land. Lynmouth hangs by its toes onto what those waters left, a low shelf between sea and moor. It's almost entirely a resort town now. Its original purpose was lost when the herring stopped running in the channel, the lime kilns became uneconomic and travel switched from boat to road.

To the west, a two kilometre walk along a cliff-hugging, vertigo-inducing metalled path, is the celebrated Valley of Rocks. This is a Switzerland-like display of meltwater-abandoned boulders jammed against each other and towering in splintered intemperance as if these were the dry valleys of Mars. As an attraction the Valley is much celebrated. The romantic poets, in their endless search for the wild and the real all came here. Wordsworth, Coleridge, and Southey, notebooks in hand as they rambled. Like me, except I make no notes and, as it turns out, write no poems either. The rocks are splendid but the layered fissures of the Glamorgan coast across the Channel waters are somehow more unexpected and uplifting. Wordsworth never went there.

From the coast path the view is a long look west into the breadth of the Atlantic, in all its greyness and squalling winds. Out there the real sea runs, the stuff that covers two thirds of the planet and has desires on what's left. Even here, high on my Devonian rocks, there is an incipient threat, a feeling that the Estuary, river origins a forgotten memory, is rising towards me, will catch me one day, will do it soon.

Lynton, a town of hotels and guest houses and shops selling just about everything any visitor could ever want, is Lynmouth's high-level twin. The cliff-face funicular railway is closed for winter repairs. Instead we climb the Westerway. On the way we pass lamp standards powered by solar light, paid for, it seems, through the sale of 1500 books[13]. At the top I find a second-hand record store. Amazingly it is open this winter's Sunday morning. I browse the jazz and soul, the guitar rock, the almost folk. I buy old Booker T and David Axelrod albums. It's often still the 60s in the back of my head.

Like much of the English coast here the tourist trade appears to have been in place for centuries and the land littered with small hotels, neat guest houses, working public toilets and lace curtained shops which sell tea. Unlike Wales where the tourist is often still regarded as a foreign intrusion, the visitor here is encouraged and has been so since the days when the Romantics, held back from their European adventures by the threat of revolution, turned their attention to their own land.

Back down in Lynmouth, CDs under my arm, I find it impossible to buy a single piece of fruit or a vegetable, fresh or not. Boxes of fudge and tooth-extracting toffee are everywhere. Mid-winter tourism shows no signs of abating. The streets are thick with Exmoor walkers and couples here for the air, the sea and the diverting sights. On Watersmeet Road the Lyn Model Railway, a large LNER 1935-40 period layout, offers its dusty self to visitors in exchange for a donation. Its cardboard houses emit grey, cotton-wool smoke. Its goods trains haul vans of Palethorpes Sausages, tanks of Insulated Milk and trucks carrying toy coal from Robert Jenks of Cardiff. The bright green Sandringham Class loco rolls on round the room-filling track.

Next door at the St John the Baptist Anglican church, Tim Prosser's giant model of pre-1952 Lynmouth is housed in a series of glass-fronted cases. Pre-1952 because that was the year of Lynmouth's great natural disaster, the year when the cloud-burst and drenching rain running down from the moors combined to overwhelm the channels of both Lyn rivers. The West Lyn, channelled for the benefit of house building, reverted to its natural course. A ten-foot high wall of water burst through the town. Flood banks crumbled and boulders shifted with monumental force. Overnight the resort changed from village to World War I battlefield. Ninety-three buildings were destroyed, one hundred and thirty-two cars wrecked, twenty-eight bridges brought down and thirty-four lives lost.

As it turned out it was largely new build that had been swept to sea. Through history such floods had happened before. In the eighteenth century Lynmouth inhabitants rebuilt their cottages out of the flood's track. Those structures still stand. It was the later dwellings that failed. Prosser, a Welshman from Newport, moved to Lynmouth in the 1990s and the flood became his obsession. He wrote the definitive study, *The Lynmouth Flood Disaster* (Lyndale Photographic, 2001) and then created the model of how the town once was. It looks an older, cluttered place with its narrow rivers not quite where they are today.

Outside there's a sign which reads *The Seagulls Are Dangerous. Please Do Not Feed.* It's been put there by the local council who are clearly worried by the threat. I can't see any. Lynmouth seabirds have paid heed. The Severn out there has receded as it does right along this coast. Atlantic or not, the tidal range remains impressive. The shingle and pebble shore stretches out towards the single passing ship. Only one I've seen all day. A dredger drifting slowly. Beyond it is just water. And then the distant coast of Wales.

This is it, then, as far as I go. Time to turn back.

Out in the Waters

The Islands

Today, as every day, the channel runs with brown water. The tide is flowing downriver. If you recognise this stretch as river, that is. It's a sliding mass that would defeat anything in its path that it didn't like, wash it down, make it pulp. And out there are the islands. The magic islands. What is it with these places that pulls me? Why do I need to reach them, to land myself on their shores and explore their surfaces?

As estuaries go this one has its fair share. They flake off the end of Pembrokeshire, a trail of fragmented rock pointing on towards America. Skokholm, Skomer, Ramsey, Caldey, Gateholm[1]. Further out, the guano-drenched peak of Ynys Gwales – Grassholm. South of here, edging a place the maps hopefully call the Celtic Sea, is Lundy. The Estuary's Jupiter. So far off land and so large, compared to the others, that it could declare independence and probably survive.

There are also the islands that are not quite islands. Sully, connected to the shore twice a day by a fat land bridge. Barry, not been an island for centuries now. Birnbeck held hard to Weston-Super-Mare's side by a raggedy wood and metal pier. Brean Down, a peninsula almost separated from its motherland, but not quite. The English Stones, a rough steppe off Severn Beach that emerges from the tides to beckon and then, at speed, to the deep returns. The Wolves, two rocks a mile northwest of Flat Holm, wreckers of ships, regularly overwhelmed by waves but still elevated enough to be named. Mumbles Head and Middle Head, hanging to the town that named them by sea-drowned concrete threads. Inner Head and Outer Head trailing off into the water at the far Worm's end of Gower. Tusker Rock off Porthcawl where local memory swears cattle were once grazed.

And there is also any amount, out there, of tidal mud, and sand, and further mud. Streaks of it in bars, and banks and ellipses, marked on maps, played cricket on by larking lads when the sea recedes, but gone again when it flows. Islands? Once.

Denny Island[2], at the end of the Bedwin Sands, mid-channel between Avonmouth and the sewage works at Magor Pill, has a southern foreshore that marks the boundary between England and Wales. Island resources here are pretty much nil. Rocks, scrub vegetation, no fresh water, no buildings or even remains. Administration is handled by Monmouthshire, which makes it the county's South Georgia. Its rocky bulk also marks the start of the Denny Island Fault Zone. This is a 155 kilometre long geological fracture between Avon and the Solent. It gives rise to hot springs at Bristol and at Bath and to geothermal wells at Southampton. In geological terms it is still active. Deep down, plate shifts and earth stumbles continue although we shouldn't expect quake or shake any time soon. Put your hand in the Denny shoreline sea. Is it warm? No.

But as channel islands go, it's the line that runs from Sully Island and Lavernock Point through Flat Holm and then Steep Holm to the penile wave that is Brean Down which catches the eye. Back before the Mesolithic when the seas were so much lower than they are now – a good 160 feet down – this line of islands were the peaks of hills in an extended Mendips. The limestone ridge was drowned when the last ice age finished and the ice sheet retreated. 15,000 years back. The Holms became limestone islands. They sit in the channel today, reminders of a gone past and, as our waters warm and globally rise, predictors of the future.

It's here that most Severn barrage builders suggest that they'll run their walls. See p.267 for Gareth Woodham's take on the prospects. There'll be dams and bridges, walkways, prefabricated caissons, bunds of earth, heaps of rock, mounds of stone, concrete in quantity enough to hold back the Atlantic. No small task. If the builders actually start. If. Projects of this magnitude rarely start with speed and ease.

I've visited these places, every one. No, that's not quite true. Denny I have circled and admired and considered just how I might get myself onto it. But have so far failed.

The Holms, Flat and Steep, are the two most visible Estuary islands. Ynys Echni and Ynys Ronech in Welsh. They mark, say some, the end of the Severn River and the start of the Bristol Channel. Or the end of the Severn Sea and the beginning of the Estuary. Or the place where the tides start to break on their long inward flow. They seem, both of them, almost touchable and so easy to get to. But most who live within their sight have never visited and reaching them can be a major effort.

Flat Holm is Welsh, administratively part of Cardiff, and is being developed as an educational, tourist and leisure facility. In the summer of 2011 the Mayor of Cardiff sailed out to open the island's new pub, The Gull and Leek, first drinkery in this, the most southern part of Wales there is, since at least 1900. The pub offers bottled beer but not draught. Much the same as the nearby tavern on Steep Holm. When I was on the island a few years ago the first person off the boat and the one who streaked up the long sloping path ahead of the crowd was the landlord. Saw him on the boat all the way out and then, there he was, smiling and pouring pints behind the Steep Holm bar. This island drinking has something of the make-believe about it. There have been no recorded incidents of stag nights at either establishment. No binge drinkers in action, not yet.

Access was once from Barry but now goes in season on the *Lewis Alexander* from the Cardiff Bay Barrage. If the sea is rough then stay at home. Health and Safety considerations have been on the rise this past decade. Landings only happen when the sea is calm. Can visitors leap from boat to quay while the waves whip as they have done for centuries? Not anymore.

Flat Holm is half council leisure and half nature reserve[3]. It's home to more than five thousand pairs of breeding seabirds, the ones that roam the streets of Cardiff, some of them. In season you land on the island at your peril, walk with a stick held above your head to ward off their diving, wear clothing that you don't mind removing the guano from later.

The limestone of Flat Holm's eighty-six acres rises softly east. There's a lighthouse and a fog horn station, the remains of a cholera isolation hospital, a farm, army barracks, gun emplacements from almost every war that used cannon, a World War two radar station, Bronze Age and early Christian burial sites, places where ancient axe heads have been found, middens full of medieval potsherds, a contemporary memorial to Guglielmo Marconi and George Kemp's famous first over-water radio signal of 1897, and a small shop selling souvenir pencils, bookmarks and bottled water. Offshore are the sites of shipwrecks. This tiny island is not the world's safest place.

But you can stay here. You can rent space and spend a long weekend in the bunkhouse, drinking cans of lager at the Gull and Leek, walking the grass-covered acres, checking the rain-driven present and inspecting the abundant past. The Council's Harbour Authority, which handle administration, even offers children's birthday parties. Sail out, enjoy burger and chips outdoors, wear hats and do some shrieking, sail back.

Steep Holm, much nearer the Weston shore, is entirely English. There are no extant Welsh claims that I know of although I am sure we could work one up if we had to. At forty-nine acres it's almost half the size of its Estuary rival. But what it loses in size it gains in height and in mystery. You can sail easily from the pier at Weston but I got the pleasure steamer out of Penarth. Off the Steep Holm shore I was taken from the Estuary liner by lighter. Exit was through a hatch halfway along the vessel's side then a clamber down a swaying walkway and into the smaller boat. The island bobbed enticingly before me.

Actual landing was a gangplank leap of faith as the small

motor launch I was on lurched violently alongside Steep Holm's greasy shore. You need to be reasonably fit, reads the promotional brochure. You do. A stiff climb later and I was among the ferns and furze and wild peonies of the top. Here, again, are the scattered remains of war. Abandoned gun batteries, searchlight emplacements, Ferro-concrete walkways, a barracks converted now for use by visitors and the island's warden. The island is managed by the Kenneth Allsop Trust, which is far less gung-ho than Cardiff in its marketing. On Flat Holm is fun, on Steep is wonder; on Flat Holm we shriek and whoop, on Steep we smile and admire. Among the remains of the twelfth century Augustinian priory, the World War II rocket launchers and the wreckage of Victorian war, I can't throw off the feeling that I am going, somehow, to lose balance and fall. To tumble from up here on land that is really Brean Down pushing up towards Wales, the home of St Gildas back in the sixth, and two hundred and sixty recorded species of plant. You can do that with the nature of these places surrounded by water. You can map them and list what's there. Boundaries are hard, they rarely seep. Steep Holm, one of those places that pulls, winner of the Estuary Island Award. First prize for enigma.

The Barrage

I've come down Fort Road at Lavernock again for another look. Yesterday I was out at the Victorian Barracks on Brean Down in Somerset, on the other side of the water. Out there on the islands – Flat Holm and Steep Holm – are the remains of Napoleonic War gun emplacements and the Palmerston Forts which once guarded the approaches. There are World War One batteries and World War Two searchlights. The Estuary here is a defended place.

Gareth Woodham reckons that the rich residents of Lavernock would resist any attempt to run a highway through their hamlet. He's changed his mind about building a motorway across the top of the Severn Lake causeway which will run from Lavernock Point to Brean Down. Instead it'll be service access only. And his enormous engineering wonder – artificial islands, free-flow shipping channels, lifeboat station, four marinas, fishing reserves, industrial-grade composter, waste storage and 200 hydro-electric turbines generating more power than anything the nuclear industry can come up with – will be constructed entirely from the sea. No land-based cranes or cliff-side excavation. Fourteen billion to build and ready by 2020. Fort Road and Lavernock can sleep tight.

Gareth, a self-styled maverick entrepreneur, lives on the hills, high above Neath. He's run a garage, worked for Aberthaw Power Station and for Costain Concrete but made his money as a speculative property developer. Working for himself. He's currently turning the ancient 112 acre farm of Pen Rhiw Angharad Uchaf into an up-market holiday village. Lodges cost £300,000 and have the best views in Wales. His core belief is that Wales has far too many layers of government. Seven, at least, who mess with his causeway proposal. He battles valiantly against local planning departments and their incompetent governance. He appears in public at the drop of a hat and speaks out for those who distrust a Welsh Government riddled, as he sees it, with bureaucracy and lack of vision.

Gareth's Severn Lake, as he styles it, proposes a causeway to run right across the massively tidal Severn Estuary at its widest economically feasible point creating a vast calmed lake of some 145,000 hectares. There have been proposals for dams further west including an enormous outer barrage to run from Minehead to Aberthaw, but most of these have never got much further than idea stage. It's obvious, really, in fact it would be stupid not to build it, he tells me. Renewable energy, free forever. Enough to cover at least 5% of the country's needs. Non-polluting, safer than nuclear and with a myriad of side-benefits. The massive tidal rise and fall on this Estuary is a gift. We must make it work for us.

So why hasn't a barrage been built already, I wondered? "Same reason that they didn't dig the Channel Tunnel to France in 1802," says Gareth. That was when engineer Albert Mathieu proposed an oil-lamp illuminated tunnel which used horse-drawn carriages and had an artificial island mid-channel on which the animals could be changed. They didn't dig it then because nobody believed they could get a quick enough return on their investment and the man in the street thought that such a tunnel would compromise national security. Substitute the words "wildlife habitat" for "national security" and you pretty much have the situation in the Severn Estuary today.

We are sitting in Pen Rhiw Angharad Uchaf next to a notice which reads *If you've not been invited you'd better have a damn good reason for calling here.* There's another on the wall that says *It's Business not Personal.* This is a place of slogans. Gareth is detailing his proposals. He is careful to call his project the Severn Lake and the river barrier a causeway rather than a barrage. "We'd need four years to do the environmental assessment and cover the rest of the paperwork and then we'd need seven more for actual construction. Crown estates, who own the coastal land we'll need, are keen because they see the causeway as an income generator." "What sort of income?" I ask. "Rentals from the residential islands, leisure use charges, retail of biomass generated by waste storage underneath the caissons, fishing licences, sales of ice cream at the visitor centre." There's an artist's impression of this on the Severn Lake website[4]. It reminds me of a conference centre on the front at Llandudno.

Unlike the majority of entrepreneurs, Gareth is also a poet. He writes under the unforgettable ffugenw[5] of Lewas ap Foote, a name chosen to bolster his Welsh credentials. Not, given his accent and his birthplace, Wick in the Vale, that they really need bolstering. In 2004 ap Foote came up with a poem about turbines and floating wave-power generators. Two years later he included this in a new collection[6] and, in an attempt to generate publicity, decided he might have a go at turning the poetic dream into hard reality. With considerable entrepreneurial flair he submitted two planning applications for Change of Use. These were sent simultaneously to both the Vale of Glamorgan and Somerset Councils on St David's Day 2006. The applications proposed changing the use of the Severn from river to lake. "Simple. You don't have to own things in order to put in planning apps," Gareth tells me. "People do this kind of thing all the time." That may be but the scale of Gareth's proposals were breathtaking.

The results are history. The Vale sent him a nine-page letter requesting more detail. Somerset thought for a moment.

Nobody had ever submitted anything like this before. Then they referred the application to the Department of Trade and Industry. After a period of consideration the Government demanded to see the proposal's principals. Financiers, business-men, fellow entrepreneurs, Sky TV trucks and the rest of the world's media beat a path to Gareth's door. This is turning out to be more than a stunt, Gareth decided. I'd best get serious.

The resulting Severn Tidal Power Feasibility study, which the government tried to get Gareth to pay for but ended up financing themselves, was launched in 2008 under a Labour administration. It reported in 2010[7] under the coalition. It contained details of a number of proposals including barrages, reefs, walls, lagoons, lakes, floating generators, wave platforms, and turbines. Its conclusions were damningly negative. Newspapers, in a bidding war, put the cost, eventually, at £34 billion. "You couldn't make it up," said Gareth. Environmental concerns were enormous. Nuclear power would be far cheaper. The then Energy Secretary, Chris Huhne, described the costs as "excessive" and ruled that there was no strategic case for building. No Government subsidy would therefore be forth-coming. However, if private business chose to construct a tidal-power scheme, then the government would not stand in their way.

The environmental lobby, fearful of loss of habitat, feeding ground pollution, groundwater rise, flood, fish death, and the wrecking of avian migration routes, breathed again. The Severn Tidal Power Group (STPG)[8], a consortium of major construc-tion companies who had got together first in the early 80s, faded away. The independents with their plans for tidal reefs, Severn fences and seabed power generators sited in new lagoons all turned their attention to other things. But Gareth is undeterred. Game on, he confidently writes, on the Severn Lake website. Green light. Go. "It'll be built, of that I am absolutely certain," he says.

His closest supporters, or at least those who have not yet totally abandoned their plans and taken down their websites, appear to be Corlan Hafren[9]. This is a consortium which includes Ove Arup and KPMG and numbers Lord Deben, the former Tory Minister John Gummer, among its directors.

Corlan Hafren plan a causeway similar to Gareth's Severn Lake proposal. They'll trade on leisure charges, boat facilities and massive power generation. They plan a circular rail link running across the barrage and returning via the existing Severn Tunnel. As an economic region this part of Wales and England will merge.

They also present some clever ideas concerning the Severn's port facilities. Existing docks on the empounded side of their barrage – Cardiff, Newport, Bristol – will continue to operate as at present. Future growth in Ultra Large Container Vessels (ULCV) traffic, however, will be facilitated elsewhere. These new 2020 giant ships will need very wide berths and very deep water. Corlan Hafren will sort this by demolishing half of the Sandfields Estate, moving Aberavon Beach south to Margam Sands or more likely north to Swansea Bay and putting in a brand new ULCV deep water port at Port Talbot. It's an amazing Wales-bending future that may well hit a few bumps if and when it gets debated at the Senedd, never mind at Neath Port Talbot Council.

They can move ahead, they say, without the need for significant investment of public money. Game on, as Gareth says. But despite all the uptalk, fluid optimism and the consortium's manoeuvring it may never come to this. The environmental difficulties the group face are more than huge and build will require some significant shift in public attitude as well as a change in the way that protection regulations are applied.

Recently the Shadow Welsh Secretary, Peter Hain, has stood down from his shadow cabinet role and, denying hotly that his actions are anything to do with upcoming retirement, put his weight firmly behind the Barrage proposals. Port Talbot will be regenerated, Wales and the world will be saved. He and Gareth need to get together.

There's another framed slogan on the wall at Gareth's valley-top eyrie. *Does it look like I care,* it reads. Maybe he didn't in the past but, trouble is, I think now he actually does.

Sailing

I have the Nikon in my pack. Hanging it round my neck would make me a tourist. Letting it dangle there on its black and yellow lettered strap. Around me they are all taking snaps. Compacts, phones, video cams. Holding up their recorders of joy, squinting through the sunlight at the flickering images on the screens on their backs. Back in 1995 Bill Gates told us we were approaching a totally interconnected world where every breathing thing we did would be recorded[10]. Everything would be logged and kept. Out here on the Severn's not yet choppy sea it's happening around me. We're on the *Balmoral* pleasure steamer sailing out of Penarth. Queued with the hordes on the refurbished pier. Families, retirees with white Welsh moustaches, ship spotters, the overweight in trackies, sea voyeurs, fans of the deep, loungers with little else to do. Recognised no one. Would have been amazed if I had.

Pleasure steamers have been ploughing these waters since Victorian times. First as a transport link managed by the railway companies taking holidaymakers from Wales to the West of England resorts. Later as ferries for those who couldn't face the road haul up through Gloucester. And finally as a way to waste time cruising the slate grey sea simply for the pleasure of setting out and then coming back. The operator everyone remembers was P & A Campbell with its White Funnel Fleet. *The Bristol Queen, The Britannia, The Ravenswood, The Cardiff Queen, The Sea Breeze, The Devonia, The Waverley, The Vectra.*

They were paddle steamers, flat-bottomed boats with great steam-operated blades like mill wheels set halfway down the sides. They'd hit the waves and bang over their tops rather than cut through. They'd bounce and rock and thwack. Seasickness, even on short Channel trips, was a constant. P & A Campbell operated from the 1890s until the failing economics for this sort of boat saw them give up a century on. Who wanted to set to sea in such antiquated ships? Wooden decks, bar and cafeteria in the saloon below, face full of sea salt and breeze, an hour and you'd be there. Penarth Pier to Weston. Who would want to go?

Many, as it turned out. A few years down the road and with the aid of grants from the Heritage Lottery Fund, the new

Waverley Steam Navigation Company, salvaged and refurbished both the steamer, *The Balmoral,* and the world's last seagoing paddle ship, *The Waverley,* and put them to work around the coasts of Britain. Today they run a season in the Bristol Channel – connecting Penarth with Ilfracombe, sailing to Lundy, up the Avon to Bristol, the mouth of the Wye, round the Holms, from Penarth to Minehead, to Newport, to Swansea, to Porthcawl. All for pleasure. No one does this because they want to get where the ships go.

It's a fragile operation too, delayed by storm and tide and the whims of the ancient ship's motors. But mostly it works, in a half decent summer. A pint and pie below deck. Views of receding Wales and advancing England on top.

The author Tom Davies worked the steamers in the 1950s. As a young man with a desire to become a sailor, he began here as an apprentice steward working the holiday routes from Cardiff to the Edwardian piers of the West of England's Coast. According to *Testament*[10,] where he unravels his life story, the crews spent most of their time drunk, the piers got regularly dented and the ships grounded on the Estuary's regularly emerging mud banks. It was on the paddle steamers that Davies "first learned about feckless, desperate men making their erratic way in a hostile world". The great scam, led by the Chief Steward, was to dump the official menus overboard as soon as the steamer had cast off. The galley's advertised 6/6d plaice and chips would then be sold for 7/6d a go, netting a shilling profit for the steward each time. You had to take part, Davies, ever the honest man, reasoned. If you didn't then the punters might talk among themselves and the whole scam would go down.

Davies did two seasons dealing with pilots who were too drunk to manage and with the endless roll and pitch of the decks as the ships smacked their ways across confused and churning seas. Campbells operated six steamers in that decade. Trade was brisk. Tom eventually went to sea, the big sea, the real sea, with the Union Castle Line, sailing round the coasts of Africa and through the Suez Canal before becoming a reporter and, later, a successful novelist. Sea in your blood. In his but certainly not mine.

My first experience was a crossing from Cardiff to

Ilfracombe in 1956 on board *The Cardiff Queen*. It was a salient experience too. I was being taken on holiday. Suitcase in the hold. "It will be great," my father had told me. "Cricket on the beach, funfairs, loads of sun. On the crossing we'll see fish. And we'll have sarsparilla and crisps in the saloon." There were none of these things, as far as I can remember. There were, instead, desperate men and a world that turned out to be extremely hostile. A storm blew up as soon we got out of port and onto the Cardiff Roads which veer west to avoid the great sandbanks of Cefn y Wrach. The deck began to buck with increasing violence. Great sheets of water poured across its boards. Ahead the waves climbed like mountains. Things continued like this for the whole three hours it took us to cross to Devon. I was ill. I was ill so much that I ran out things to be ill with. I was an empty moaning vessel full of pain and gut wrenching despair. So was everyone else.

Ilfracombe did not have a fun fair. And I didn't see much of the beach. I can't remember any cricket. Just the train we took to get home, my father complaining about the cost of the entire and, it has to be said, lovely journey. Smuts, cows in fields, whizzing telegraph poles. I swore I'd never go to sea again after that.

Paddle Steaming was never much of a cultural affair. Although there were sea-borne jazz dances that ran right through until the 1990s. Mike Harries and his Jazzmen, the Cardiff stalwarts, would blow in the saloon. Beer would be consumed in huge quantity and drunken Dixie dancing would follow. The steamers would sail in circles. Passengers, crisp packets and plastic-glassed pints in hand, were there to have a good time. Some enjoyed themselves so much that they fell off the pier and into the sea when they disembarked.

In its heyday as a promoter of the old guard Anglo-Welsh, the Welsh Academy organised a ship-borne poetry reading in the 1980s. Like a jazz dance but with bards instead of bands. The ship would leave Penarth Pier and describe a great circle in the Channel before reluctantly coming back. It was a great idea, live literature with the Welsh coast as a backdrop. Poetry with added salt. Helen Dunmore guested. Dannie Abse was the star. He stood next to the funnel with his audience, those who could be extracted from the saloon bar, respectfully clustered on the slowly pitching deck. As he began the ship's hooter sounded, a long low moan drowning his verses. Campbells commentary on culture. Maybe poetry just doesn't work out of doors.

The Balmoral[12], which disappointingly has no paddles, does most of the Bristol Channel legwork now. Built originally in 1949 it's been doing so since it returned after refurbishment in 1986. New engines, replaced decks, a self-service restaurant now avoiding Tom's tricks, and two bars. It's big enough to accommodate 750 passengers. Today we are not that number but we are still a load.

As we sail, Cardiff recedes and begins to resemble the port it actually is. The coast merges with the sea as distance intervenes. The waters of this Estuary now seem more vast than any view from bridge, path or headland has hitherto revealed. The coasts themselves cease to run in the straight lines I'd imagined them to follow. Instead the curves of the Heritage Coast and the promontory of Brean Down begin to dominate. Come up here mid-channel, heading east, and ahead would be Newport or Bristol. You'd need to know Cardiff was there in order to arrive.

Around us are gulls, the ship's wake full of them. In the distance are yachts, a group of them circling. And a dredger, slowly moving mid-waters. More ships in one go than I've habitually seen from my coastal walks. Maybe you've got to be part of this ship sailing stuff to see what's really happening. The smell of brine. The engines throbbing. The decks as smooth as the sky. I steam on. Calm prevails. I put some more pixels onto my storage card. Severn experience finally complete.

Afterword – Wales Again

Walking through the Mill Park, Roath on a spring morning I feel as if the desire to travel has been somewhat satiated. The setting out and the arriving, the motorway thrum, the hills on my right hand, my head full of whatever music the iPod was that day dispensing. The landscape constantly rocking and rolling, spinning before me as I interrogated, explored, exclaimed, pontificated and then moved west. Always west again.

In the park the local archeological society are spending the day looking for the remains of the mill that had stood by the Roath Brook, its wheel slowly turning, since at least 1102. Men with geophys arrays like elaborate TV aerials and walking slowly across the ribbon-marked grass. At their tent the members of the society are patiently explaining to passers-by that the mill ground corn for the landowners at Roath Court and that it predated local house build. "My house was built in 1907," interjects a woman in a knitted black hat and long knitted black coat. "What's left?" asks someone else. Not much. The stonework that held the wheel still sits in the stream but we're looking for the mill's actual foundations. What else was here? Those devices out there use magnetometry and measure ground resistivity. Around us the grass shows no signs of ever having a building upon it. The geophys men have reached the end of their furrow and are now slowly ploughing back.

They pulled the mill down, without ceremony, in 1897. The past had ceased to be important. Cardiff was booming, its population expanding, its moneymen turning many a buck. The Mill Gardens in which I am standing opened in 1912. The mill pond was drained, the Goosler, the land on which generations had kept fowl, was turfed. A paddling pool was dug and a green wooden hut for the use of leisure seekers erected. Cardiff expanded. Roath dissolved.

Where I am is certainly at the edge of something. A place of uncertainty. That's such a fashionable thing now. Edges, ends, interzones, waste spaces, conclusions of territory, irregularities, unfinished areas, awkwardnesses, things that should be but are not quite, things that given time may be altered but time is never on their side. Things where the centre ceases to hold. These places are trending. There are books by the dozen written about them. They are no longer ignored or avoided. The worst to cross, the hardest to love and the least engaging have moved right on up.

My trip, right along the southern edge of Wales, where the tectonic plate of difference from England slips slowly into the water, has told me more about my country than any Eisteddfod or historical lecture, and I've been to loads of both of those. Is Wales different? Somedays you look and it's not. On others it's significantly so. Along the coast, crossing that stretched-out version of Cardiff imagined by the Tudors, I experienced moments that made me certain I was in a country that was not a mere appendage of its much larger neighbour. The insistence among the West Country accented lave fishermen that they were not from Gloucestershire but from Cymru. The bilingual nature of almost every directional and information sign I passed. The administration. The flags. The sense of Wales that rose around me from the path I trod. The greenness of the hills.

As I crossed England's Welsh mirror along the Estuary's edge things may have seemed bigger, more suited to turning profit, and with more facilities and grander designs but I don't think they were ultimately better. My quest was to find out where the line between the two territories ran. I guess I never actually discovered it. Things do not finish at lines in the sand. They fade and dissolve. They shift and shift. They merge with moving abandon. They are how they are one day and different the next. Subatomic Wales, particle England. Quarks of charm and strangeness. Anglicised Bosons. Anglo-Welsh Neutrinos. Fermionau Gymreig.

Some of the things I didn't do:

Break anything
Get arrested
Fly along the water's edge

Exit the Bay Barrage at high speed on an inflatable
Get to Lundy
Sail down the Severn on a freighter and like Bronislav
Korchinsky in the film of *Tiger Bay* be brought back by police
boat.
Crack access to Scottish & Southern's coal-fired Uskmouth B
By kayak enter the sea cave at the end of Worm's Head
Surf the bore
Get lost

But I did, despite many privations, get myself from Chepstow
to Worm's Head. 138 miles[1]. A mere bagatelle in these days of
boy-next-door triathlon winners, marathon runners in every
street and people known to me personally who have been to
every one of earth's continents, including Antarctica and
especially the lost Welsh colony in Patagonia.

Should others do the same? Given the newly established All
Wales Footpath such a project would now be a pushover.
Except that the route of that path is not the one I always used.
In fact I found myself not on it more often than on. There were
gates which I opened, fences I crossed and deviations I ignored.
The leisure way was not my way. I wasn't doing the trip to get
a rambler's medal. I was a psychogeographer and that meant
engaging in geography, social geography, topographical geography, fantasy geography and geography that I created by tossing
dice in the air.

How many ways are there to move from Chepstow to Worm's
Head, the Tudor port of Cardiff writ deep in the landscape? As
Cardiff grows it may well spin out to become this again, fling-
ing its suburbs and new builds out along the water-facing coast.
Cities of the future will not need to cluster in balls or wedge
themselves into defensible declivities. They will sprawl where
the money takes them. Where the living will be good and deprivation small. Allow the developers unregulated access and this
may well be what we'll get. But that's the future. For now I
simply wish to consider in all this just how many ways there are
to make the transit. How many routes? How many methods? I
check the maps again just to be sure. More than one? More than
ten? Many, I guess. As many as you like.

Thanks and Acknowledgements

William Ayot; Des Barry; John Briggs; Don Brooks; Robin Campbell; Martyn Clark – *G24i*; Dave Coombs; Tony Curtis; Ceri Cope – *Siemens*; Tricia Cottnam – *Cardiff Council*; Ian Crummack – *DONG*; Grahame Davies; Joanne Gossage – *Newport City Council*; Chris Green – *APB*; Russell Higgins; Nigel Jenkins; Glyn Jones – *BARS*; Pete Marlow; Brian Miller – *DONG*; Robert Minhinnick; Martin Morgan – *Black Rock Lave Fishermen*; Edward Nightingale; Paul Parker – *Severn Estuary Partnership*; Paul Rebhan – *G24i*; Lynne Rees; Paul Ridley; Heike Roms; Janet Rzezniczek; Daryl Sindle – *G24i*; Amy Sherborne – *Aberthaw Power Station*; Meic Stephens; Chris Torrance; John Williams; Barbara Wilshere; Sue Wilshere; Kevin Wilson – *Chepstow Rifle Club*; Gareth & Ann Woodham – *Severn Lake Ltd*; Sarah Woolley – *DONG*. And, of course, to Mick Felton at Seren for his close and supportive editing.

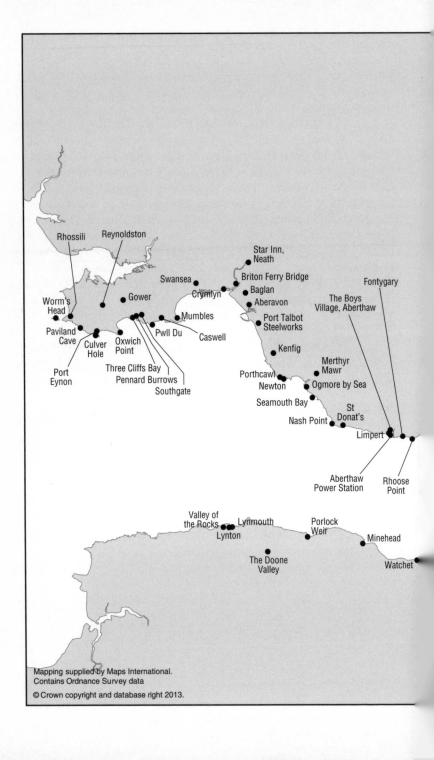

Rhossili   Reynoldston

Star Inn,
Neath

Swansea   Crymlyn   Briton Ferry Bridge

Baglan

Aberavon

Fontygary

Gower

The Boys
Village, Aberthaw

Worm's
Head

Mumbles

Port Talbot
Steelworks

Paviland
Cave

Pwll Du

Caswell

Culver
Hole

Oxwich
Point

Kenfig

Port
Eynon

Three Cliffs Bay

Merthyr
Mawr

Pennard Burrows

Porthcawl

Southgate

Newton

Ogmore by Sea

Seamouth Bay

St
Donat's

Nash Point

Limpert

Aberthaw
Power Station

Rhoose
Point

Valley of
the Rocks   Lynmouth

Porlock
Weir

Lynton

Minehead

The Doone
Valley

Watchet

Mapping supplied by Maps International.
Contains Ordnance Survey data

© Crown copyright and database right 2013.

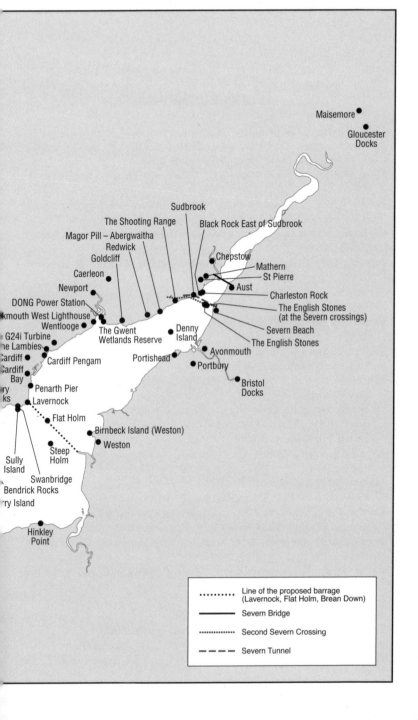

Maisemore

Gloucester
Docks

Sudbrook

The Shooting Range

Black Rock East of Sudbrook

Magor Pill – Abergwaitha

Redwick

Chepstow

Goldcliff

Mathern

Caerleon

St Pierre

Newport

Aust

DONG Power Station

Charleston Rock

kmouth West Lighthouse

The English Stones
(at the Severn crossings)

Wentlooge

Denny
Island

Severn Beach

G24i Turbine

The Gwent
Wetlands Reserve

The English Stones

he Lambies

Avonmouth

Cardiff

Cardiff Pengam

Portishead

Portbury

Cardiff
Bay

ry
ks

Penarth Pier

Bristol
Docks

Lavernock

Flat Holm

Sully
Island

Birnbeck Island (Weston)

Weston

Steep
Holm

Swanbridge

Bendrick Rocks

ry Island

Hinkley
Point

··········	Line of the proposed barrage (Lavernock, Flat Holm, Brean Down)
———	Severn Bridge
···············	Second Severn Crossing
– – –	Severn Tunnel

Works Consulted

Amis, Kingsley, *The Old Devils*, Hutchinson, 1986

Ap Foote, Lewas, *The Grumpy OldWelshman*, Lifestory Services, 2012

Ayot, William, *The Inheritance*, PS Avalon, 2011

Ayot, William, *Moynes Court – A Contextual History*, unpublished, 2011

Barber, Chris, *A Guidebook to Arthurian Caerleon – History and Legend in the True Land of King Arthur*, Blorenge Books, 2010

Benjamin, E. Alwyn, *Penarth 1841-71 A Glimpse of the Past*, D Brown & Sons, 1980

Bowen, E.G., *Britain And the Western Seaways*, Thames & Hudson, 1972

Breverton, Terry, *Glamorgan Seascape Pathways*, Glyndwr Publishing, 2003

Breverton, Terry, *The Secret Vale of Glamorgan*, Glyndwr Publishing, 2000

Brewer, Richard J, *Caerleon And The Roman Army*, National Museums & Galleries of Wales, 1987

Campbell, Robin, *Sites: Public Art In Swansea 1985-1990*, Swansea City Council, 1993

Chappell, Edgar L., *History of the Port of Cardiff*, Priory Press, 1939

Conway Jones, Hugh, *Gloucester Docks An Historical Guide*, Black Dwarf Publications, 2009

Croxford, Colin, *Lynton & Lynmouth A Shortish Guide*, Bossiney Books, 2008

Davies, John and others, *The Welsh Academy Encyclopaedia of Wales*, University of Wales Press, 2008

Davies, Tom, *Testament*, Berwyn Mountain Press, 2008

Edmunds, George, *The Gower Coast*, Regional Publications, 1979

Evans, Stuart, *Wales Fisheries Strategy*, Welsh Assembly Government, 2008

Ferris, Paul, *Gower In History – Myth, People, Landscape*, Armanleg Books, 2009

Finch, Peter, *Real Cardiff*, Seren, 2002

Finch, Peter, *Real Cardiff Two*, Seren, 2004

Finch, Peter, *The Welsh Poems*, Shearsman Books, 2006

Fry, Trevor, *Return To Severn Beach* (DVD), 1st Take Video.

Gillham, Mary E., *A Natural History of Cardiff – Exploring Along the*

Rivers Rhymney and Roath, Dinefwr Publishers, 2006

Gillham, Mary E., *The Glamorgan Heritage Coast Wildlife Series Volume 1 – Sand Dunes*, Glamorgan Heritage Coast Project, 1987

Gillham, Mary E., *The Glamorgan Heritage Coast Wildlife Series Volume 2 – Rivers*, Glamorgan Heritage Coast Project, 1989

Gillham, Mary E., *The Glamorgan Heritage Coast Wildlife Series Volume 4 – Coastal Downs Ogmore and Dunraven*, Glamorgan Heritage Coast Project, 1993

Gillham, Mary E., *The Glamorgan Heritage Coast Wildlife Series Volume 5 – Sea Cliffs Cwm Mawr to Gileston*, Glamorgan Heritage Coast Project, 1994

Griffiths, Barrie, *Kenfig Folk: Part 1. The First Borough of Kenfig, 1147-1439*, Kenfig Society, 2011

Griffiths, Barrie, *Welcome to Kenfig, The Kenfig Society Monograph No 20*, The Kenfig Society, 2002

Griffiths, Barrie, *The House At Sker Point – The Kenfig Society Monograph No 19*, The Kenfig Society, 2001

Hall, Alan, *St Donat's Castle – A Guide and Brief History*, Atlantic College, 2002

Holmes, Richard, *Shelley The Pursuit*, Weidenfeld & Nicholson, 1974

Holt, Heather, *Pwlldu Remembered*, Heather Holt, 1996

Howden, J.C.W., *Theme Gardens at Dunraven*, Glamorgan Heritage Coast Project

Hudson, Rob, *From East to West & Dawn to Dusk – Photographs of the Glamorgan Heritage Coast*, Church Row Books, 2007

Hutton, John, *An Illustrated History of Cardiff Docks*, Silver Link, 2008

Jenkins, Nigel, *Real Swansea*, Seren, 2008

Jenkins, Nigel, *Real Swansea Two*, Seren, 2012

Jenkins, Nigel & Pearl, David, *Gower*, Gomer, 2009

Jones, Neville, *A Roam Through Swansea and Gower*, Neville Jones, 1992

Jones, Sally Roberts, *The History of Port Talbot*, Goldleaf Publishing, 1991

King, Robert, *Haunted Neath*, The History Press, 2009

Knight, Jeremy K, *Caerleon, Roman Fortress*, CADW, 1988

The Leys Golfing Society – *Members' Handbook 2006-2007*

McCall, Bernard, *Still Passing The Point*, Coastal Shipping Publications, 2010

Minhinnick, Robert, *Sea Holly*, Seren, 2007

Minhinnick, Robert and Bourke, Eamon, *Fairground Music – The World of Porthcawl Funfair*, Gomer Press, 2010

Morgan, Alun, *Porthcawl Newton & Nottage – A Concise Illustrated History*, D Brown & Sons Ltd., 1987

Morgan, Dennis, *An Illustrated History of Cardiff's Suburbs*, Breedon Books, 2003

Morgan, Keith, *Images of Wales – Around Porthcawl, Newton And Nottage*, Tempus, 1996

National Trust, *Exploring Gower – A Selection Of Walks*, National Trust, 2008

Neal, Marjorie and others, compiler, *Rumney & St. Mellons – A History of Two Villages*, Rumney and District Local History Society, 2005

Newman, John, *The Buildings of Wales – Glamorgan*, Penguin, 1995

Perkins, J.W. and others, *The Glamorgan heritage Coast – A Guide to its Geology*, Glamorgan Heritage Coast, 1975

Pierce, Gwynedd O., *Place-Names In Glamorgan*, Merton Priory Press, 2002

Porch, Richard, *Swansea's Heritage*, The History Press, 2008

Proser, Tim, *The Lynmouth Flood Disaster*, Lyndale Photographic Ltd, 2001

Punter, John (editor), *Urban Design And the British Urban Renaissance*, Routledge, 2010

Rainsbury, Anne, *Chepstow And the River Wye* – Britain in Old Photographs Series, The History Press, 1989

Rhys, Ernest, *The South Wales Coast – From Chepstow to Aberystwyth*, Frederick A. Stokes, Co., 1911

Richards, John, *Cardiff – A Maritime History*, Tempus, 2005

Riopelle, Christopher & Sumner, Ann, *Sisley In England Wales*, National Gallery Company, London, 2008

Robbins, Terry, *Digging Up Kenfig – The Kenfig Society Monograph No 22*, The Kenfig Society, 2002

Rowson, Stephen & Wright, Ian L., *The Glamorganshire and Aberdare Canals Volume Two, Pontypridd to Cardiff*, Black Dwarf Publications, 2004

Rubens, Bernice, *I Sent A Letter To My Love*, W H Allen, 1975

Rzezniczek, Janet, *Echoes From The Past – A Family History*, unpublished, 1998.

Schweitzer, Deirdre, *A Guide to St Donat's Church*, The Rector and Churchwardens of St Donat's Church

Severn Estuary Partnership, *Severn Estuary – Joint Issues Report, May 1997*, Environment Agency, 1997

Severn Estuary Partnership, *Strategy For The Severn Estuary*, Severn Estuary Partnership, 2001

Severn Estuary Partnership, *State of the Severn Estuary Report, Autumn, 2011*, Severn Estuary Partnership, 2012

Shipsides, Frank and Wall, Robert, *Bristol: Maritime City*, The Redcliffe Press, 1981

Takel, R., *The Story of Ports and Shipping along the Glamorgan Heritage Coast*, Takel, 1982

Tames, Richard, *Isambard Kingdom Brunel*, Shire Publications, 2009

Taylor, Duncan, *The Maritime Trade of the Smaller Bristol Channel Ports In the Sixteen Century*, Phd Thesis, University of Bristol, 2010

Thorne, A.R., *Place Names of Penarth, Historical and Colloquial*, D Brown & Sons, 1997

Valeways, *The Valeways Millennium Heritage Trail*, Valeways, 2005

Waters, Brian, *The Bristol Channel*, J.M.Dent, 1955

Weston-Super-Mare's Seafront Enhancements – The Beauty of Engineering, North Somerset Council, 2010

White, Jon Manchip, *The Journeying Boy*, The Atlantic Monthly Press, 1991

Williams, Allan and others, *Coastal Processes and Landforms – The Glamorgan Heritage Coast*, Glamorgan Heritage Coast, 1997

Williams, Diane M., *Gower – A Guide to Ancient and Historic Monuments On The Gower Peninsula*, CADW, 1998

Williams, Glanmor (editor), *Swansea An Illustrated History*, Christopher Davies, 1990

Williams, John, *Bloody Valentine – A Killing In Cardiff*, Harper Collins, 1994

Maps

Ordnance Survey 1:25 000 scale Explorer series
The Tudor Port of Cardiff:
OL14 Wye Valley & Forest of Dean
154 Bristol West & Portishead
152 Newport & Pontypool
151 Cardiff & Bridgend
165 Swansea
164 Gower

England:
179 Gloucester, Cheltenham & Stroud
154 Bristol West & Portishead
153 Weston-Super-Mare & Bleadon Hill
140 Quantock Hills & Bridgewater
OL9 Exmoor
139 Bideford, Ilfracombe & Barnstaple

Notes

The Land and the Water

1. Ballard, J.G., *The Drowned World*, Gollancz, 1962
2. Baxter, Stephen, *The Flood*, Gollancz, 2008
3. I paraphrase. The formal Welsh Government strategy is to a) Reduce the consequences for individuals, communities, businesses and the environment from flooding and coastal erosion, b) Raise awareness of, and engage people in the response to flood and coastal erosion risk, c) Provide an effective and sustained response to flood and coastal erosion events, and, d) Prioritise investment in the most at risk communities.
4. Environment Agency Wales is in a special position – it is an Assembly Government Sponsored Body (AGSB), while also being part of the corporate Environment Agency for England and Wales.
5. There's a lot more information on the Partnership on their web site and in their Business Plan at http://www.severnestuary.net/sep/partnership.html
6. *Severn Estuary – Joint Issues Report*, Environment Agency, 1997
7. *Strategy For The Severn Estuary*, Severn Estuary Partnership, September, 2001
8. *State of the Severn Estuary Report – An Initial Overview of the Estuary's Uses and Features*, Severn Estuary Partnership, 2012.
9. The ports at Bristol are owned and managed by the Bristol Port Company. Those at Cardiff, Newport, Swansea, Barry and Port Talbot by ABP, Associated British Ports. The smallest port in size is Swansea at 521 acres. In trade it's Barry with 281,000 tonnes annually.
10. Source: *Department for Transport Port Freight Statistics*, 2010
11. The 2010 Harbour Revision Order grants permission for the construction of a port capable of handling future generations of ultra-large container vessels carrying up to 18,000 containers. There will be a new 1.2km quay and 100 acres of storage facility. Source: *State of the Severn Estuary Report*, 2011
12. Tamion – Taff. Fluvius Sabrina – River Severn
13. Although maybe without the same degree of sleaze. Leek was constantly threatened, assaulted and held against his will by those not wishing to pay duty. Eventually he gave in. He was dismissed from his post for gross corruption in 1571.

The East: Chepstow to Redwick

1. Nor in the *Geiriadur Prifysgol Cymru*, last word in words at the time of writing
2. See also p. 40 for a description of Ayot's castle, Moynes Court, in the village of Mathern and the *On the Border* series itself.
3. St Tecla came to the rocks off the southern tip of Beachley in the fourth

century. The chapel she founded there is long gone. A chapel dedicated to St Twrog was built on the same site but by the eighteenth century was in ruins. The rocks hold a holy well and a navigation light. Access is dangerous and can only be made at low tide.

4. The gout is the preferred method for draining landwater into the sea. A flap is installed in the seawall that only opens outwards. When the tide ebbs the gout opens, when it flows the seawater presses the flap back.

5. The (invented) science of what lies beyond metaphysics first expounded by Alfred Jarry in 1893. Ionesco was a fervent adherent.

6. Some historians suggest that this inlet was known as Porthiscoed, the harbour below the woods, the original Portskewett or Porth Ysgewin y Gwent, one of the Chief Ports of the island of Britain, according to *Trioedd Ynys Prydein*. The place was significant enough to be used as one of the island of Britain's measuring points (as in from Land's End to John O'Groats). An ancient ridgeway bound for Monmouth passed nearby.

7. *Coflein*, which sounded to me like the surname of a minority language French researcher, is one of those wonderful pronounceable (just) by people who don't speak Welsh word amalgamations. This one welds *cof* (memory) with *lein* (line). Timeline. Neat. http://www.coflein.gov.uk/.

8. *Iron John* was poet Robert Bly's analysis of the Brothers Grimm tale of the same name. Against a backdrop of rising feminism, Bly demonstrates who men are and the place of masculinity in a rapidly changing world. *Iron John*, Addison-Wesley, 1990.

9. A number are collected in *Small Things That Matter*, The Well at Olivier Mythodrama Publishing, 2003, and others in *The Inheritance*, PS Avalon, 2011. Further information on William Ayot's website:, www.williamayot.com.

10. Most extraordinary 20 minute reading in the entire series, Ayot tells me.

11. According to oral testimony given to the local historian Fred Hando (*Out and About in Monmouthshire*, R.H. Johns, 1958) the stone coffin is still there. In 1881 it was seen by a local resident, skeleton extant with a hole in the skull made by the point of a spear still visible.

12. Published in Latin in 1616 as *Rerum Anglicarum, Henrico VIII., Edwardo VI. et Maria regnantibus, Annales* and translated in the English by Godwin's son, Morgan, as *Annales of England* in 1630

13. *The Man in the Moone* was written by Godwin in the late 1620s and published posthumously under the pseudonym Domingo Gonsales in 1638.

14. Owen, an American, believed that Shakespeare's plays had actually been written under a nom de plume by Francis Bacon. He came to this conclusion while decoding secret messages in the plays themselves. Nothing was found.

15. *Fishtraps In the Middle Severn Estuary: Air-Photographic Evidence From the Mid Twentieth Century*, J.R.L. Allen. *Archaeology In the Severn Estuary*, 2004 (Annual report of the Severn Estuary Levels Research Committee)

16. The Severn Estuary Research Committee (SELRC) founded in 1985. An organisation which promotes archeological research into the Estuary levels. http://www.selrc.org.uk/.

17. That, too, has stopped trading. Operations ceased in 2006.

18. Bromwich, Rachael, *Trioedd Ynys Prydein*, UWP, 2006.

19. Take the kissing gate 150 metres from main road towards Leechpool. Kissing gate in hedge fence, short hill climb. Pudding stones on top of the rise.
20. Further details are at http://www.channel4.com/history/microsites/T/timeteam/2008/portskewett/portskewett-more.html.
21. There are many histories available. One of the swiftest is at http://www.greatwestern.org.uk/severn1.htm.
22. Webb, Harri, *Collected Poems*, Gwasg Gomer, 1995
23. Power, christened Raymond Leslie Howard, was renamed in 1959 in order to make headway in a rock and roll scene dominated by Wilde, Pride, Fury and Steele. He didn't.
24. A Pill: a creek or inlet. Derived from the Welsh for pool, *pwll*.
25. Palaeochannel – an ancient, currently inactive river or stream channel system. Archaeologists of the Levels have discovered many in the muds, just off the current shore. They are indicators of how these flatlands were once drained.
26. *RESTD 1875* is engraved over the porch along with an additional marker which indicates a restoration update in 1996. The 1875 restoration was by John Norton.
27. The Great Flood of 1607 is a feature of these levels. See p.85.
28. Founded and endowed in 1113 by Robert de Chandos. First an alien priory of Bec, Normandy. Later a cell of Tewkesbury. Dissolved in 1450.
29. "High above the water and not far from Caerleon there stands a rocky eminence which dominates the River Severn. In the English language it is called Goldcliff, the Golden Rock. When the sun's rays strike it the stone shines very bright and takes on a golden sheen." Gerald of Wales, *The Journey through Wales and the Description of Wales*, trans. Lewis Thorpe, Penguin, 1978.
30. The Hounds of Annwfn – dogs of the otherworld – from the Welsh Mabinogion.

Newport

1. *Quatermass* was originally a BBC TV science fiction serial from 1953, set in the near future against a background of the British Space programme. The series spawned a series of successful Hammer film productions. The BBC produced a live TV digital remake of *Quatermass* in 2005.
2. DONG's Severn Power Station has the capacity to generate up to 824 megawatts of electricity. It uses combined gas turbine technology making it one of the most efficient natural gas-fired power stations of its type. Over 1200 people worked on its construction. The plant is operated by Siemens on behalf of DONG. It has a staff of around forty.
3. At this time WPG traded under the name Carron Energy.
4. DONG's efficiency rate is so much higher due to the fact that at Severn Power it has a brand new state-of-the-art power station.
5. *Tak* – Danish for thanks
6. *Forbrydelsen* (lit. the crime) is a cult Danish TV serial broadcast in the UK as *The Killing*. The original Danish production is undubed and uses subtitles. Its twenty episodes of rainy landscape, miserable fast food and Thor-like characterisation beat the American ten-episode remake hands down.

7. Pill – inlet, tidal creek or stream. A common place name along the Welsh coast. Newport has a whole district bearing the same name.
8. See Branch in *Real Cardiff Three*, Seren, 2009, which describes a walk Briggs and I took tracking the route of the now vanished Roath Branch railway.
9. APB – Associated British Ports – http://www.abports.co.uk/.
10. In 1911 these were The Newport (Mon) Shipway Dry Dock and Engineering Company operating two dry docks – the Channel and the Union.
11. There have been at least eighteen transporter bridges in the world, based on Ferdinand Arondin's nineteenth century design for an aerial ferry. Eight still stand and six remain in use. The Newport Bridge has a direction sign showing locations and distances to all eight.
12. Newport's City Bridge on what is known locally as East Dock Road but is now the Southern Distributor opened in 2004.
13. WAG – Welsh Assembly Government, pronounced much like the thing dogs do. In 2011 redesignated by the incoming Labour administration as Welsh Government, WG, pronounced *oog*, more something Inuit or North American Indian.
14. 'Newport State of Mind'. Lyrics by M J Delaney, Tom Williams and Leo Sloley.
15. The Second Aeon Travelling Circus, poetry and music band circa 1970, was a performance spin-off from Peter Finch's second aeon poetry publishing enterprises of the period. The band featured variously Geraint Jarman, Heather Jones, Geoff Sherlock, Dave Reid, Huw Morgan, Christopher Morgan, Dave Mercer and Will Parfitt.
16. This was the country of the Silures, a Welsh tribe not easy to control.
17. Geoffrey of Monmouth: *History of the Kings of Britain*.
18. The National Roman Legion Museum, a branch of the National Museum of Wales.
19. http://www.caerleon.net/intro/heritage.htm.
20, Newman, John, *The Buildings of Wales – Gwent/Monmouthshire*, Pevsner's Architectural Guides, 2000.
21. Finch, Peter, *The Way It Grows*. http://www.youtube.com/watch?v=lED7 QLDLz9E.
22. 'The Way It Grows', included in Finch, Peter, *Selected Later Poems*, Seren 2007.

Cardiff

1. Ecotricity – http://www.ecotricity.co.uk/ – turning electricity bills into windmills – founded by Dale Vince, eco warrior and Peace Convoy engineer turned business victor – now one of the UK's fastest-rising green tech operators.
2 *Archaeology in the Severn Estuary*, 2002.
3. "In order to generate a 3-4 m tsunami at a distance of several hundred kilometres as implied by the tsunami explanation, an earthquake of magnitude 7.5 or higher (i.e., around 200 times more energy than the largest known earthquake in northwestern Europe) would have occurred. An earthquake of magnitude 6 or higher anywhere along the Atlantic margin of Ireland in 1607 would have been felt and reported across the whole of

northwestern Europe, including Ireland, great Britain, and France." *1607 Bristol Channel Floods: 400-Year Retrospective*, RMS report, Risk Management Solutions, Inc., 2007. http://www.rms.com/Reports/1607 _Bristol_Flood.pdf

4. *Lamentable newes out of Monmouthshire*, 1607.
5. Sources can be read on the Great Flood of 1607 website at http://website.lineone.net/~mike.kohnstamm/flood/.
6. From *Another Poem on the Flood. To William Stradling, Kinsman and Friend*, an epigram written originally in Latin. http://website.lineone.net/~mike. kohnstamm/flood/.
7. As described in *Records of the County Borough of Cardiff*, edited by John Hobson Matthews, Vol. 111, 1901.
8. Herman Melville wrote *Moby Dick*.
9. *Real Cardiff* – Seren, 2002.
10. CBAT – Cardiff Bay Arts Trust. Subsumed by Safle in 2007 when that public art organisation was formed by merging CBAT with Cywaith Cymru / Artworks Wales. Safle lost its Arts Council of Wales funding and closed in 2010.
11. Text for the poem appears in *The Welsh Poems*, Peter Finch. Shearsman Books, 2006. A description of its composition and installation appears in *Real Cardiff Two*, Peter Finch, Seren, 2004.
12. http://www.realandpresent.org/.
13. http://www.far-south.org/.
14. QR – Quick Response code – a matrix barcode the size of a fingernail consisting of black modules arranged in a square pattern on a white background – developed for use with camera phones.
15. Cortázar, Julio, *Hop Scotch*. Pantheon, 1966.
16. Barry, Des, *The Chivalry of Crime*, Jonathan Cape, 2001.
17. *Secret Station*, bronze, fibre optics & steam, 1992.
18. See p. 92.
19. *Stalker*, 1979, directed by Andrei Tarkovsky and based on Boris and Arkady Stugatsky's novel *Roadside Picnic* (Gollancz).
20. *Atlantic Echo* Dan Archer, 2000.
21. *Miss Shirley Bassey* by John L. Williams. Quercus, 2010.
22. On the air as I write reporting on the BBC journalists' strike.
23. Named after 'After Hours', the final song on the Velvet Underground's third, self-titled album *The Velvet Underground* which appeared in 1968.
24. 'Don't Give The Lifeguard a Second Chance' / 'White Tiger Burning (WTB)', Z. Block Records, 1979.
25. Pierre Vivant's 'Landmark', a publically funded art installation using road signs that sits on a roundabout at one of Cardiff Bay's eastern approaches. The work is known locally as 'The Magic Roundabout'.
26. The Dutch barge built in 1910 by Cornelis Hijstek and used initially for transporting cow dung used as a fertilizer for the Dutch tulip industry.
27. Williams, John L, *Into the Badlands*, Paladin 1991.
28. *The Cardiff Trilogy* which combined *Five Pubs, Two Bars and a Nightclub* (1999) with *Cardiff Dead* (2000) and *The Prince of Wales* (2003) was published by Bloomsbury in 2006. John Williams published a further Cardiff novel, *Temperance Town* in 2004.
29. Kerouac, Jack, *The Dharma Bums*, Viking Press, 1958.

30. *ibid.*
31. Humphreys, Christmas, *Buddhism*, Penguin Books, 1951.
32. Kerouac, Jack, *op. cit.*
33. *Porth Teigr*, a direct translation into Welsh of Tiger Port, something Cardiff was never actually called.
34. The Igloo Regeneration Fund is a partnership of pension, life and charity funds managed by Aviva Investors, which invests in sustainable urban regeneration across the UK. http://www.igloo.uk.net/projects/cardiff-tiger-bay. The Welsh Assembly Government (WAG) has now redesignated itself as the Welsh Government (WG). WAG WG WAG WG. There's a sound poem here.
35. Designed by Studio Bednarski and Flint & Neill from a winning competition entry.
36. 'Doomsday', a *Dr Who* episode featuring him returning to the Earth of the Cybermen Army was recorded in the Square in 2005.
37. Cardiff Barrage Skatepark – all persons using this facility do so at their own risk.
38. See 'The Billy Banks' in *Real Cardiff Two*, Seren, 2004.

The Beaches Everyone Vistits: Lavernock to Fontygary
1. Taff Vale railway Company – Barry to Cardiff http://www.webcitation.org/query?url=http://www.geocities.com/cardiffrail/TVR-Cadoxton-to-Penarth.html&date=2009-10-25+16:57:36.
2. For years the three towers of Guest's Glassworks were used by arriving mariners as markers for the safe sea channel into what was then no more than a small town. The towers stood on the site presently occupied by Mount Stuart House in Cardiff Bay.
3. St Lawrence's Church was founded in 1291 and became redundant in 2002. The Honorary Chaplain, as the Vicar is formally known, maintains three or four services annually.
4. These were 7 ton RML guns firing armour-piercing Palliser shells, the first in the world. They were capable of knocking a hole in the side of Napoleon III's iron-clad ships, which threatened but never came. The Victorian guns were never fired in anger.
5. In 1964 The Who changed their name to The High Numbers. They recorded 'Zoot Suit'/'I'm the Face' which wasn't a great success. For their next record, 'I Can't Explain', they changed their name back again.
6. The Gary Edwards Combo, formerly The Solid Six, were the houseband for school dances at Caer Castell in the early 1960s. Caer Castell was at the top of Rumney Hill in Cardiff, on the border between old village Rumney and brash housing estate Llanrumney. This was the school I went to. Gary Edwards is actually Gary 'Duffy' Cooper, Charlotte Church's grandfather, and still occasionally plays at the Robin Hood in Canton, Cardiff. *The Method*, complete with pull-out dance instructions, appeared in 1962.
7. In the thirteenth century Alfredo de Marisco, a Norman pirate known as the Nighthawk, established a base here.
8. A tontine is a complex scheme for raising capital which combines features of both group annuity and lottery. Tontines feature in *The Wrong Box*, both a British 1966 comedy film and a novel by Robert Louis Stevenson.
9. *Abersili* lit. the Mouth of the Sully, a rather infelicitous description. The

nearest watercourse would be the Sully Brook, which is currently a tributary of the Cadoxton River further to the west.

10. *HMS Cambria* – commissioned in 1947 – has operated from the former Service Married Quarters near Sully since 1980. It is primarily a training base for Royal Navy reservists.

11. The Cadoxton River which rises north of Dinas Powys originally reached the sea where the lock gates to Barry Docks now stand. When those docks were being constructed in 1884 engineers diverted the Cadoxton to its present course, channelling it to reach the sea through a damn-and-flap valve at Bendrick Rock. The Cadoxton's original riverbed now forms Barry's Number One dock.

12. Archaeology Cymru Director Karl-James Langford claims to have identified the site as a 3500 year old settlement twenty-five years ago. There are visible remains of Bronze-age roundhouses, postholes and edge stones but they are fast being eroded by off-road bikers. A nearby Viking settlement has been completely destroyed. The Vale of Glamorgan Council, who own the site, have said that they will look into the matter (May, 2011). It might be that they should have done this when Langford made his discoveries in 1985.

13. Vale of Glamorgan Council Inventory 2007.

14. The former Dock Offices and one-time headquarters of the Barry Railway Company were designed by the Cardiff architect Arthur E. Bell and opened in 1898. The building is currently used as the headquarters of the local authority, the Vale of Glamorgan Council.

15. In his day Gilbert was one of Britain's leading sculptors. It was he that fashioned the Duke of Clarence Tomb at Windsor, and Eros for the centre of Piccadilly Circus.

16. At the time of writing Whitbread has at last started work on its new £7.5 million Premier Inn Hotel and Brewers Fayre Restaurant. "A crucial step in plans to attract long-stay tourists to the town and Barry Island", says the Council.

17. A Mk 101 DMU called Iris II. More information is at http://www.valeof glamorgan.gov.uk/enjoying/visit_the_vale/places_to_go/boats,_trains__trip s/barry_tourist_railway.aspx.

18. Professor Dai Smith, eminent historian, TV programme maker and Chairman of the Arts Council of Wales.

19. Tony Curtis, poet, critic, anthologist, Fellow of the Royal Society of Literature, D.Litt, Cholmondeley Award winner and well-practised reader of poetry. His many books include *Heaven's Gate*, Seren, 2001 and *Crossing Over*, Seren, 2007.

20. The local authority, the Vale of Glamorgan Council, in 2004 had completed a feasibility study earmarking the site for a possible University campus for UWIC to be called *The Wales International Centre for Hospitality, Tourism and Leisure Management*. TC thought the space could be better utilised by the establishment of an art gallery.

21. After protracted negotiation plans for redevelopment of the whole four and a half acre site were approved by Barry Council in February, 2012. The rebuilt will include restaurants, cafes, a cinema, a bowling alley and, inevitably, 124 flats. How much actual fairground will remain or even be renewed is unclear.

22. Maintained by the Vale of Glamorgan Council as "one of the best examples of calcareous, cowslip dominated hay meadow in south-east Wales".
23. Originally known as the Marine Hotel "for the more select Victorian visitor" and built in 1858 by Francis Crawshay.
24. See p.89, Lambies.
25. See p.122, Bendrick.
26. WDA – Welsh Development Agency. Abolished in 2006 as part of First Minister Rhodri Morgan's bonfire of the quangos. Its functions are continued today by the Welsh Government.
27. Fonmon Castle – late thirteenth century keep, later extensions, Georgian interiors, fine gardens. One of the few Welsh buildings with Norman origins still in private hands. Owned by Sir Brooke Boothby, Baronet.
28. It was when I passed in the summer of 2011 but at the end of October a section three metres deep and one hundred an eight wide slipped dramatically into the sea. This left fifteen caravans overhanging the cliff edge. Pitches have now been found for them further back in the 300 caravan site. Fonty shrinks as the coastline recedes. Geotechnical surveys show that erosion, bar iron-cladding the entire cliff face, is progressive and unstoppable.
29. *Journey to the Surface of the Earth* – Mark Boyle's atlas and manual. http://www.boylefamily.co.uk/boyle/texts/index.html.

The Heritage Coast: Aberthaw to Porthcawl

1. John also gave me this splendid Friedlander quote. It's worth repeating here: "I only wanted Uncle Vern standing by his new car (a Hudson) on a clear day. I got him and the car. I also got a bit of Aunt Mary's laundry, and Beau Jack, the dog, peeing on a fence, and a row of potted tuberous begonias on the porch and 78 trees and a million pebbles in the driveway and more. It's a generous medium, photography."
2. In 1897 the nine-hole Barry Golf Club at the Leys was established by Scottish and English engineers building Barry Docks. It closed when the Central Electricity Generating Board compulsorily purchased the land in 1956 to build Aberthaw A. Efforts to re-establish a gold course nearby at Summerhouse Point failed. As The Leys Golfing Society, however, the club still exists. It represents 16 golf clubs in South Wales and averages 70 members. It is based at Cardiff Golf Club and meets three times a year.
3. Lavisher, Antony, *Whispers of a Storm*, Authorhouse, 2011.
4. I long ago gave up telling people that I ran Academi, the Welsh National Literature Promotion Agency. The majority had no idea what this was. They thought, if they thought at all, that this might be some sort of Reader's Digest Condensed Book Club or a Welsh Language company dedicated to promoting the work of druids.
5. ACE2 – Aberthaw Centre for Energy and the Environment.
6. Leaked reports show that Aberthaw has been identified as a suitable location for a future nuclear power station. The report bases its recommendation on the technical case rather than the political impact. http://www.walesonline.co.uk/expats/expats-newsletter/page.cfm?objectid=16753509&method=full&siteid=50082.
7. *A Walk In the Woods* is Bill Bryson's 1998 account of traversing the two thousand mile trail that runs the length of America's eastern mountains.

Unlike our own ridge pathways, which are generally clear of foliage and offer extensive views of the countryside you are crossing, the American examples are closed in by native woods. Views of the mountains are scarce and it is quite normal to walk for ten miles or more without seeing anything other than scrub oak and pine. My attempt, in 2003, to follow in Bryson's footsteps was a disaster. I inadvertently accessed the trail at the point where he came off and managed to cross none of the country nor visit any of the places he describes in his book.

8. Coflein's technical description is worth repeating: "A strongly defended site, set on the E end of a spur between a defile to the N and an eroding cliff-line on the S. A subrectangular inner enclosure, c.60m WNW-ESE, defined by a bank and ditch, is set within a similar, larger enclosure, c.126m WNW-ESE, defined by triple ramparts and ditches. There is a possible annex, c.52m WNW-ESE, on the E. The whole complex is cut by the E-W cliffs, being from c.82-46m N-S." Iron Age forts are a feature of this coast. Starting with the Bulwarks at Porthkerry they run all the way to Gower.

9. Roger Seys of Cowbridge Attorney General for the Principality of Wales under Elizabeth I acquired Boverton land by marriage. He died in 1600.

10. Boverton Place, built in 1587.

11. Cor Tewdws, or possibly Bangor Tewdws, was the College of Theodosius (named after the Roman Emperor who originally founded it). It burned down in AD 446. Illtud re-established it as part of his monastery in AD 508 and the university flourished with at least two thousand students in attendance. Cor Tewdwas went down with the dissolution. Henry VIII, the British MaoTse-tung, in action again.

12. Nash after the ash trees that once grew here. No sign of them now.

13. Nash point Lighthouse – designed by James Walker and built in 1832. Electrified in 1968 it was the last manned lighthouse in Wales. It was automated in 1998. The fog horn is disused. "But when the sun spots predicted for next year knock out the gps then we'll sound them," John smiles.

14. 'Breath, after Philip Glass'. Finch, Peter, *Selected Poems*, Poetry Wales Press, 1987.

15. These were created by Morgan Williams at the start of the twentieth century. Among the animals are a royal lion, a unicorn, two versions of the white greyhound, and a griffin. These are all heraldic emblems which the monarch is entitled to use. There are also statues of a panther and an antelope. Each animal occurs several times.

16. A fifteenth century structure, now roofless, erected by Sir Harry Stradling as a lookout for pirates and other marauders.

17. Plus *The George* (1770), *The Industry* (1786), *The Thomas* (1806), *The Bee* (1820), *The Harriet* (1827), *The Jessie Orasie* (1831), *The Frolic* (1831), *The Providence* (1832), *The Mayflower* (1841), *The New Felicity* (1841), *The Vigo* (1842), *The Betsey* (1849), *The Lucie* (1854), *The Williams* (1854), *The Mary & Deffus* (1861), *The Gillies* (1862), *The Elphis* (1865), *The Amelie* (1870), *The New Dominion* (1872), *The Bessie* (1872), *The John & Eliza* (1876), *The Jane & Susan* (1882), *The Ben-y-gloe* (1886), *The Malleny* (1886), *The Caterina Camogle* (1887), *The Denbigh* (1888), *The Tilburnia* (1888), *The Claymore* (1892), *The Lizzie* (1892), *The Elizabeth Couch* (1913), *The Narcissus* (1916), *The Pollensa* (1919) and *The Cato*

(1951). Just inland is the village of Wick, home of the wreckers who showed false lights along this coast. The Plough and Harrow pub at Monknash, in former life, was a monastic farmhouse for Neath Abbey. Here the monks would prepare the bodies of drowned sailors for burial.

18. Ogmore Castle, one of the most western of Norman castles. Built in 1106 near the confluence of the rivers Ogwr and Ewenny. Possibly erected on the foundations of an earlier Welsh Castle. Given by Robert Fitzhamon to William de Londres, one of the twelve knights of Glamorgan.

19. So described on Bridgend Council's website.

20. Medieval origin. Buried first in the sixteen century, revealed by storm in 1822 then lost again until the mid-twentieth century when its low walls were once again dug free by Police cadets.

21. Gillham, Mary – *The Glamorgan Heritage Coast Wildlife Series Volume 1 – Sand Dunes*, Heritage Coast Joint Management and Advisory Committee, 1987, p.4.

22. *The Itinerary of John Leland in or about the Years 1535-1543*, Southern Illinois University Press, 1906.

23. Minhinnick, Robert and Bourke, Eamon, *Fairground Music – The World of Porthcawl Funfair*, Gomer Press, 2010.

24. Thruster, Flying Fish, Freerider, Fusion, Bilbo, Custard Point. Prices start at £195 and go up to £395.

25 Iwan Llwyd Williams, 1957-2010.

26. *Llwybro â Llafur at Lynllifon*, 1990.

The West: Kenfig to Swansea

1. *Gwely'r Misgl* – mussel bed – first century BC footprints were found in the peat here in 2007.

2. Rhys, Ernest, *The South Wales Coast – From Chepstow to Aberystwyth*, Frederick A. Stokes, Co., 1911.

3. Withdrawn from stock, Normal College Library, Bangor.

4. Aberafan, Baglan, Bryn, Cwmafan, Margam, Oakwood and Taibach.

5. *Real Cardiff*, which I wrote in 2002 was where it all started. *Real South Bank* and *Real Bangor* are currently in planning. *Real Los Angles* later. *Real Sands of Mars* after that.

6. http://www.lynnerees.com/.

7. Junction 38, M4.

8. Morfa Colliery. Opened in 1849 to feed the nearby copper smelter at Taibach. Closed 1913.

9. Losing significant buildings to fire does seem to be a Port Talbot feature. I've suggested to Lynne Rees that she might write this up as a *Real Port Talbot* feature. Buy the book to see where that idea goes.

10. 'Kitetail and Taper'. Erected July, 2008.

11. Sustrans, the British charity promoting sustainable transport. Sustrans flagship project is its 10,000 miles of signed UK cycle routes. http://www.sustrans.org.uk/.

12. Yr Hen Gastell was excavated in 1991-1992 by a team led by P F Wilkinson for the Glamorgan Gwent archeological Trust. Their finds revealed high status occupation between the sixth and the tenth centuries. A report is available at http://ads.ahds.ac.uk/catalogue/adsdata/arch-769-1/ahds/ dissemination/pdf/vol39/39_001_050.pdf. The M4 bridge was completed in

the mid-1990s.

13. Or maybe it's not. See p.196, Swansea.

14. We imagine things to persist but they don't. Enterprises that outlast their operator are few. Structures that stand and stay stood are far fewer that we think. That the Romans persisted for more than four centuries is amazing. Sir Humphrey Mackworth, squire of the Gnoll Estate, was in at the dawn of the Industrial Revolution. The furnaces he built on the north bank of the Cryddan brook, to reduce copper ores and using coal from his own mines, were erected in 1695. They began smelting copper ore from Cornwall and expanded to work with lead mined in Cardigan. Silver and zinc followed. By 1766, seventy years down the line, the works had doubled in size. But by 1796 it was all over. A hundred years of enterprise and then collapse. The roof of the works was sold in 1797. The OS map of 1877 shows only slag heaps on the ground. By the twentieth century these too had gone. It all makes the window frame fight I engage in against the advancing rot along the bottom edge of my writing room windows fade into insignificance. Here the wooden 60s frames, added in the early 70s to a between the wars structure and already showing signs of crumble by the time I acquired them in 1980, have been dug out and re-filled at least five times. I've used indoor filler, exterior filler, high performance filler, plastic wood, mortar mix, plaster, wood hardener and crushed nylon fronted with paste all to no eventual avail. The prevailing water-bearing westerlies settle like acid. They seep and dissolve. I fix and wait, then fix again. Shift and flux. The world as emulsion. Everything is everything. Nothing for long stays the same.

15. SSSI – Site of Special Scientific Interest.

16. From *Sea-Sounds of the Pacific Ocean at Big Sur* – Jack Kerouac, 1962.

17. Carr is a type of waterlogged, wooded terrain that, typically, represents a succession stage between the original reedy swamp and the eventual formation of a forest in a sub-maritime climate (Wiki entry).

18. Formerly half of the duo OutKast but now solo. Check his 2010 masterpiece Sir Lucious Left Foot: the Son of Chico Dusty.

19. In 2011, following the exposure of its inappropriate validation of bogus degrees awarded by foreign institutions, a number of the University of Wales's constituent colleges left the federation to strike out on their own. The rump of the University rebranded itself as University of Wales Trinity St David's, a name slickly shortened to University of Wales, the institution's new brand. How this now actually represents the whole of the nation, which is what its name implies, I do not know.

20. Spelter – zinc and zinc alloy.

21. 'Ecliptica' – a nude cast by the artist Rob Conybear of his then girlfriend Uta Molling's body form. The clothes were added later to enable the figure to turn with the wind.

22. Nigel Jenkins original commission was for 'Six short texts on the cosmos', one of the most creative official orders ever issued by the local council. The resultant poem is based on the three-line englyn penfyr. It appears in both English and Menna Elfyn's Welsh translation.

23. As I visit, in 2012 for sale. Interested parties, say the council, have been asked to submit proposals and financial offers for the building. "We'd like to see a mixed-use development that incorporates features of the existing

observatory building but we invite any developers with other imaginative design ideas to get in touch because we don't want to preclude innovative proposals." The future may not be in the stars.
24. Famous for its crawls along a run of more than twenty pubs, the drinking centre of the south Wales coast until the arrival of the 1990s and the rise of binge culture. The bars and clubs of the cities hold the honour now.

Gower: Oystermouth to Worm's Head

1. In response to a call the archaeologists tell us that they had not lifted the track at the time of my visit and that it had probably been temporarily covered by shifting sands. Worryingly they report that there does remain the possibility that the sea had actually destroyed it. However, in March 2012 the remains are located, uncovered and some of them lifted. More detail can be found in Nigel Jenkins's *Real Swansea Two* (Seren, 2012).
2. First Book of Esdras, Chapter II, verse 12. A book from the Bible's Apocrypha.
3. Spirit of the Sea.
4. The owners, AMECO (Amusement Equipment Co. Ltd.), estimate Pier redevelopment costs to be above £3m. To fund this they need to build a hotel along with, possibly, an old people's home at the landward end. Swansea Council has approved the plan in principle, in spite of concerns about architectural appropriateness and a sense of scale. These are both qualities, in the world of Welsh architecture, that are often lacking.
5. *The Child On The Cliffs*, 1915.
6. As described by Dylan Thomas biographer Paul Ferris, in *Gower In History – Myth, People, Landscape*. Armanaleg Books, 2009.
7. *The Gower Coast – A coastline walk and guide to the history, legends, shipwrecks & rescues, smuggling, castles & caves, including the story of the Dollar Ship* (Regional Publications, Bristol, 1979) but mostly ship wrecks.
8. Song on Whitney Houston's final studio album, *I Look To You*, in 2007. The song was a minor hit in Korea where it got to number 56. Not on my iPod.
9. http://penricecastle.co.uk/.
10. Upstairs there's a room known as Little Tor. It's probably not big enough for a bed and you have to sleep on the floor.
11. Oxwich Castle – built by Sir Rice Mansel in 1520 on the site of an earlier castle recorded as being in the possession of Philip Mansel in 1459. The present structure was considerable enlarged ("re-edified or repaired") by Sir Rice's son Sir Edward between 1538 and 1580.
12. Actually a licensed restaurant and pizzeria http://www.smugglers haunt.com/
13. The 870 mile (1400 kilometre) Wales Coast Path opened officially on 5th May, 2012.
14. *Wales, A History*, made by Green bay Media for BBC Wales, 2012
15. Lit. Relics of the Flood – 'Observations on the Organic Remains Contained in Caves, Fissures, and Diluvial Gravel, and on Other Geological Phenomena, Attesting the Action of an Universal Deluge', 1823.
16. Thomas, Dylan, *Portrait Of the Artist As A Young Dog*, 1940.
17. "There is a wonderfull Hole at the poyant of Worme Heade, but few dare entre it, and Men fable there that a Dore within the spatius Hole hathe be sene withe great Nayles on it."

England: The Tidal Limits to Lynmouth

1. Ynys Echni – Flat Holm.
2. The Severn Way long distance footpath. Runs 223.9 miles from the river's source in Plynlimon to its defined end, as a river anyway, at estuary mouth near Bristol.
3. 'Hills' in Finch, Peter, *Selected Later Poems, op. cit.*
4. Plans to barrage the Severn may compromise this venture with new ULCV facilities being established at Port Talbot. The economic drivers are the time and cost it may take a ship to pass through barrage lock gates vs. the extra road time on the difficult M4 from Port Talbot to that road's inter-change with the M5 at Bristol.
5. ULCV – ships of a length greater than 397 metres and capable of carrying in excess of 14,500 containers. Regular container ships, those capable of using the Panama Canal, carry no more than 5000.
6. Birnbeck Pier was damaged by the storms of 1990 and closed for safety reasons in 1994. It was sold in 2008 to Manchester developers Urban Splash. In its heyday visitors arriving by steamer often never left the pier, spending their time enjoying its amusements, cafés, pavilion and funfair on Birnbeck Island itself.
7. The Wonders of Weston is an art project created between 2008 and 2010. It is part of the much larger Sea Change Department for Culture Media and Sport £45 million Initiative which attempts to "drive cultural and creative regeneration and economic growth in seaside resorts by funding inspiring, creative and innovative projects, bringing a sense of pride, enjoy-ment and celebration". The Weston component has put public artworks throughout the town. These include at least forty poem-like tangential state-ments with a forty-first over the water on the Cardiff Bay Barrage. That one reads *PERHAPS YOU CAN SEE WESTON-SUPER-MARE TEN MILES TO THE SOUTH-EAST. A CENTURY AGO YOU COULD HAVE CAUGHT A WHITE FUNNEL FLEET STEAMER TO WESTON'S BIRNBECK PIER TO VISIT THE THEATRE OF WONDERS, THE FLYING MACHINE OR THE BIOSCOPE. FORGET PLANS FOR THE CARDIFF-WESTON BARRAGE. WALK ON WATER INSTEAD.*
8. AONB – Area of Outstanding Natural Beauty as designated by Natural England (the successor body to the UK's Countryside Agency). AONB's are National Parks without their own authority and with far more liberal planning laws.
9. 'The Pylons', Stephen Spender.
10. Shelley described the property as "The poverty and humbleness of the apartments is compensated for by their number, & we can invite our friends with a consciousness that there is enclosed space wherein they may sleep" (as quoted in Richard Holmes excellent Shelley biography, *Shelly, The Pursuit*, Weidenfeld & Nicolson, 1974.
11. "Government has no rights; it is a delegation from several individuals for the purpose of securing their own…. The rights of man are liberty, and all equal participation of the commonage of nature.. Awake!-arise!-or be for ever fallen." Shelley was a supporter of disaffected revolutionary Irishmen, of Catholic emancipation, of the French Revolution, of atheism over forced Christianity, of vegetarianism. In fact of most things anathema to the civil society of the day.

12. From 'On Launching Some Bottles Filled with Knowledge into the Bristol Channel' – a sonnet by Shelley.
13. "Donated by Lyn Valley Society. 1500 books were sold to pay for this solar light." – sign on lamp standard.

Out in the Waters

1. Gateholm, *Goteholme*, Goat island in Old Norse, snakes out from the Pembrokeshire Coast Path near Marloes. On shore is a three embankment Iron Age fort, huts to the sea, ditches towards the land. It's another place with a pull. I've spent half my life in its thrall. Waiting for low tide to cross the narrow, sea-weed and rock-pooled strait, clambering on, pulling myself up the island's near vertical faces, taking that deep breath that sufferers of vertigo always need, to access the grassy top.

   I'd done this as a young man with not a care anywhere, as a family man with kids in tow, got them up there too, and later with my skin buckling and my ascetic look in disarray I'd done it again. I'd crossed its grass hummocks so many times, looked for the reputed postholes but never found them, hoped to find the remains of something, anything, but never did. Felt the winds blow on me. Tried to work out just what it was that was making me come here. Never could.

   It transpires that this place was never the Christian settlement as some maps show it. Monks did not build their cells here, tight to the rock, facing the Atlantic storms down. The god that flowed along Gateholm's rocky sides was a pagan one. For pagan read anything that is not Jehovah. Instead this island held three successive waves of occupants, living in huts in the Bronze Age, in Celtic roundhouses when iron arrived and then in terraced rows at the time of the Romans. Geophysics and exploratory trenches have revealed the island to be home to hundreds. The island is abandoned now, totally. The rain, the winds and nature's predictable, ever-reliable re-encroachment is returning Gateholm to a pristine state. Its magic is back below its surface. Back on shore I salute. Been on you, Gateholm, in 2010, missed 2011 somehow. Be back again in 2012. Will have done it by the time you read this. Finch standing there among the magnetism, pulled by forces he never believed in, attracted by things at the edge of reason, where the world really is.
2. Denny Island – the name comes from *Duyne* (1373) 'island shaped like a down'.
3. SSSI, Special Protection Area – Rock Sea Lavender, Wild Leek, Lesser Black-Backed Gull, Great Black-Backed Gull, Herring Gull, Slow Worms. No herring.
4. www.severnlake.co.uk.
5. *Ffugenw*, Welsh – nom-de-plume.
6. Ap Foote, Lewis, *The Grumpy Old Welshman,* Lifestory Services, 2006
7. http://www.decc.gov.uk/assets/decc/what%20we%20do/uk%20energy%20supply/energy%20mix/renewable%20energy/severn-tp/621-severn-tidal-power-feasibility-study-conclusions-a.pdf.
8. STPG – The Severn Tidal Power Group members are: Sir Robert McAlpine Ltd, Balfour Beatty Major Projects Ltd, ALSTOM Hydro Ltd, Rolls Royce Power Engineering Ltd, Taylor Woodrow Construction Ltd, and Tarmac Construction Ltd.

9. Corlan Hafren, Welsh – Severn Group. The group includes Halcrow Group Ltd, Ove Arup & Partners Ltd, KPMG LLP, Sancroft International Ltd, Marks Barfield Architects LLP, Hannah & Mould Solicitors and Professor Roger A Falconer FREng.
10. Gates, Bill, *The Road Ahead*, Viking, 1995
11. Davies, Tom, *Testament*, Berwyn Mountain Press, 2008.
12. Built as a ferry by John Thornycroft and Company at Woolston in 1949. Operated by the Southampton, Isle of Wight and South of England Royal Mail Steam Packet Company (the Red Funnel Line). Acquired by P&A Campbell in 1968 until their White Funnel Fleet ceased trading in 1980. Used as floating restaurant at Dundee until 1985. Purchased by her present owners, the Waverley Steam Navigation Company and brought to the Bristol Channel in 1986.

Afterword – Wales Again

1. How do I reach this figure? I measure the route I walked using a Silva 'get out there' Map Measurer Plus. This is a wheel and scale you roll across your OS map. You do it twice to ensure accuracy as you follow the path around the inlets, over the bridges, around the diversions, along the roads, over the cliffs, across the sands, and through the cities. You end up with a mere 138 miles. But this is Wales, don't forget. And as a country we are not famous for being big.

For more on *Edging the Estuary* visit:
www.peterfinch.co.uk/Estuary/estuary.htm